CLOSER
TO
LOVE

CLOSER
TO
LOVE

HOW TO ATTRACT THE RIGHT RELATIONSHIPS
AND DEEPEN YOUR CONNECTIONS

VEX KING

bluebird
books for life

First published 2023 by Bluebird
an imprint of Pan Macmillan
The Smithson, 6 Briset Street, London EC1M 5NR

EU representative: Macmillan Publishers Ireland Ltd, 1st Floor,
The Liffey Trust Centre, 117–126 Sheriff Street Upper,
Dublin 1, D01 YC43
Associated companies throughout the world
www.panmacmillan.com

978-1-5290-8784-0 HB
978-1-5290-8785-7 TPB
978-1-0350-1531-3 PB

1 3 5 7 9 8 6 4 2

A CIP catalogue record for this book is available from the British Library.

Typeset by Palimpsest Book Production Ltd, Falkirk, Stirlingshire
Printed and bound by CPI Group (UK) Ltd, Croydon, CR0 4YY

MIX
Paper | Supporting
responsible forestry
FSC® C116313

CONTENTS

I deeply admire your capacity to love.
If only I and others could love as purely as you,
the world would be a better place.

Thank you for being my greatest teacher.

Share images or videos of your favourite pages, quotes, and experiences related to this book on social media using #CloserToLove so I can see them and share them across my platforms.

For more inspiration, follow my social media platforms (all @vexking) and sign up to my mailing list using the QR code below.

INTRODUCTION

How can you share your life with someone else if you are disconnected from yourself?
How can you establish closeness if you are emotionally distant from your own emotions?
The truth is, it is virtually impossible to build a healthy relationship with another person if you haven't built one with yourself first.

It hit me like a ton of bricks.

I felt as though the wind had been knocked out of me. And even though I could see it coming from a mile away, I was still staggered by the impact of my first heartbreak. In a single moment, all I had known of love was wiped away and the future I created in my mind dissipated. For some time, I became a shell of my former self.

You could say it was a brutal, painful, but absolutely necessary wake-up call for my spiritual and emotional expansion. If it wasn't for the ending of multiple important relationships, I may have never learned to sit with my own darkness and crawl my way back to love.

When relationships fall apart, so does the illusion of the joint future you had mapped out in your mind. And the tighter you cling to those hopes, the harder you fall.

But despite the isolating feeling of heartache, I soon realized that there was nothing unique about the earth-shattering sensation I was experiencing. Most of us have gone through a break-up and lost someone we're attached to or in love with. And if you find yourself in that position now, I know how lost, hurt, and hopeless you must be feeling. You might not see the rainbow at the end of the storm yet – but I have. And I'll usher you there.

During every post-break-up healing process, I would roll my eyes at the sight of happy couples who seemed privy to the meaning of love and the secret to lasting relationships. What did they know or have that I didn't? This confusion and jealousy was a knee-jerk reaction because of my lack of self-awareness.

But everything changes when we become empowered by our role in a relationship. Many of us don't take the time to recover and, instead of doing a deep-dive self-inquiry about how we may have contributed to our own heartache, we seek out another person to help alleviate our longing for love. Then we repeat the cycle.

As some of you might already know, I'm not a psychologist or professional marriage counsellor, and some of what I write may not align with you. The way you interpret anything you read also depends on your current emotional state, past experiences, and the context in which you are reading this book. That said, I've spent most of my adult life learning about self-development and looking into different approaches to building strong relationships, and I'll share all of that with you here.

I've always been motivated by my own belief that we are capable of living full, blissful lives if we are given the tools to do so. Love is a basic human need, but it's also our greatest superpower. A life lived with love is rich, abundant, and rewarding, and if we can share that with someone special, all the better.

You may carry wounds from a decade ago that have begun

to open up again in your current relationship. You feel the love slipping away but have no idea how to save what's so important to you. Or perhaps your relationship lacks the emotional depth and intimacy you desire, and you want to be closer to the one you love.

The most important thing I can share with you is not to wait. Don't let one more month, year, or decade go by without a heart-centred self-reckoning. By becoming radically honest about your relationship patterns, aware of your needs and attachments, and closer to understanding how to nurture and love yourself, you will liberate your heart and know how to experience authentic connection, intimacy, and true love.

When you are able to collect all the little pieces of your heart and show up fully in a relationship, the deep connection and bond you can experience are supreme. Often, modern relationships suffer from a lack of loyalty, fulfilment, and depth. That makes a lot of sense because our relationships can only meet us in the place we're at emotionally, mentally, and spiritually. But it is possible to grow and move on to a more authentic way to love.

This book is an invitation to do something different; to pause, reflect, and liberate yourself from troubling relationship patterns.

The following chapters will help you to evaluate how and why you love, learn how to do so in healthy and unconditional ways, develop new relationship habits, and deepen your connection to self so that all shared love comes from a place of authenticity and self-knowing.

Use your heartbreak as a catalyst for your growth.

Discover why you keep repeating unhealthy relationship dynamics.

Actualize your ability to build thriving relationships, romantic and otherwise.

With every page you read, welcome new ideas about your capacity to give and receive love. Insecurities, fears, and doubts may rise to the surface as your heart and mind are exposed to what relationships can be and how they can look. But understand that, **no matter how much loss you may have endured, unconditional love awaits you.** It is nestled within the healing and restorative process offered in each chapter.

By traversing this journey of self-healing, I was eventually able to restore my heart, make peace with my past, and build a life with the most joy-filled human. And because I trusted the healing process, I let go of what I thought love was and found a new understanding about relationships that allowed me to give and receive the love she and I both deserved. Now is your chance to do the same.

This book will take you on a journey to self-awareness as we explore fresh possibilities for healing, love, and relationships. You will need to consider what to leave behind as you set out for a new destination – one that will lead you into the unwavering arms of unconditional love.

What are you dealing with?

People are struggling. For years, I have heard from so many who are going through so much emotional pain and are looking for answers to the problems they are facing.

Much of what I hear has to do with people trying to make their relationships work. I get asked often about how to change someone, what to do when they won't change, and how to protect themselves from being hurt or from hurting the other. The issues stem from a lack of communication or feelings of being undervalued in some way. Many have been burned in a past relationship and are afraid to start a new one. Others want to know more about unconditional love and whether it really exists. They wonder how loving someone without conditions plays out in practice and are looking for ways to take their relationship to the next level. A lot of people feel like failures when their relationship breaks down, blaming themselves for not doing enough or not 'being' enough.

We've got a lot to talk about!

It makes sense that people are struggling, because there's no handbook on what to do when your partner cheats on you, or how to nurture a relationship based on non-attachment. **Schools don't teach us about codependency, trauma, or self-awareness, so how can we be expected to work through the quagmire of building a meaningful relationship today?** My goal in writing this book is to speak to you directly. We can change the way we connect with each other and form lasting, loving, healing, and life-giving bonds.

A lot of us have to learn through trial and error, painful experiences, confusion, and guesswork. And even then, we don't all succeed.

Like every couple, my wife and I have disagreements. Our wounds can get the better of us, and we often allow the waves of our emotional turmoil to drown each other out. Nevertheless, we keep showing up, ready to resolve and evolve. Even when we're acting not-so-loveable, deep down we know we are loved by one another.

I'm not here to boast about our love. While I'm proud of the woman I'm married to, I know how hard we've worked to get to where we are, and how much effort we are willing to invest so we can keep growing. However, this growth can only take place if we are committed to loving ourselves in the first instance.

Recognizing you're already whole will make you a better half.

Before meeting Kaushal, I hadn't had many long-term relationships, especially after the devastating one that I wrote about in the Introduction to *Healing Is the New High*. After that, I had to stop and think about what was really important to me. I realized that I needed to feel aligned with the other person, but in order to do so, I had to be aligned within myself first. When I met Kaushal, I felt deeply connected to her very quickly but wasn't able to express it properly because I was protecting myself from getting hurt. Although I had already embarked on a journey of self-love, I really stepped it up, because by being with her, so much was revealed about my past, conditioning, expectations, fears, insecurities, and so on.

Let's face it: we are all looking for someone who understands where we are coming from, and they are looking for the same thing, too. It's magic when you meet that one person who just 'gets' you. But, you have to know how to share, open up, and be vulnerable. This 'not knowing how' is one of the reasons people find it difficult to begin or maintain relationships, and it makes absolute sense.

We can't get close to someone if we aren't able to get close to ourselves. When I wrote *Good Vibes, Good Life*, my aim was to help readers get in touch with their inner self and to begin practising self-love. I mention it here because before we take a seat on the roller coaster of relationships, it really helps if we've ousted our demons, got rid of that excess baggage, and come from a place of true self-awareness and authenticity. Even if you haven't been able to do that completely, as long as you are on a path towards self-love, it's all good.

You can enjoy fulfilment within a relationship if you create the space to do so. I know you may find yourself confronted by deeply painful experiences with a partner because you haven't been able to do the hard work first. That's the path of learning more about yourself, who you are, what you want, and being willing to grow. But you can mature during a loving, caring relationship, and there's nothing more wonderful in life than that. Even so, you might keep making the same mistakes, go through the same range of negative emotions and pain, and can't seem to find a way out.

Feeling close to someone is a lovely experience. It makes us all warm and fuzzy inside just to be with them and seems to restore and renew us. To establish this closeness with someone else, we need to have something called 'reciprocal self-disclosure' – this means being able to communicate often with each other, without fear or criticism, in an accepting way.[1] When you hear people saying that they are 'very close' to someone else, this is usually what they mean. Their relationship is based on care, warmth, acceptance, and support, making it a mutual intimate connection.

By sharing your personal feelings, thoughts, and memories, you are allowing the other person to get to know you. If you are reserved and less likely to share these things, it's much more difficult for them to get closer to you. Having a high level of self-disclosure is one of the most important building blocks in an intimate relationship, as well as in social ones, too. The more you share about yourself, the easier you make it for the other person to share their inner self, and this becomes a mutual exchange that can lead to greater closeness.

When you do feel close to someone, it's easier to maintain positive emotions about each other and to express any negative feelings without fear. It takes two to tango and both of you need to have this trust if the relationship is going to thrive. If you can't communicate how you feel, if you send confusing messages, aren't honest, or are emotionally shut down, it's highly unlikely that the other person is going to be able to help you. You need to help yourself first.

You can also live quite happily on your own, without having any particular partner or special person in your life, and still give love to others and be loved. There are just as many happy singles out there as there are happy couples, and it's not a one-size-fits-all thing here. In this book, I'll be writing a lot about romantic relationships, but much of what I say covers all kinds of intimate ties.

Self-love doesn't require a partner, and I know many people who choose to be single for a variety of reasons but still have caring, loving relationships with others. You have to do what feels right to you and pursue your own life goals, whatever path that creates.

Most of us jump into relationships from a relatively young age, without even knowing what we want or how to go about getting it. No one told us that we need to connect with ourselves before we can connect with others. I bet you know a few people (perhaps yourself included) who met someone in their late teens or early twenties and then broke up later on because they 'grew apart'. You'll have heard that expression many times, right? What they are actually saying, in most cases, is that the relationship didn't work for them because they aren't the same people now as they were when they first met.

Could it also mean that they discovered who they really are at a later stage of their relationship? Maybe one person matured while the other stayed stunted and unable or unwilling to grow. Any of these explanations is possible, as well as other variants.

It's completely normal to change, grow, mature, want different things in life, feel a need to start over, or reassess our needs as we grow older. Not all relationships will work out for these very reasons, although some will if they are flexible and resilient enough.

If you don't know who you are when you walk into a relationship, how can you make it work? When you have never thought about what is compatible, acceptable, or desirable, how can you spot the incompatibilities, know what is unacceptable, and define what is undesirable? If you have no yardstick, how can you measure anything?

You deserve a relationship where you are seen, heard, understood, and accepted for who you really are.

PART 1

The Self: Mastering the role you play within your connections

Love is the bridge between you
and everything.

– Rumi

You're never single.
You're always in a relationship with
yourself; so stay committed to loving
yourself and evolving.

HOW IT STARTED

My wife and I went to the same school from the ages of nine to thirteen, although she was in the year below me. We only discovered this fact when we entered into a relationship together.

We looked back at our time at that school and tried to remember one another, but just couldn't paint a strong image of each other during that period. My long-term memory is pretty good, but I couldn't form a clear picture of her in my head, no matter how hard I tried.

It wasn't until I saw a school photo of Kaushal that I remembered her. I was then taken back to a particular moment in the school playground where I looked at her and was intrigued. It was a vivid memory.

I recall her being with two other girls, who she confirmed were her best friends (actually her cousins). I was staring at Kaushal in particular, just wondering who she was and if she had the same origins as me. I'm not going to pretend that I was in love with her at this age or that I was observing her romantically; I just remember there being something about her that captivated me and left me wanting to know more. She was a total stranger to me at school, among many students, but I wondered about her during that time and the memory came back to me. It's strange, I know, but it's also true. Even at such a young age, her energy was a catalyst for emotions that felt very foreign but very visceral.

When Kaushal was thirteen, she moved to America, only to return to the UK in her late teens. One night, I spotted her out for the first time, not knowing she was the same girl as the one in the playground all those years ago. We shared a brief smile but then she disappeared again for a while. Her face was different, but that same feeling from the playground returned. Who was this being?

At the age of nineteen, I was on the social networking website Myspace and I saw her profile pop up through a mutual friend. I remembered that moment when I saw her a few years before and I just knew there was something about her. I was tempted to add her but I didn't, although I did hover over the 'add friend' button for an unmentionable amount of time.

I only ever saw her once over a period of seven years or so after she returned from the States, despite both of us being from the same town. We knew of each other but never seemed to meet. I was naturally drawn to her, even though I tried to play it cool. This only began to make sense after our first real interaction and conversation, which occurred just before I'd finished university. It felt like we had known each other for a lifetime. At this point, our connection consisted primarily of a handful of glances and a single conversation. But I had a feeling it would be the first of many.

It was weird because when we got talking, we also randomly started seeing the same signs. We were both big believers in having a Positive Mental Attitude (PMA) after experiencing hardships we had both gone through in life. Before we entered into a relationship, we'd see PMA written everywhere, even on takeaway leaflets.

Perhaps this was our Reticular Activating System (RAS) in action – a grouping of neurons in the brain that's hard-wired to focus on what's important and filter out what's unnecessary. It essentially focuses on what your brain finds relevant or highlights what you already believe (along with other functions such as regulating arousal and our sleep–wake cycles).

We're inundated with millions of bits of information every second from all of our senses. If we were paying attention to every piece of information, it would feel like we're going to explode. Our RAS filters out irrelevant details and only permits data into our consciousness that will keep us safe and be of interest to us.

But our coming together, perhaps that's synchronicity. Now that she is my wife, I feel like I was always gravitating towards her. The signs were guiding me to Kaushal, even if I ignored them for a while. In fact, she also remembers the night she saw me for the first time, many moons ago; she had enquired about me to her best friend, who knew me. We have since learned that these weren't rom-com coincidences. This was energy.

In quantum mechanics, there's a phenomenon called quantum entanglement, which is where two sub-atomic particles become intimately linked across time and space, with a change in one particle affecting the other, no matter how far apart they are.

This concept makes me think of the way people are inexplicably drawn together – and perhaps in the future there will be discoveries about how our own sub-atomic particles are somehow linked. I feel that my wife and I were linked long before we said 'I do', and the brief encounters were the natural ebb and flow of our energies colliding and separating.

It may not be scientifically accurate but I like to think that those who are meant for you, will find you, because there is already a bond that exists between you and them. An ancient

Chinese proverb says: 'An invisible red thread connects those destined to meet, despite the time, the place, and the circumstances. The thread can be tightened or tangled, but will never be broken.'

Nevertheless, even when you find someone that you feel aligned with, there's no guarantee it will always work out.

Some relationships will feel like the big bang that creates worlds of wonder and magic within you. Others will feel like a meteor, zipping through your life with burning passion but disappearing as fast as they came. Some will be like a dying star that vanishes but leaves you wishing for more. But all experiences of love can be used for your greater good and deeper self-knowing. The energy of love is found in all things and surrounds you even now.

As variable as the opportunities and ways in which we can experience love, so are the degrees and kinds of relationships possible. In this book, I will feature a few fictitious and real-life relationship examples. But I want to be clear that these scenarios apply to all gender roles and different couplings. Love is love. And these practices and examples span all relationship types.

I hope I can offer you clarity on past experiences, help you to renew your perspective on current relationships, and to master your heart so that you may foster as much authentic love as possible in all connections.

Chapter 1

CLOSER TO ME, CLOSER TO YOU

Do you know who will never leave your side?
You.
Perhaps this is the relationship you need to
nurture the most.

Love.

We can't live without it. And we shouldn't.

Unfortunately, most of us look for love in all the wrong places. This may be a book about relationships, but make no mistake: the love you experience with others will be a direct reflection of the love you share with yourself. Wherever this text takes you, and in whatever place in life it has found you, I want you to understand, above all else, that love is an internal experience. It is found and felt from within. **A relationship can help you cultivate more love but, essentially, it will amplify the abundance or lack of love you carry towards yourself.** So, let's talk about where that comes from.

The need to be loved is so strong that from day one of our existence, we demand it. That basic emotional need doesn't disappear as we get older, instead it grows even stronger.

Which one of us doesn't want to find their soulmate, or thinks they have found them? The one, the love of our life, the person we can't live without?

Modern relationships are more complex than ever and our approach to love often comes from a place of lack rather than an outpouring of a cup that is already filled.

Understanding how to love is complex. From a psychological perspective, the way we learn to feel and express love starts from a very young age. Most child development specialists will tell you that newborn babies have two emotional responses: attraction and withdrawal.[2] They are attracted by whatever brings them pleasure, comfort, and stimulation, while withdrawing from anything unpleasant, like bitter tastes or physical discomfort. Depending on the care that an infant is given, its consistency and its predictability can contribute to the type of **attachment style** it develops, or the way it relates to others. In adulthood, it is critical to meet your attachment style with grace and healing so that you do not try to seek a partner who will 'fix' or 'complete' you. We'll talk more about attachment styles in Chapter 2.

As babies, we want to be soothed, rocked, or comforted by our caregivers, because we can't yet regulate our emotions ourselves. Without realizing it, the way we experience and express love is influenced by how others responded to our emotional cues. In our adult relationships, many of us mirror what we learned at a young age, having formed specific attachment styles.

Beyond basic needs, you are a unique individual with experiences, memories, likes, dislikes, habits, and preferences. How you were raised is only a portion of what teaches you how to love – along with your personality and one-of-a-kind perspective. The more intimately you craft yourself through personal development and expansion, the more aligned you remain with the love you have to offer others. As the ancient Greek aphorism goes, 'Know thyself'.

Many people don't take the time to explore themselves and so forget who they really are. As life goes by, they accumulate false ideas about themselves or assume thought patterns that aren't really their own. In effect, they live without having a deep sense of self, which stops them from forming genuine connections with others.

Acquiring that deep sense of self-knowledge is how you invite conscious, happy, healthy, and fulfilling relationships. Navigating relationships is challenging enough, but to not be rooted in your deepest values and beliefs will make it feel impossible.

Whatever you bring to a relationship, you can be certain that the other person is also carrying their own baggage, and that's a lot to grapple with. How do you navigate what is right or wrong for you if you aren't crystal clear about what that means?

We often enter connections with people wondering if they will like us. But do we like them? Discernment is incredibly important when seeking a compatible partner. But it's also a trait of those who seek love from a higher awareness and not from the unmet, unconscious needs dictated by our early attachment figures.

I think Rumi was spot on when he said that love can be a bridge between you and everything else, no matter what form it takes. How you create that bridge is up to you, but it has to start with a solid base, right? You have to begin from a sound starting point and know that the crossing will be secure enough to prevent you from falling. It's the same with love: if you aren't grounded in your own self-love, it's tricky to manoeuvre yourself in relationships with new partners.

Knowing who you are is a good starting point. I don't just mean your name, what you do for a living, or what your favourite colour is, but REALLY having a strong sense of self-awareness and identity. This begins with self-inquiry – raising questions in a mindful way that will help you to rediscover who you are. As a taster, I want you to read the questions below and give yourself some time to reflect on them:

1. How do you see yourself?

2. What makes you who you are?

3. What do you offer?

4. What do you need?

5. What are your deepest values?

6. How do you handle criticism, rejection, or failure?

7. What are your non-negotiables with yourself and within a relationship?

8. Are you capable of giving without expecting to receive anything in return?

9. What does your ideal relationship look like? How do you contribute to that image?

10. How do you respond to interpersonal challenges?

You don't have to answer these right away – I'm putting them out there so you can think about them a little bit. You might find some of them tricky or that they take you down a path you aren't ready to explore, and that's OK. I do want to say, though, that if you are looking for meaningful connections, you've got to do some self-discovery first. You can't expect a doctor to cure an illness if they don't look at what's causing it – or prescribe the right treatment without any idea of what's wrong in the first place. In the same way, **life doesn't get any better if you are stuck in a pattern of thought and behaviour that isn't serving you, or is leading you nowhere.**

What do you want and what do you bring to the table?

Are you willing to challenge the stories about relationships that you maintain? Is it worth thinking of things differently to shed light on new ways of connecting with others?

Your idea about what you need from a relationship is the culmination of your past, as well as projected expectations about your future. Beyond answering a few hard questions posed in this chapter, understand what you need from your relationships by observing current ones and auditing past ones. What did you like about them? What absolutely didn't work for you? What parts of you do they amplify? How do you feel about life, love, and possibilities when you're around them?

Love isn't about operating from a headspace, and you'll soon learn that I'm not a fan of entering a connection with a checklist. However, these practices are great for the journey within. **If you are looking to completely transform your life, heal, and feel whole, I emphasize that the first relationship you must honour and nurture is the one with yourself**.

When we are in love with ourselves and in love with life, it becomes apparent which people and spaces lack love. When love first comes from within, it acts as a compass moving you towards a person who can mirror and sustain that love from within themselves in harmony.

You are a very complex person, but underneath all the layers, you just want to be loved, right? At the same time, you have a massive potential to give love. But do you really know how to give and receive it?

Common blockages to receiving love

- Feelings of unworthiness

- A lack of belief in it

- A belief that it will always end

- An unwillingness to work at it

- General insecurities

Much of who you are is made up of past experiences and some of these experiences may have left you guarded. Many hurt people are still able to give love, despite inconsistency in receiving it.

Common blockages to giving love

- Fear of vulnerability

- Uncertainty of what it means to love (often due to lack of positive examples)

- A belief that everyone leaves

- Fear of rejection

- Discomfort with intimacy

If you find it hard to give love, it's often because you don't see the value in it. You may not directly associate giving love with happiness or fulfilment. Perhaps you've experienced love being weaponized against you – used as emotional blackmail, or manipulation.

Most of us can think of at least one life experience that was painful enough to give up on love. Hurt can cause you to wonder if it's worth the risk.

As you go through life, love usually grows organically in your close connections with your parents, relatives, children, pets and those within your immediate circle. It's as if you enter into an unspoken agreement that these relationships are based on giving and receiving love. You can even express it on a wider scale, such as a love for art, poetry, nature, music, sport, and so on. Love is boundless.

Everyone uses the word 'love', but when it comes to more intimate relationships, we all have a unique take on what it means and what it looks like. My idea of love may not be the same as yours because we are two different people. Your understanding could also be linked to positivity, negativity, trauma, pain, bliss, happiness, fulfilment, struggle, salvation, or any number of emotional states.

The relationships that we form naturally through blood ties or at work aren't so much a matter of choice but more about who we are stuck with. These are different from relationships we choose that may be based on romantic love, platonic love, or even pure sexual attraction. We can face difficulties in all types of relationships, but we can't always end them. The 'natural' ties with relatives, or even our community, can be problematic, and even if we try to withdraw from them, those ties might still remain in some way. As they say, 'You can choose your friends but you can't choose your family.'

On the other hand, the relationships we choose to have, such as those with a girlfriend, boyfriend, lover, husband, wife, or friend, are maintained through our own volition. That is to say, we decide whether to keep or end these relationships (unless some outside forces are controlling our choices for us, such as cultural norms or family pressures). This is a unique and powerful responsibility. When we consciously choose healthy, positive relationships, we can create heaven on earth. When done poorly, we can cause ourselves and others an incredible amount of suffering.

It's also possible that a past trauma prevents us from being able to change the way we approach relationships. A strong attachment to a certain kind of behaviour pattern can make us feel that we are incapable of developing healthy relationships or breaking free from unhealthy ones. I understand how challenging that might seem and sympathize with anyone who feels unable to walk away.

Some people may not feel that they have love in their lives, for a number of reasons. They might have lost touch with family or have differences that keep them apart. There are those who don't have close ties with anyone they can call friends; others who live an isolated life, suffer from social anxiety, or are completely estranged from their partner, spouse, children, and so on. All of these situations can lead to loneliness and a sense of isolation, especially if the person involved finds themself in that position unwillingly.

I believe that when we feel empowered enough to realize that it's up to us how we handle our intimate relationships, the decision to stay or leave will become a lot easier. Some of these relationships might be deeply meaningful to us or, in contrast, totally superficial. They could be lifelong partnerships that we work hard to invest in or one-night stands that we forget about the day after. There's no right or wrong here, and everyone has their own cache of personal experiences to refer to and talk about.

Many people throw themselves into intimate relationships without having any idea of how to actually handle them. These people don't know themselves yet, so haven't a clue what they are bringing to the table. They could be carrying past traumas or unhealthy expectations, and be seeking connections for all the wrong reasons. When this happens, they probably struggle to form solid, healthy relationships and will quickly move on to the next one, taking with them the same unresolved issues.

Trauma, past conditioning, or unprocessed emotions will just become more magnified within a relationship. Pain and unmet needs that you didn't even know you had can be easily triggered because the relationship, by its very nature, is expecting you to open up and be examined. It can be unbearably painful. But love has the capacity to bring light to the dark corridors of any heart that has been avoiding it for so long. That's why it's important to explore ourselves beforehand so we don't feel blinded and dazed by the brightness of love when it does appear.

What I've come to realize over the years is that nothing is, or ever will be, perfect in a relationship, and that's OK. Each one of us is constantly changing, growing, transforming, and discovering more about ourselves every day. There's no secret formula that says, 'If I do this, everything will be perfect,' because there are so many variables to consider. But knowing where the goalposts are really helps. From there, it takes a willingness and readiness on both sides to move forward.

ALL ABOARD

I like to think of these personal relationships as a train journey you embark on together, without any idea of where you are going. Once you decide to buy those tickets, it's a given that you enjoy being with each other and want to take this trip hand in hand. There's no better feeling in the world than having that important person by your side as you speed past the landscapes of life. You can enjoy the scenery together and discover new horizons. You might stop off somewhere you don't particularly like, or find a hidden gem you never knew existed. You may go through dark tunnels, only to come out into brilliant sunlight, and often notice the pace slowing down before picking up again. There could be periods of monotony or exciting revelations as you speed along the tracks together, and the trip itself will bring something valuable to you both.

It's difficult to navigate when you start such a journey if you don't know where you are in the first place – where is your north, your south? Which direction is east or west? When you begin your 'journey' with someone else, you can't predict how or when it will end. All you know initially is that you have chosen a travel buddy and want to sit next to them until you reach the end of the line, wherever that may be. If they also have no sense of where they are coming from, it's going to be a bit disorientating for both of you.

Most of us get on that train with a lot of baggage created from past experiences. No one embarks on a relationship with a clean slate – we all have a past, which forms a large part of how we act and think today. It could be how we were brought up, childhood memories, cultural beliefs, personal relationship experiences, the job we do, our self-perception, or even because of what we have read on the internet. Our luggage is absolutely stuffed with a lot of preconceptions based on what we've experienced so far.

If only we made strict choices about what we need and what can be left behind while packing before that journey so we travel light but still enjoy the trip.

That's the secret really for starting any new relationship – **to bring only what you need and not be weighed down by unnecessary stuff**. It's also one of the hardest things to do – much harder than packing your suitcase – because it's all tied up with deep-seated emotions, memories, and patterns of behaviour.

> **It's pretty impossible to enter a relationship without some baggage, but a good connection with someone can actually be a beautiful place to unpack if you have the right support. However, if you go into a relationship badly wounded, you will likely continue to irritate your wounds and hurt your partner in the process. In other words, it's important to embark on the healing process first.**

IT BEGINS WITH US

Before I met Kaushal, I didn't really know what a mature, meaningful relationship meant. Although I knew what I wanted, I had no idea how to build or maintain it, so that was a learning and unlearning process from day one. Firstly, I had to unlearn those old thought patterns that had built up from former experiences, and then I had to learn how to be fully committed to something that would benefit us both. It wasn't easy.

In truth, my relationship with my wife is a result of everything we have both experienced in life up to now, both as individuals and as a couple. We bring every single little thing that has made us who we are into our relationship, good or bad. We've had our ups and downs just like everyone else and I would never say that we have the perfect relationship, although it's something we are continuously working at. As long as we're both going in the same direction, I think we are on the right track.

We continue to surprise each other every so often with gifts. We still go on date nights together even though we're married. We regularly flirt and tease in the same sentences. We feed one another's mind, body, and soul. We pray for each other's wellbeing while the other person isn't around. But not every day in our love story is glamorous.

Sure, you can unload everything on them, but wouldn't it be fairer and better if you begin with a whole heart, an expanded mind, and the spirit of awareness and self-acceptance? If you can manage that, you will attract a partner who can offer the same or similar emotional maturity. When your desire to give and receive love is fulfilled without being blocked by pain, fear, or a trauma response, that's the way to attract and develop a fruitful relationship.

LET GO

No relationship is a total waste. Despite how painful they may be, they teach you about what you want and what you don't want. They can remind you that you deserve better. And if it's painful enough, a bad relationship can be the catalyst for a journey inward. But no relationship, either with a past lover or friend or family member, is worth damaging future opportunities to connect with others or yourself.

Every day starts anew, bringing its own chapter, and what you carry around with you is a choice. I encourage you to end each night and start each day freeing yourself from the suffering and unhelpful stories you may have about love. Invite a new version of possibilities and trust that you are worthy of love and others are worthy of receiving it.

THE MYTH OF TRUE LOVE

Even when we feel tremendously healed, love can still become complicated. After all, we're human and have incredible ways of messing things up. For starters, we've built idealistic notions surrounding true love. With these impossible expectations, modern relationships rarely stand a chance.

We've come to believe the popular myth that when we find true love, all of our problems will be solved. When we meet 'the one', we'll experience fulfilment, contentment, and happiness. I wish it were that simple. The reality is that divorce still happens, couples still break up, and there are a lot of people out there desperately searching for the next 'one'. It's a lot to expect of another person to fix all of your worries and fulfil all of your dreams. How would you feel if your partner expected that from you? Intimidated? Pressurized? Overwhelmed? Uncomfortable? Responsible?

We'll come back to the subject of expectations a bit later on, because it's one I know many people struggle with. For now, I want to remind you about the need to build that solid base, forming a sound relationship with yourself first, before you set off making the same mistakes you have made time and time again.

Just like emotional baggage, unreasonable expectations crowd our hearts and suffocate relationships. **True love feels like freedom, emotional liberation, a chance to be loved exactly as you are and to love another for exactly who they are.**

I want you to think about the beliefs you have that prevent you from being able to connect. I know these are tough questions and it's not easy to delve into some issues of your life that make you feel uncomfortable. What I will stress, though, is that by doing this type of inquiry, you will learn a lot about yourself, and that's worth every ounce of effort. You can start by asking yourself things like:

- How were you brought up? (place, culture, society, rules, beliefs, parental influence . . .)

- What conditioning was imposed on you by outside forces? (family beliefs, traditions, customs, norms, expectations . . .)

- How many of those are you still living by?

- Who told you what is right or wrong for you?

- If your caregivers told you what is right or wrong, who told them and how was that confirmed?

Once you start thinking about these questions, how does it make you feel? What thoughts come into your mind? How much is your self-identity tied up with societal norms, upbringing, and conditioning?

It's a big subject, and one that needs time to work through. We are all creatures of our environment to a large extent. Your family might include Christians, Hindus, Muslims and so on, so the chances are that you have been brought up in the same faith. The society you live in could be based on white male privilege, and that's shaped your view of the world. Homosexuality may be illegal in your country, so you live within the framework of that law, or your community may be very diverse, which feeds into your experience of what is normal.

All of the above go towards shaping who you are, although nothing is written in stone. You can, and should, be able to live by the personal value system that feels right for you, whether that goes against the current trend or not. When you live in accordance with your deepest values, they act like a satnav as you journey through life and relationships. Hopefully, you'll meet someone who shares those values, but that's not always the case, and you need to know how to respond if that occurs.

Growing up in a community where you're expected to prepare for marriage as soon as you begin to show some facial hair (very early in my case), and where marriage talks happen as soon as you date someone, I'm glad Kaushal and I waited and never let any pressures dictate the pace. We wanted to be in a place not to have a wedding, but a marriage. You can't arrange, force, or rush this type of commitment. You can only show up each and every moment, ready to create harmony in the next, despite whatever you may be facing.

We've been through an incredible journey: from meeting as kids who were merely attracted to each other to a place where we have learned to create organic happiness individually but express it as one. It's taken a lot of work to get here and it's going to take even more work to get to the next stage of our evolution, where we continually and selflessly give the love we've cultivated together to the rest of the world. But this love, this union, and this desire to improve the world in correlation to our growth, will always be worth working for.

For any couple out there, remember it's your journey, and there's no timeline or opinion that you need to follow to pursue it correctly. Live, learn, love, and grow – together.

The more self-awareness you have, the better you will be at putting yourself out there and going on to be a stable partner. Sometimes, one half of a couple may have found that inner balance while the other half has unresolved issues. That's OK, because one can help the other to grow if they are also ready and willing to do so. Even if you have issues you are still grappling with, you can work through them with a partner and create a stronger bond if there is a supportive space in the relationship to do so.

'I feel kind of bad when I go out every Friday evening with my mates because my girlfriend complains about it all the time.'

One thing I hear from many people is that they feel they are losing their identity in a particular relationship. It's not something that happens overnight, but more of a gradual shift that creeps up on you. One minute, you are free to do whatever you want and before you know it, you feel guilty if you go out with your friends. You start feeling like you're doing something wrong and gradually lose your independence and your sense of 'I'. Even if your partner is the sweetest, kindest, most loving person in the world, it can seem like everything you do in life has to include them, otherwise, what kind of couple are you? On the other hand, you may internally begin to feel restricted, constrained, and resentful.

This is probably because you haven't been able to establish the right kind of boundaries yet, or are following the type of relationship pattern you are used to. If you deal with these issues beforehand and have a partner who can understand and accept where you are coming from, it is possible to avoid these pitfalls. That's why I say that mastering your inner map is crucial if you want to enjoy a healthy, happy relationship in the future.

We are complicated, for sure, but if you can decode everything that has been piled on top of you in life, you will get a better understanding of your self-identity. Why is this important? Well, imagine striking up a relationship with someone who has amnesia and no memory of who they are. How would that work?

In effect, a lot of us are going through life with some kind of identity amnesia – totally disconnected from who we really are. We behave according to learned habits and respond to emotional triggers without knowing why. Often, we interpret the way in which someone responds to us as an image of who we really are, even though this isn't the case. And yet, we expect others to understand us. Hold on a minute, though – do we even understand ourselves?

It's worth pausing here and thinking about that.

- Do you know why you react the way you do to certain triggers?

- Can you explain your thoughts?

- Are they all justified?

- Are you being honest with yourself?

- Do you feel like you have reached your potential?

- Do your negative feelings about yourself affect how you see others?

- What about how they see you?

These are questions that I think we should all be able to answer.

Often, the person we think we need to be in order to feel safe, validated, successful, and happy is essentially a personality that we form to fit in and avoid pain and danger. It's based on other people's impositions, their expectations, and our trauma.

In other words, it's created through fear, control, and emotional pain. Ultimately, we become this person to feel and receive love – even though it's mostly conditional because it's given based on what we do and how we act.

Our authentic self is found beyond that, when we express ourselves as we are. Imagine who and how you would be if you had never been hurt in the past, for example. What if other people's opinions didn't matter or if you lived alone on a desert island? You might discover a joyful, curious, loving, liberated individual who is free to express their own views, meet their own needs, stay true to their intuition, living in line with their own current beliefs and values.

Living in line with your authentic self will look different as you go through each stage of your life. What was once 'fact' to you as a teenager won't always apply in your adult life, and this is all part of adhering to your current belief systems while accepting previous versions of you. It can also include how you see yourself in the future. When people love you as you are and express their love unconditionally, it's much purer, because, it's accepting of your past, present, and future.

> **If you stop trying to get people to like you for who you aren't but for who you really are instead, you will notice how authentic people and experiences align with you naturally.**

For those who lean towards a spiritual outlook on life, the concept of authenticity might look different. We might say it's your truth – but the truth is absolute, which means it doesn't change. It's true whether you believe it or not, but your identity can always change throughout life. Therefore, seeing life through a spiritual lens might mean considering the former description of authenticity more like a true-for-now type of personality that isn't limited by fear, expectations, and trauma.

However, the unchanging you is different. It will remain, regardless of how your life changes. You might call it soul or pure consciousness. In ancient Indian texts called the Upanishads,[3] it's known as the Atman, and it's basically Self with a capital S. It's a timeless, steady, and blissful centre that is connected to everyone and everything around us. In a way, when we remove the fear and conditioning, the closer we get to it and can express it in our everyday lives.

When you start to look at all of the things you have gone through in the past, how you've been brought up, and what kind of conditioning has been imposed on you, you will see yourself differently. It's like a fog lifting, allowing you to have a clearer picture. It's not easy to do because it means meeting some scars or pain on the way. You may have gone through intense heartbreak and could be still holding on to intense feelings of fear, doubt, and insecurity. These are all normal reactions to whatever you have dealt with, but it's important to heal and move on. Bringing them into your new relationships can deepen the scars and intensify those negative feelings you are harbouring. It's time to let go of anything that prevents you from enjoying loving, fulfilled relationships with those special people in your life.

The way we connect with each other in our relationships will continue to evolve, but that inherent need to give and receive love is as true today as it was at the dawn of time. Everything we do in this life is a means to an end and, ultimately, we are all looking for love. Being able to establish closeness with someone can bring a great sense of comfort, belonging, fulfilment and contentment, so it's definitely worth pursuing. You can begin by connecting with your inner self, exploring your boundaries, and getting to know the real you. After all, the more you know yourself, the more you have to share with someone else.

Once you get back in touch with the person you really are and have understood how to reframe your past experiences in a more uplifting way, you will be in a much better place to stretch out your hand to another. Next, we'll explore the art of having an open heart – one that is truly ready to receive and give love without the fear of losing yourself in the process or seeking something in return.

GETTING CLOSER TO YOURSELF

Here are some more tools to help you return to yourself. You can practise a few or all of them daily on your path to self-awareness.

- **Keep a journal.** Writing down your thoughts and feelings each day is a great way to raise your consciousness about who you really are and identify areas of healing. Note how you feel about something that happened or didn't happen to you. Express your worries, doubts, fears, or the pain you have experienced, as well as including any joy, gratitude, or hope you felt. Reflect on what you have written and think about how you can bring greater positivity and love into your life. Look back often on what you have written. Journaling records changes in thoughts and emotions to track progress and direction while allowing you to connect with your own voice. If you prefer a little more direction than a blank notebook, check out *The Greatest Self-Help Book (is the one written by you)*, a journal where you'll find lots of prompts and exercises.

- **Spiritual, physical, and mental self-care.** Looking after all these aspects is crucial if you want to enjoy a healthy relationship with someone else. Take care of your spiritual needs by spending some time meditating or simply sitting quietly and observing your breath. Look after your physical wellness with healthy eating and regular exercise. Nourish your mind with some light reading. You will find plenty of ways to practise self-care in my book *Good Vibes, Good Life*, which you can check out if you haven't read it yet.

- **Maintain hobbies/interests.** Follow your passions and do what you love. Whether that's playing football, dancing, writing, travelling, painting, or DIY, immerse yourself in activities that bring you personal freedom and a sense of accomplishment. These will feed your sense of self-worth and help you to rediscover joy in your life – something we all need.

- **Self-regulation.** During turbulent moments, acknowledge any emotions and observe them from a distance. According to Harvard-trained author and neuroanatomist Dr Jill Bolte Taylor, it takes less than 90 seconds for emotions to dissipate.[4] Failing to acknowledge them will allow the same thoughts to trigger the emotions repeatedly. Attempting to resist them will give them further influence over you. The simple act of noticing them tamps down activity in the part of the brain called the amygdala, reducing their charge. Therefore, if you are feeling anger, pause for 90 seconds, take a deep breath and notice how it is a feeling, but it's not who you are. Let it float on by, and then strongly exhale. Finally, decide which feeling you would prefer to have in those moments and lean towards that trajectory. If the anger continues, inspect the thoughts which may be restimulating the circuitry by journaling.

Audit your heart and mind regularly.

Where have you contributed to the breakdown of your relationships?

What false beliefs about love are putting you at risk of unfulfillment?

As challenging as this first chapter may have been, it is filled with opportunities for you to design and define love for yourself. Removing the influence of trauma, failed relationships, and a broken family system, find what love is to you through confrontational self-discovery. Love yourself whole. This is the best glow-up you can have. Your journey towards more fulfilling connections has begun.

KEY INSIGHTS

- We learn a particular way to love from the moment we are born.

- When you ask yourself who you are and what you need, the answers may surprise you.

- Learning to unblock the ability to truly love is crucial.

- Self-awareness and self-knowledge allow you to love others completely.

- Starting a relationship is like a journey in which you don't always know the destination.

- Unblocking past pain and negative experiences can be done.

- Make space in your heart for yourself and your partner.

- Society's common view of true love is a myth, but deep connection is a real possibility.

- By rediscovering your authentic self, you can nurture greater closeness with others.

Chapter 2

CLOSED HEART, OPEN HEART

A relationship forms a trinity – you, the other person, and the connection. The trajectory of the relationship will depend on the direction in which the individuals are heading.

Rory's parents split up when he was five. He grew up never seeing his dad much after that, and his mum was always working a lot of hours to support the family, so he spent most of his early childhood pretty much alone. His mum often had different boyfriends coming and going and he didn't feel secure with the instability going on around him. He found it hard to make friends as they were always moving house, and by the time he got to his late teens, those emotions had developed into resentment and anger. When it came to relationships, he would usually dump the girl after seeing her a couple of times, and didn't feel like he was capable of loving anyone enough to have a serious thing with them.

When I met Rory and spoke about all of this, he was completely shut down emotionally, which was a pity as he is such a nice guy with a lot of tucked-away love to offer others. I could understand why he behaved the way he did, but could also see that he had never sat down to really think about what was going on underneath the surface. Those strong emotions of anger, resentment, and even a sense of insecurity, were actually making him miserable. Not only that: they were blocking him from moving forward to enjoy a warm, close relationship with anyone.

No one can change Rory's past. It happened years ago and is gone. It's the after-effects that linger, seeping into his every being and making him believe that his past is to blame for the way his life is now. Obviously, our past moulds us to a great extent, and we are products of that. But that doesn't mean it has to shape our present, or even our future. I'm not a psychologist, so I'm not going to try to make any kind of psychological analysis here about Rory and his upbringing. What I can do, though, is to work through some of his issues with him and help him to reset the balance.

Instead of saying, 'I'm like this because such and such happened to me,' I prefer the statement, 'This happened to me, but I'm not going to let it stop me from finding happiness.'

Through self-love, you can shatter the parts of your ego and personality that were formed through pain – the bits of emotional armour that were meant to protect your heart after it was hurt. When you carry this old, heavy armour into every relationship, it's as if you're preparing for battle. It's time to disarm, letting your body, mind, and spirit know that you are inviting love not war. The first step in doing so is to let go.

ARE YOU AN EMOTIONAL HOARDER?

Rory is one of those people I would describe as an emotional hoarder, just in the same way that people hoard clothes, rubbish, or even cats. We all hoard things from our past to a certain degree, but some of us are full to the brim of stuff that we really, really don't need. This is a kind of habit we get into that we think serves some kind of need or purpose but, in reality, it suffocates us.

Hoarding is a mental disorder recognized by health professionals as the inability to get rid of or part with (often quite trivial) possessions due to a perceived need to save the items. The idea of letting go of these possessions or making decisions about what to keep can cause considerable distress. I think that, in many ways, emotional hoarding is similar. Our desire to hold on to our past can create so much unhappiness and discomfort, and prevent us from living fulfilling lives. When it comes to relationships, just think about which emotions from your past you are bringing to the present.

How many times have you heard parents, friends, or even work colleagues bickering about what was said or done yesterday, last week, or even years ago? You might recognize this kind of habit in your own relationship with your girlfriend, boyfriend, partner, or spouse, where things get dragged up into the conversation that happened in the past. The reason you keep up this kind of interaction is because you've been hoarding your thoughts and feelings surrounding them. Constantly reminding your boyfriend of how he forgot your birthday last year and rubbing it in his face every chance you get isn't going to make anybody happy – not you, not him, nobody. Instead, this will lead to resentment on both sides, which most therapists agree is a prime suspect for relationship ruin.

What are you really trying to say when you bring up things from the past that upset you? That he doesn't care about you or love you? Why do you really feel like that? What else is going on inside you and how many of those feelings are actually attached to something much, much deeper?

I get it – forgetting someone's birthday can be a big thing, but an oversight doesn't necessarily mean your boyfriend doesn't love you or care about you. Often, it has more to do with the expectations within a relationship, which are closely linked to what you have experienced in the past and the needs that spring from that. When you remind your partner all the time of this or any 'crime', you are actually dwelling on your own past disappointments and pain. It's not that you want to; you just haven't found a way to stop doing it. The way we interact, have conversations, and argue reveals a lot about our emotional hoarding habit, and understanding new ways to communicate will help.

The cat-loving woman down the road who lives with fifty felines can't possibly look after all of them. After beginning with one or two, she keeps adopting more and more until she gets to the point where she feels overwhelmed. The cats keep breeding at will, do their business everywhere, and there's a lot of cross-infection. The poor woman can't cope and someone needs to step in and help her. No one can live healthily in such conditions – but it's hard for her to accept because she loves all of her cats so much.

Some of us may cling to pain because we think it's a part of who we are, while others might attach themselves to people who trigger negative feelings from their past because they think that's the normal state to be in. When you hoard all of those emotions, they keep resurfacing without being resolved.

When Rory talks about his inability to connect emotionally with someone, it isn't because he is unfeeling or uncaring. It's more likely that he is letting his insecurity and resentment affect his behaviour. These are real, valid emotions, but that doesn't mean that he needs to cling on to them any more. It can play out in the opposite way with someone who has a past similar to Rory's – he could end up being too clingy, attaching himself to anyone who shows the slightest interest in him, and desperately trying to form relationships for all the wrong reasons.

There's no blueprint for how we interpret our past or use our experiences in the present. Everyone is different, but we all act in response to what we have gone through, no matter what that response is.

Imagine where the cat lady would be if she had just one or two cats. Their home would be so much cleaner, with plenty of space to roam. The pets would likely be happy and healthy and the woman would be relieved of all that excess pressure. Similarly, **when we relinquish painful memories, we create space in our heart, decluttering it of resentment, anger, fear, and pain.** But it can be easier said than done if you are unconsciously attached to maintaining these feelings.

HOW ATTACHED ARE YOU?

Your memories and experiences of when you were a child may be vague, or it could be that you can't access them at all. Psychologists often talk about 'attachment issues', but it can be hard to be aware of any that you may have. That's why it's difficult to know why you or someone you know acts the way they do as a grown adult. I honestly never understood what the problem was with me when I was going through a phase of not being able to commit to a relationship, and today I see many people struggling with things like conflict, insecurity, jealousy, possessiveness, or even controlling behaviour. Many of these behaviours are triggered by our attachment style.

> **Going into any relationship is a minefield because there are so many hidden challenges that might come up. Two people with totally different stories trying to make a new one together can be explosive.**

You might have very specific expectations of how your partner should behave and also expect them to accept the way you are. If these patterns are old, ingrained habits, they could stunt the relationship from the start and that's obviously not what you want.

I get to hear about a lot of people's stories in my work and, sure enough, many of them remind me of the type of attachment styles that are well known and talked about by wellness coaches, psychologists, and relationship experts. Sometimes, we just can't understand why we don't feel fulfilled in our relationships, but attachment styles provide us with a clue.

The concept of attachment theory was first introduced by the psychologists John Bowlby and Mary Ainsworth in the 1970s, and since then, a lot of research has been done on the subject. To put it briefly, your attachment style is the specific way that you relate to others in relationships. It's something that was shaped in your early childhood in response to your relationship with your caregivers. Your adult attachment style is, essentially, a mirror of the earlier dynamic you developed with your caregivers as an infant. Just in the way you learned (or didn't) to love, you also learned to what degree to attach or not attach to another person, regardless of how important and valued their role in your life.

It's pretty clear that attachment is an emotional bond with another person, and we all exhibit one kind of attachment or another in our relationships.

According to attachment theory,[5] there are four different attachment styles:

1. **Secure.** You find it easy to love and be loved, and to trust others. You're not afraid of intimacy or of your partner needing/wanting space from you. You are better able to enjoy stable, fulfilling relationships and have healthy responses and coping mechanisms for relationship conflict.

2. **Anxious.** You have a tendency to feel insecure and to worry about your relationship a lot. You might feel like your partner doesn't care enough about you or find it hard to trust them and often have dramatic relationship experiences. When conflicts arise, you tend to cling to your partner more tightly in fear of them leaving and are more likely to forgo your own needs for the sake of the relationship.

3. **Dismissive Avoidant.** You struggle to get close to others and have a fear of intimacy that you may not even be aware of. Relationships can feel suffocating and prevent you from making a commitment. You may miss important emotional cues within yourself and others and are often considered cold and uncaring, even though you are thoughtful but fail to express it.

4. **Fearful Avoidant.** This is a combination of avoidant and anxious attachment styles. You might crave affection and love but also avoid relationships to minimize your chances of getting hurt. Your response to relationship conflict varies and you are prone to creating a push–pull dynamic with your partner.

Attachment styles apply to all of our relationships, and not just the romantic ones. Understanding them can be helpful when it comes to building more supportive, peaceful relationships with family, friends, and partners. Although we can never completely understand another person or be in control of our own responses to emotional triggers, we can gain some awareness of where those reactions come from and be more compassionate with ourselves and the other person.

I mention compassion because it's an essential part of any relationship. If you look solely at someone's reaction to a situation, a lot of misunderstanding can follow. You might misinterpret their behaviour towards you, think they are deliberately trying to hurt you, or don't love you enough. By having some compassion, you will see them through a totally different lens and have a much better chance of working things out together as a team.

Many of us will have a mixture of attachment styles, with one more dominant than the other – and we could also show different attachment styles in different kinds of relationships. As I said in Chapter 1, we are already developing these attachment styles as babies, but that doesn't mean we are incapable of changing them.

How is your attachment style affecting your relationship? First of all, you need to know which attachment style refers to you, and this is something a therapist or health professional can help you with. Once you are more aware of which attachment style seems to be the most dominant, you can learn to work through it and find ways to change it if it's causing you to experience unhealthy relationships.

There are plenty of attachment style tests online and the one currently on www.attachmentproject.com is quite fun to do, plus it's free. It's worth bearing in mind that you can always seek professional help if you really want to get to the root of your emotions and reactions in your relationships. There's also a great book on the subject by Amir Levine and Rachel Heller called *Attached: Are you Anxious, Avoidant or Secure? How the science of adult attachment can help you find – and keep – love*.

Here are some examples of the three problematic attachment styles that you might be able to relate to:

• **Sam & Keisha**

Sam can be so distant sometimes and she's one of those people who doesn't open up very easily. Her girlfriend, Keisha, complains that they don't talk through their problems and it's like Sam just shuts down. She'll even walk out when Keisha tries to start any kind of conversation about an issue. Sam will do anything to avoid confrontation. Keisha is often left feeling like Sam doesn't care enough about her. **Sam may be exhibiting a dismissive/avoidant attachment style.**

- **Max & Isla**

  Isla recently met Max, who seems like a nice guy, but because Isla is very insecure, she goes over the top when she thinks Max is looking at other girls. She threw a tantrum at a party the other day, accusing him of not paying enough attention to her because he was talking to his mates. Even though she is really keen on him, she constantly questions how much he really likes her. **Isla may be exhibiting an anxious attachment style.**

- **Charlie & Mia**

  Mia loves Charlie, who she's been dating for a few months, but she has recently started to feel panicky. After being hurt in the past, she's afraid to express her feelings and can't let herself enjoy the relationship to the fullest. When Charlie tries to approach her about it, she ends up snapping back at him and goes into a mood. It's really hard for Charlie to understand what's going on with her. **Mia may be exhibiting a fearful/avoidant attachment style.**

We all have that need for intimate connection, but can't always achieve it with everyone we meet. What is important to realize is that all of the above examples are behaviours, and don't describe someone's exact personality. These behaviours are a way of coping after previous (bad) experiences, rather than true personality traits. Your emotions aren't always true and are often based on unconscious assumptions about your relationship, which is not the same as the one before that or those of your childhood. You do have the strength to exercise choice and can use agency when dealing with your life today, even if you aren't used to doing that.

If you see yourself in Sam, Isla, or Mia, at least you know that lots of people handle relationships in the same way as you do. You aren't the only one who finds it difficult to face conflict, or has been burned in a past relationship and is trying to avoid the same thing happening again.

What would the ideal scenario be? I guess, something like the couple Shah & Laura, who have **a secure attachment style**.

- Shah has been with his partner, Laura, for over five years now. You can tell that they are still pretty connected to each other while both of them work and maintain their independence. Even though they've had their fair share of problems, it's obvious from how they behave that they support each other immensely and are still very much in love. **They feel secure, independent, supported, and emotionally connected.**

Most of us have secure attachments that keep us safe, make us feel concern for our loved ones, and enable us to help others. You don't need to feel bad if you haven't found the person who can help you get over your insecurities or if you feel uncomfortable about getting emotionally intimate with them.

There is another kind of attachment that you might have come across if you are more spiritually orientated, like me, and that's the idea of clinging to or obsessing over sensory objects that ultimately lead to suffering. These include a fixation on self-related concepts, thoughts, feelings, goals, and possessions. The more we try to keep hold of them, the more they have hold of us. It's a type of Eastern philosophy found in Buddhism that has been made popular recently by people such as the writer and speaker Alan Watts, and has been embodied into many mindfulness, positive thinking, and wellness platforms today.

In spiritual philosophy, attachment describes bondage, which inevitably leads to disappointment. Attachment Theory, by contrast, stresses the need for human bonding to thrive.

Going back to the psychological attachments I was talking about, there will be triggers that stimulate your psychological attachment style when you begin a relationship and are reminded of past experiences. It's all normal and even healthy, to a certain degree. I even maintain that it's a real opportunity for you to grow and overcome whatever you are carrying around with you from the past.

Your nervous system has been used to reacting in a certain way and it's going to take some time to create new neural pathways that resonate with love instead of fear. But it is possible when the relationship allows for space to do so.

If you have a loving, understanding partner and you are prepared to do some self-work, you can have your needs met and feel secure. It's not impossible, but requires a willingness to recognize your vulnerabilities, to lay them out on the table, and decide which ones you don't need any more.

FREE YOURSELF FROM ATTACHMENTS

No one attachment style is worse than another. The majority are rooted in insecurity, fear, and a lack of love – given or received. But no matter how damaging, you can overcome your attachment through self-compassion, consistent effort, and support.

If you feel insecure within a relationship, it could be that your partner isn't right for you or ready to grow and get over their own issues. You'll know when you meet someone who lets you work through your worries in a safe, loving space. It is important to avoid scenarios or people that trigger your attachment and, instead, to seek supportive and healthy relationship dynamics. In the meantime, it's good to remember that there's no shame to your inability to cope within an intimate relationship. It doesn't make you a failure or a bad person – you are on a healing journey, that's all.

Try to honour your emotional needs and express when you feel afraid, hurt, worried, incapable, or stressed. Keeping them inside may seem like the easy answer, but you recall what I said about hoarding, right? And you know, if you aren't honest and open with your partner, they will never be able to understand what's eating you. You can't expect them to guess, have a crystal ball, or be a mind reader – you've got to explain stuff to them.

When you can accept yourself, it will be a lot easier for the other person to accept you, and they will feel secure, knowing that you are comfortable with who you are. It's nothing to do with finding fault or berating yourself and everything to do with saying, 'This is the behaviour pattern I've been following so far, and I would like to change that.'

CUT-OFF LINES

Sometimes, all it takes is for us to draw a line – I like to call them cut-off lines. If someone like Rory, who I talked about earlier, looks at what his problems are now, they are most likely linked to his past. But there's got to be a cut-off point –

a time when he says to himself, 'Okay, that was then and this is now.' It's not as simple as it sounds, obviously, because it means sorting through a lot of things that he has been hanging on to without even realizing it.

Some might call this 'tough love', but it's absolutely necessary for us to ditch the things that we know are cutting us off from love, through self-compassion. Process it. Let it go. Do this as many times as you need to. Write a farewell letter and burn it if you must. But make a conscious effort to free yourself of the negativity that poisons your opportunities to connect with yourself and others.

Consider what conditioning or hard lessons from your past are serving you and which ones aren't. Being dumped by a boyfriend may have hurt a lot, but how much of that was about you and how much of it was just a natural end to your relationship? Do you associate that feeling of rejection with past failures and amplify them, or look at the case in isolation and move on? As humans, we tend to connect the dots and fail to see unpleasant experiences as singular. The habit of creating a dialogue around what happens to you deepens your attachment and identification with it. You are only reinforcing those negative perceptions when you say things like, 'Of course he left. They always do. Everyone I start to love disappears.'

If you are emotionally hoarding past pain and trauma, no doubt being rejected today is twice as painful, even triple, because it feels like a build-up of previous unresolved emotions. That's why the cut-off line works – separating what is going on in your life now from what happened to you in the past. Having as your point of reference something that happened way back, when you were more vulnerable or impressionable, is understandable. But it's time to shift that point of reference and set your compass to a new location – to today. Focus on what you want, not what you've had. It is very difficult to resurrect dead love, although you are offered the opportunity to create it within yourself and share it with others many times in any given day.

You are here in the present, armed with what you know now. **Use your past to propel you forward, rather than letting it drag you down.** It's the difference between war and peace, a famine or a feast, hate and love, sadness and bliss – which one do you prefer? Draw up the anchor of your past and sail forth into a brighter future where you can create the relationships your spirit craves. The beautiful thing about having a natural appetite for love, despite having relationships that have starved us of it, is that you will continue to seek it out. And the search for love is one of life's greatest journeys. But as with every journey, there are bound to be a few wrong turns and hiccups.

DEALING WITH HEARTBREAK

Most people talk about experiencing some kind of heartbreak after a relationship ends and feel like they are victims of an extremely painful event. It does hurt to suffer from loss or rejection and there's no denying that. Depending on how attached you are to another, a break-up can feel like the death of a loved one. These are perfectly natural emotions and no one can blame you for feeling them. The downfall of future relationships happens when that heartbreak is carried from one connection to another. But how differently would you love if your heart had never been broken? Who were you before the heartbreak? You can be that person again, and more, and love like you've never lost. It is possible to learn from your experiences and forgive, heal, and move on. Honestly, it is.

Ask any cardiologist, and they'll tell you that your heart is just part of your anatomy. It's the main organ of your cardiovascular system and pumps blood throughout your body, as well as affecting blood pressure. So why do we talk about the heart as if it's part of our emotional state? Well, I guess there are many answers to that.

Being in love can make us feel alive, so losing love can feel like our life has come to an end (metaphorically speaking). Having a broken heart simply means that we feel intense emotions like stress or pain; a deep longing for something we have lost. And often, intense emotional pain or stress can literally feel like a tightness or weight on our chest. Matsyasana, or Fish Pose, is a yoga position often recommended by yogis to those suffering heartache. In the position, you open up the chest space and breathe into the heart centre. This honours both the physiological and emotional heart. In yoga, the belief is that there is no separation between the two.

The ancients recognized the heart as the centre of our life force. In Chinese medicine, it is the 'emperor of all the organs'.[6] In Vedantic philosophy, the heart holds the Self and is a place for unity and connection with cosmic energy. In Christianity, the heart is where the true character of a person lies, as pointed out in Proverbs 4:23: 'Keep your heart with all diligence, for out of it spring the issues of life.'[7] Many others today believe that the heart is the centre of healing, wellbeing, and wellness. In that respect, it's obvious why we talk about the heart as if it is the singular most important thing in our whole existence.

We aren't really referring to the physical organ, though, but to our emotions and feelings. It's true that stress can have a negative effect on our heart, while being happy can impact our cardiovascular health, so there is definitely a connection between what we feel emotionally, and the workings of our heart. The heart is also a symbol of wisdom and intuition and is often talked about as being the centre of our being – sometimes our consciousness, or true Self.

In our culture especially, love is very much tied up with the workings of the heart. Matters of the heart, affairs of the heart – there's no shortage of phrases we use that include references to the heart. We all understand that we're talking about intense feelings that are reciprocated or rejected. The concept of romance itself is built on the 'state' of our heart, and such relationships are one of the most precious gifts of our existence. They allow us to engage with another person on a physical, mental, emotional, and spiritual level. They can be empowering and life-changing. Ironically, they can also be the source of intense distress, anguish, and emotional pain if they go wrong.

In that respect, carrying around sadness and negative memories, or being tied to harmful habits and unrealistic expectations, can lead to heartbreak. It can be truly soul-destroying to suffer a break-up, a divorce, or a separation, and equally painful to be trapped in an unhappy, unfulfilling relationship.

It's no wonder that you feel your world is coming to an end when you suffer heartbreak. If you aren't fully in tune with your emotions or have a lack of self-awareness, your heart is going to take some knocks, because it becomes completely exposed. But protecting it doesn't mean shutting down your emotions or being cold. It actually means the opposite – opening up to explore your fears, hopes, doubts, or worries, and resolving whatever has been keeping you locked in the past. This takes guts, but it can be done if you practise self-love, first and foremost. Being in a caring, supportive relationship can also allow you to confront your issues and lead you on a path of total self-transformation. You don't need to do it alone, but it is important that you raise your awareness of your behaviour and reactions at all times.

HEALING THE HEART

'Being deeply loved by someone gives you strength while loving someone deeply gives you courage.' – Lao Tzu

If you are suffering from heartbreak, you might be wondering what you did wrong, why your partner broke up with you, how they could be so cruel. I feel for you and know it can be a torturous experience. People often say it takes time to heal and, in some ways, that's true. What usually happens, though, is that the sands of time slowly sweep over the wounds, without them ever healing. This happens when we don't address what we have been through and, instead, allow all of that pain to sink into the deepest, darkest parts of our psyche without addressing it.

No one can heal without tending to their wounds with care and compassion. In a way, rejections are invitations to love yourself more.

If you really think about it, your heartbreak is closely linked to how you see the world. That view may be defined by mistrust, fear, self-sabotage, disempowerment, or a victim mentality. These aren't obvious things that will come to your mind when you are crying over a broken relationship, but they do alter your perspective.

Everyone has suffered rejection, hurt, and pain in the past in some way, whether those elements were very subtle or extremely dramatic. Every time you had a knock-back, received negative comments, were disappointed by someone, or witnessed harmful behaviour, you stored an interpretation of them. These go on to colour the lens of anything that happens to you. They aren't necessarily who you are, just the lens through which you interpret what you experience.

When you start a new relationship, no doubt you are on a high. You feel great about yourself because you are loved, admired, appreciated, and wanted. Your self-worth rises to new levels because someone loves you. It's all music and roses. When the relationship ends, you take a nosedive, experiencing feelings of failure and self-doubt, thinking there's something wrong with you, or that you're not 'good enough'. That's a terrible penance to pay, and one we inflict on ourselves without mercy.

It's funny how, when we are in love, our attention shifts fully to the other person as they become the centre of our world. On the other hand, after a painful break-up, we turn in on ourselves and over-obsess on our failures.

This shift in attention or focus, from the 'one' to ourselves, is like experiencing a tectonic earthquake, unsettling our very existence. If we don't feel balanced within ourselves before entering into a relationship, it's easy for us to become disorientated when things don't work out. You may even be the one to instigate the break-up, and leave it carrying the burden of guilt, shame, or great sadness. This could seriously stop you investing in other relationships in the future because you want to avoid such harmful emotions recurring.

It doesn't need to be that way.

It is possible to enjoy all that an intimate relationship has to offer without bringing your past into it. You can also grow and cultivate healthier behaviour patterns within a relationship, despite your past, if you are willing to embark on it with an open heart.

Here's an example of what I mean:

Sarah separated from her husband after an eight-year marriage. It was a dramatic break-up because they were always fighting with each other and, in the end, things got out of hand. Her husband began drinking and being physically abusive, so she had to leave him. After a couple of years, Sarah met Guy and they started dating. She was extremely critical of him when they went out if he had more than one drink, and she couldn't relax. She kept remembering those awful moments with her ex, where he would belittle and threaten her when he was drunk. She was terrified of experiencing the same thing with Guy.

On the other hand, Guy had grown up in a household with an alcoholic father and had vowed never to drink to the extent that he would abuse his wife or kids. He couldn't understand Sarah's nervousness whenever they went out together and started thinking that she simply didn't want him to have a good time. He liked her a lot but felt that she was a bit of a wet blanket and her nagging started to get on his nerves.

Two different people, both bringing their own experiences to the table, but unable to communicate well enough to overcome their issues. The thing is, Sarah was coming into the relationship with very specific preconceived expectations – she believed that Guy was no different from her husband. The template that she had in her head could prove to be disastrous.

HOW CAN WE BUILD NEW RELATIONSHIPS AFTER HEARTBREAK?

The heart can harbour pain, which leads us to behave, think, and feel a certain way. We can go into self-protection overload or even avoidance. But the heart can also offer us the chance to experience love, to be brave, willing, and curious. Being locked down to emotions also means being locked out of love, and no one wants that.

The solution to Sarah's predicament might have been simple, but was very hard to execute. Firstly, to recognize that she wasn't responsible for her ex-husband's behaviour, so had no need to doubt her self-worth. Secondly, that Guy is a completely different person from her ex. By overcoming her own fear of experiencing the same trauma with another man, she would be able to cultivate a deeper bond with Guy and enjoy a nourishing relationship. She would need to draw that line between her past and her present, discarding those destructive thought patterns at the starting point. It's not that easy to do, I know, but at least by trying, she can look forward to a happier future.

A lot of our negative experiences leave deep wounds that seem impossible to heal. They will do, but they need to be tended to, not ignored. You can't expect someone to recover from an injury if they don't receive treatment. In the same way, you can't expect to get better after a painful break-up if you don't look at what went wrong, where your responsibility lay, and what can be done to correct it in the future. This is also a form of self-love; accepting that there are dark parts within you screaming for light and acknowledging that you need to tend to them.

This all takes some soul searching and having full awareness of who you are, strengths, weaknesses, and all. There's no such thing as a perfect person, and no need to aspire to that, thankfully. What you can do, though, is introduce some new ways of being into your life – ways to help you work through what happened and how you reacted to it.

By thinking about what your emotional response was, you will get some insight into how those thoughts and reactions are dominating the way you are behaving now. It's worth doing if you want to move on and establish a healthier relationship with yourself, before you pursue a connection with someone else.

THE HEART HAS NO LIMITS

Just as this vast Universe of ours is limitless, so too is the heart's capacity for love. You may not feel that way if you are suffering from a broken heart. Notice how we often use the word 'suffering', as if having a broken heart is some kind of illness that needs treatment. That feeling of being completely destroyed when you lose someone you love is so overwhelming that it can truly feel as if you are sick.

I really couldn't hazard a guess as to how many songs have been written about broken hearts, how many movies made or books written, and how many people have experienced that feeling. The great Chilean poet Pablo Neruda is well known for his love letters, and one of his sonnets in particular is an insightful reflection on the way we approach love. He talks of the intensity of love and the capacity to surrender to it completely as he writes:

I love you only because it's you the one I love;
I hate you deeply, and hating you
Bend to you, and the measure of my changing love for you
Is that I do not see you but love you blindly.[8]

There's nothing more magical than falling in love and discovering all the wonders that it can bring into our lives. Who doesn't want to experience it to the fullest? I'm as romantic as the next man and can honestly say that since meeting my wife, my life has become so much richer in every way. What I do think, though, is that usually we walk into a relationship completely blind. We know nothing about the other person and, as the relationship grows, their real self is slowly revealed, just in the same way that we reveal ourselves to them. Through that loving interaction and connection, it's possible to grow together and create something truly divine.

But, as Neruda so eloquently puts it, often we are in love with the idea of love, without really seeing ourselves or the person in front of us. We can be so close to the light that it blinds us to reality. We get dazed and confused by it, losing our orientation and sense of direction, only to be devastated when that love is taken away from us. We become heartsick . . . heartbroken.

Heartbreak is pain, loss, grief, and suffering, for sure. So, how will you go about things the next time around?

That's something you need to explore if you want to enter into a new relationship with greater clarity and a deeper sense of self.

- What preconceptions will you carry into it based on your past experiences?

- What expectations will you have of yourself and the other person?

- Will you be ready to honour your own needs while meeting the needs of your partner?

- Can you enter into a new relationship while protecting your boundaries?

These are difficult but worthwhile questions you could ask yourself.

IT'S OK TO GRIEVE

Grief is a very normal human emotion that serves an evolutionary purpose. It is a feeling of loss: that we no longer have something we thought belonged to us. You might experience grief when you lose a person – or when you lose other things, such as your job or plans you made that didn't come to fruition. Although it isn't a pleasant experience by any means, it can propel us into forming deeper bonds with others for our own wellness and protection.

Accepting that we are no longer with our partner is painful and heart-wrenching. It requires that we come to terms with reality and learn to live with that. This means honouring our emotions without judgement and allowing them to manifest naturally. It's OK to say, 'I feel sad', and better to avoid thinking things like, 'I'm overreacting'. You deserve to go through this period of hurt and to take the time to look at why the relationship didn't work out.

Remember that a sore won't heal if it is covered – it needs fresh air to help the cells regenerate, so don't deny yourself this process. Be kind, gentle, and encourage a deeper understanding of yourself at this time, because you need it.

SEEK INNER JOY AND PEACE

Just as things going on around you can bring you down, reconnecting with yourself can bring so much happiness and bliss. You see, within all of us is a powerful energy. It's our life force – the one thing that never fails to burn brightly while we are on this earth. We are the keepers of that life force and the masters of how brightly it glows.

You will have read books or seen movies about people who have gone through extraordinarily gruesome trials throughout history, such as the famous Papillon, who was imprisoned on the notorious Devil's Island in French Guiana. There are plenty of stories like this, where someone has suffered terrible cruelty, deprivation, torture, and isolation. Despite that, they survived, often against all the odds. You might put it down to faith, optimism, a belief in themselves . . . but all of them kept that inner light burning.

Heartbreak isn't necessarily as life-threatening as being imprisoned on Devil's Island, but the overwhelming feeling of doom and gloom can be just as overpowering and make you feel totally miserable. It's exactly when you do feel like this that you should reconnect with what makes you happy, and focus on that. Just as you need to have a regular intake of nutrients to keep your body healthy, you have to feed your emotional needs, and this could be anything from doing your favourite hobby to going out with friends. By spending some time with others, you might feel better than if you had stayed at home alone, licking your wounds.

Instead of dwelling on what your ex told you in anger – or even on purpose – to hurt you, rekindle positive affirmations about yourself. Write down your strengths and repeat them often, or note anything that makes you a good person, such as simple acts of kindness. These affirmations can be of help:

- I am radiant, wonderful, and beautiful in all ways.

- I am responsible for my actions, and my actions only.

- I am enough now, which is why I continue to attract opportunities to be more.

- I am full of love. I exude positivity and light. I am a source of goodness, which continues to come back to me in multiple ways.

- Letting go of what doesn't serve me becomes easier every day. I am constantly creating space for new and wonderful energy to enter my life.

- I am thankful for my body; for how it takes care of me, how strong it is, how intelligent it is, and how consistent it is. I eliminate all shame and forgive myself for times I didn't honour it, and commit to loving it in all of its forms.

- I am worthy of deep care, warm compassion, and pure love. I acknowledge my wholeness and welcome beautiful souls into my life who match my level of awareness.

GIVE SPACE TO YOUR PAIN

When you are trying to get over a broken heart, hearing one of your favourite love songs can make painful feelings rise to the surface. It's OK to allow that to happen and to give space for your emotions to vent. There's absolutely nothing wrong with recognizing you still feel hurt, but instead of letting those emotions put you into a state of paralysis, simply try to acknowledge them and bear witness to the fact. As your tears flow, or your heart sinks, be mindful of the experience and feel the waves of emotion pass through you before letting them go.

This may sound hard to do, but one way to handle it is to express how you feel verbally – out loud – at that moment. As the pain surfaces, with memories and thoughts flooding back to you, let your emotions take up space through words. Maybe it will go something like this:

I feel so upset. I never expected this relationship to end.

I still love them.

I can't bear being without them.

The pain is overwhelming and I can't stop feeling miserable.

I feel so angry/disappointed/frustrated.

After you have acknowledged how you feel, allow yourself to reframe the narrative slightly, if you can. If not, that's fine – these things aren't easy. But if you feel it is possible, allow yourself more space to observe your pain without harshness. What follows could be along the lines of:

It's natural to feel the way I do.

I still love them and know that love is never wasted.

I will treasure the time we had together.

I know that the pain I'm experiencing now will be replaced by happiness in time.

My anger/disappointment/frustration comes from my inability to handle things at the moment.

Self-love heals. Time helps, but it's facing those real, raw emotions that will eventually make you more able to cope with any future relationship. Trust me – you have every right to feel hurt, and every chance of coming through this with the clarity you need to enjoy a wonderful new relationship when the time is right.

INSTEAD OF CLOSING YOUR HEART, KEEP IT OPEN, BEATING, WARM, AND ALIVE

This may mean going over the relationship and looking at why it ended, but without dwelling on it. I wouldn't say that it's about apportioning blame, accusing anyone, or beating yourself up here. Sometimes, relationships fizzle out, the passion leaves, people get bored or restless, meet someone else they feel more connected with, can't handle intimacy . . . any number of things. Maybe you just weren't compatible. You might feel that you were giving more to the relationship than your partner was, or you could have sabotaged it yourself because you had some internal conflict.

Whatever the reasons, and there could be millions, maybe you will come to the conclusion that it is for the best. Then again, you might not. Both are valid outcomes and there's nothing wrong with either. You may never figure out what went wrong, and that's OK, too.

I want to tell you that although relationships are extremely important to us, not every single one is destined to be permanent. While we crave companionship, warmth, and compassion, which are all very human traits, we may not always find them in every relationship. But that shouldn't stop us from being willing to share and experience those emotions when they do come along.

We all have the gift of being able to love unconditionally and in abundance, although having a closed heart will hinder that immensely.

The pain we experience in relationships tells us something about ourselves – it tells us that we want, crave, and need love. Hold on to that thought and let love be your guide – it will never let you down.

The door to love is always open.

KEY INSIGHTS

- Letting go of the past is the key to achieving your future happiness.

- Hoarding your emotions leaves no space for positive, new ones.

- When you understand what your attachment style is, you can begin to detach from it and improve your relationships.

- Your heart may be broken but it can heal again.

- Any new relationship can trigger old wounds if you aren't grounded in your authentic self.

- Love is limitless when we learn how to overcome emotional barriers.

- Self-love creates space to love again, with an open heart.

Chapter 3

MAKING SPACE

The only thing that's greater than loving yourself is seeing someone you love finally love themselves, too.

The heart is a sacred space. It's the source of love and a vessel for holding everything that you cherish in your life. But how the heart influences your life and relationships will be based on what you store within it. When you are in love, your heart feels full, and when it's broken, you feel empty. Some say they will never love again after a broken heart, but it doesn't take long before they are seeking to fill that void once more.

When I think of the heart, I see it as a life source – both literally and metaphorically. I mean, if your heart stops beating, that's the end of your physical life. At the same time, it's through the heart that we express and receive love, which many describe as a feeling, an emotion, a craving, a need, a response, a state of being. If emotional hardening of the heart occurs, the natural rhythm of the emotional heart gets disturbed. Love struggles to flow in or out, in a similar way to a partially blocked artery.

There's a lot of talk about mindsets these days – getting into the right frame of mind and being able to deal with whatever hits you. I'm one of those people who likes the idea of thinking things through and being more mindful of how my thoughts are affecting me. But when we spend too much time in our heads, there's a good chance we lose our balance.

What about if we can move out of that headspace and into our heart space more often? How would that affect the way we interact with our partner, friends, family, and wider circle? What difference would it make to the way we experience love?

When I say move out of our headspace, this might sound kind of weird. Our ability to think, to imagine, to invent, and to shape the world is invaluable, and I'm not knocking that. The brain's capacity for innovation and intelligence is undeniable and no one in their right mind (excuse the pun) would say otherwise. As cognitive beings, our ability to solve problems, adapt to change, and thrive is what sets us apart from other beings and makes us human.

I'm not talking about letting logic fly off out of the window and succumbing to our emotions, because that would cause chaos. Imagine if everyone acted solely on impulse or cravings, seeking to satisfy their needs whenever they felt like it. It just wouldn't work. There has to be a balance. We should be seeking harmony.

What I mean when I talk about headspace is that inner voice of ours, the one that makes up stories, the one that gives a non-stop commentary on who we are or how we should be. It's the voice that tells us how to process rejection, fear, abandonment, possessiveness, jealousy, and other soul-destroying emotions. It's the voice that triggers all of our insecurities and keeps reminding us of them. It's the voice that makes us react without thinking, rather than respond with awareness.

There is another voice, or sense of knowingness, in there. One that is much quieter and softer. One that can't be heard unless we silence the chatter within our mind. This is why meditation can be so beneficial. It gives us the opportunity to fade out the incessant chatter of the brain and invite a new heart-sourced awareness to rise, sometimes referred to as the consciousness.

This place within us that you could describe as consciousness is where our thoughts and emotions can harmoniously fuse so that our actions are more aligned with our true Self. When we can tap into that, it brings benefits not only to our lives, but to the lives of those we love, too.

Try to visualize a whole spectrum of emotions that you might go through in any lifetime, from pain to bliss.

It's this spectrum of conscious existence that helps us to move into a more heartfelt space – to a place of genuine compassion for ourselves and others. By transforming the way we are, we can begin to achieve our greatest potential to love and be loved, which then has a ripple effect on how we relate to others. That's why it's important to have a clear idea of how useful the mind can be, but also of how crucial it is to tend to our heart space – the place where pure, unconditional love can truly flourish.

THE THREE LOVE SPHERES

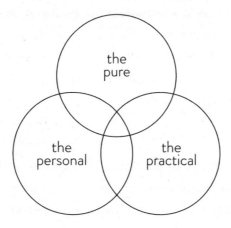

The Three Ps

You could say that there are three spheres of love: the pure, the personal, and the practical.

1. The first sphere is the idea of **love as a pure, autonomous energy or universal concept**, which I will talk about in Chapter 8. We all have the potential to generate that

love and, in a way, it's an absolute or boundless energy. It's always present, whether we are aware of it or not.

2. Then, there's **our own personal experience of love**, which is made up of layers and layers of habits, perceptions, behaviours, and preferences directed towards one particular person or thing.

3. The third sphere is **love as a practice**: an action or continuous series of actions that nurture the authentic and powerful nature of love.

You might catch glimpses of the first kind of love, absolute love, with your partner, when you are out in nature, in a sacred location, or engaged in some kind of deep introspection. The sensation you experience in those moments is what philosopher Rudolf Otto called the 'numinous' in his book *The Idea of the Holy*. It's that feeling of the divine, of rapture; a mysterious or awe-inspiring experience that takes you over for a short period of time.[9]

It can make you feel like you are having an out-of-body experience, or that there is an omnipotent energy pervading everything. It could fill you with a sense of pure peace, sending ripples through your whole body and causing it to tremble. You might experience it during lovemaking or in a time of height-ened emotions, and it can be a powerful bonding moment for you and your partner.

These flashes of numinosity can leave lasting impressions on us – ones that we remember for the rest of our lives. We usually link them to the particular person who evoked them and feel a deeper, more profound connection, even a spiritual unveiling.

The second sphere is everything we experience, from our

first kiss to being in a mature relationship. Each event, memory, feeling, and thought builds up like a giant onion, with thousands of layers. Each of these layers shapes how we act now. Our personal experience of love can make us feel unhappy, disappointed, and hurt. It's subject to change, attachments, emotions, and isn't really very reliable at all. When we lose someone we love, it makes it seem like the end of the world. But, in truth, we all have the capacity to love again, because love is an eternal energy.

The third sphere, love as a practice, is the bridge between what we thought love was to how it can really be experienced, helping us to overcome any preconceptions or limitations. When we practise love, we cultivate acceptance and compassion within ourselves and those near to us, which is a very human need. Even when we feel down, we can practise self-compassion and when we are too hard on ourselves, we can practise removing self-criticism. Loving is doing and not only feeling.

Love is all around you and within you, making it available at any time. It's not always connected to romance and you can feel love for your family, friends, animals, books, nature, or any other thing in this world. It can be expressed in a zillion ways and can overcome great difficulties and challenges. If you feel removed from the idea of love or aren't experiencing it, imagine that it's all around you like a gentle breeze or a flowing river.

Allow yourself to enjoy that breeze on your face or feel the water with your hand as it flows past you. You are simply letting love in and permitting it to surround you like a warm embrace. It's not a difficult thing to do once you open up to its energy, and you will begin to experience it more and more in every moment of tenderness, affection, and care from your partner. Love is all-powerful and lifts us up to new heights of joy and bliss.

FROM HEALING TO A HEALTHY HEART

You can't fix a broken heart if you haven't healed previous emotional wounds. Instead, you will inevitably develop multiple scars as each fresh wound covers the old ones. Love on the rebound is a great example of that. When my friend Arun fell out with his girlfriend, who I thought he was really in love with, I expected him to be moping around for ages. Surprisingly enough, one week later, he was dating someone else and it seemed to be full on. Arun had felt so hurt after his last relationship broke down that he couldn't cope with being alone, and had linked up with one of his old girlfriends almost immediately. Good for him, you might say.

The problem was that he hadn't given himself enough time to get over the past break-up – to think about what had gone wrong, evaluate the lessons he learned from the relationship and its demise, and to treat his broken heart. Instead, bam! He threw himself straight into a couple scenario again, trying to continue where he had left off.

You might have done the exact same thing yourself in the past, or know of someone else that has behaved in the same way. Or, worse, perhaps you were the rebound for someone else's broken heart. People jump into these kinds of relationships for all kinds of reasons, sometimes because they can't deal with the negative feelings of anger, guilt, hurt, and sadness. Often, these emotions are never dealt with and will be carried from one relationship to another. Imagine, then, trying to have a healthy relationship under these conditions . . . it's kinda hard to do.

Healing is non-linear with an indefinite end. You may never be fully healed before you enter a relationship. But, embarking on the journey before you start building a relationship with a new partner will ensure that the remnants of your broken heart will not cut them deeply during triggering moments.

Hopping from one relationship to the next without doing the work of processing emotions is bound to smother the connection. For some, the heartache wasn't caused by a break-up, but perhaps family trauma or other painful events that you haven't processed and let go of.

In my previous book, *Healing Is the New High*, you'll find a step-by-step guide to embarking on your healing journey and learning how to reach that point where you can embrace life with greater emotional balance and positivity. I suggest you take a look at it if you want to find a way to treat all of those old emotional wounds that are preventing you from moving on.

OK. None of us is perfect and it's natural to want to find comfort in the arms of someone else. But when you are unconsciously seeking that, you will attract a connection that is temporary by its very nature. Once you are healed and happy again, what role will this comfort have? Your need to heal and distract your heart has gone; where do you go now? You are no longer the person you were when you met, and it is possible that being with this person you chose to 'fix' you no longer seems to fit the way it once did.

You don't have to be one hundred per cent healed in order to move on to the next relationship, because that could mean waiting for ever. The truth is that it's nice to enjoy the attention of someone else, especially if you are feeling particularly low. But when you have freed yourself from the grip of heartache, you can enter new connections as your authentic self. Instead of broken pieces, you feel whole, and you will be more discerning. Moreover, you will align with someone who refuses to carry so much of their pain from one person to the next.

Most therapists talk about what they call a 'cycle of grief' when a relationship ends. The word 'grief' actually has its roots in the Latin 'gravis,' which translates as 'a heavy burden'. In that respect, grief is like the heavy burden of emotions triggered by the kind of loss you feel when someone isn't in your life any more – someone you were very attached to.

There are many models of grief, and the psychologist John Bowlby began looking at the subject during his work on attachment theory. Once an attachment has been formed, a response of fear, anger, frustration, or grief is unavoidable when that attachment or bond is broken. Bowlby developed his theory even further with the psychiatrist Colin Murray Parkes to outline the Four Phases of Grief in relation to bereavement, explaining how the feelings of grief we experience are a normal response to loss.[10]

The Four Phases of Grief

In this particular model, you can see how we go through four emotional phases as we try to come to terms with the loss of an attachment, be that to a person, a thing, or something else. For the sake of this book, I'm referring to the loss of someone who meant a lot to you in a relationship and not necessarily someone who has died.

1. **Shock and numbness:** At first, you feel in a state of shock because you weren't ready to accept the reality of a loss. This is a kind of defence mechanism that allows you to cope when a relationship first ends.

2. **Yearning and searching:** In this second phase, you might experience a range of emotions, from anger and confusion to despair and sadness. You yearn for your loved one to return and ask yourself why this had to happen.

3. **Disorganization and despair:** In the third phase, the reality of the situation begins to sink in and you might want to withdraw from everyday life as you start to realize nothing will ever be the same again. Feelings of hopelessness and despair set in.

4. **Reorganization and recovery:** In this phase, you begin to understand that your life has changed and you start to accept the new 'normal'. You will slowly begin to see things more positively and feel you have greater energy and interest in life. It doesn't mean you stop grieving, but you will rekindle more positive memories of the relationship you lost.

This grieving cycle or process can't be rushed. Everyone deals with loss differently, but taking some time out can be really helpful. It will give you the chance to get things out of your system, like a detox, where you can focus solely on yourself. During that phase, you can try to figure out who you want to be in your next relationship and what you are prepared to bring to it.

You could also call this 'making space in your heart'. Instead of moving forward with a battered one that is full of open sores, allow it to heal by working through those painful emotions that are lingering there. However long it takes – there's no right or wrong – seize this opportunity to look at yourself and your emotional, mental, spiritual, and physical condition. Before you embark on a new relationship, figure out if you are ready. You can ask yourself questions like:

- What is motivating me?

- What would be right for me?

- Can I bring my authentic self to this relationship?

These aren't easy questions to answer, but as long as you start the healing journey, you are on the right path. You might have just gone through a romance that fizzled out, or ended a relationship because you weren't happy with it. Maybe your loved one passed away or circumstances didn't allow for you to continue the relationship. Either way, what's crucial at this stage is to honour your own needs, first and foremost.

Knowing how much space there is in your heart for connection to the self, and then connection to another, involves having a heart-to-heart with yourself.

How much room can you make to accommodate all of those powerful emotions that come with truly loving someone?

How much of that space is taken up by past experiences that can block your way?

If you remember from the last chapter, I talked about emotional hoarding and the importance of being able to get rid of whatever isn't needed any more. You owe it to yourself to make room for deep love.

MAKING SPACE

When you look deep within yourself, what raw emotions can you identify? How many of these do you associate with past relationships? Find a quiet space at some point in your day to think about this – you can even make a list if it's easier for you. When you think about relationships, do you have emotions like anger, pain, guilt, or sadness rising to the surface? If you do, how would you feel if you let go of them?

Letting go isn't just trying to bury anything that is troubling us or weighing us down – it will only resurface. It's about coming to a point where you can say, 'I acknowledge this emotion and it is no longer needed in my life. It's not serving any purpose.' If you can do that and simply release it from your cache of emotions, you free up room for more positive feelings to take root in your heart. It can be very difficult to get there, because we often hold on to these emotions, afraid that if we do let go of them, we'll find a void. Often, we will have to release them many times over.

Sometimes, it's a case of 'better the devil you know', with all of those ingrained negative responses giving you a false sense of security. These are feelings you are familiar with and are used to. How will your life be if they are no longer there for you to lean on? You could have become used to being in a constant state of anger, fear, or hypervigilance, none of which are useful when you want to build a new relationship.

Many couples seeking help from a relationship specialist are unaware that they are bringing a list of issues to the therapy session that go way back to before they even met their current partner. By the time they decide to get help, many of the problems they are experiencing are so entrenched that it takes a long time to resolve them.

Some of the most common stumbling blocks that couples experience have to do with communication, intimacy, chores, money, trust, differences of opinion, and boredom. Relationships often become like battlefields, with each side adopting an attack or retreat strategy and neither being prepared to compromise or see the other's point of view.

The war of attrition that can occur between two people can be extremely painful and drawn out, with each side suffering losses. For a professional therapist to establish unilateral disarmament and get the couple to declare a truce needs a lot of skill and expertise. There's often a lot going on between two people that they can't identify by themselves, but an arbitrator or third party can help.

If you think about the way we communicate, for example, most of us aren't that good at it. We all want our voice to be heard and to be taken seriously, but might not know how to do that effectively. We've adopted a pattern of shouting, talking over the other person, being too demanding or downright stubborn. On top of that, we struggle to listen because we are so desperate to make our point that we can't allow room for that to be challenged or criticized. If people do not agree or support our perspective, we lose our sense of self. When we lose grip of our sanity, we attack who we are speaking to as a form of protection. We really aren't communicating at all a lot of the time; we're simply trying to get people to see the world in the same way as we do.

I don't want to generalize too much here, as communication means different things to different people. I can give examples, though, of very common patterns that seem to dominate the couple narrative, and they go something like this:

Passive-aggressive behaviour

You know that feeling of being angry with your partner but showing it in a kind of hidden way, instead of addressing it head on? You might make jokes about something you don't like about their behaviour, give them the silent treatment, or keep making sly, sarcastic digs at them. You aren't communicating how you really feel here, and although your partner can tell you are annoyed, they don't know exactly what about. Your behaviour definitely isn't doing anything to fix the problem that you have.

Ignoring the issues

Whenever you brush something under the carpet, that pile will only get bigger and bigger in time. Avoidance can often seem like a much easier option than having to deal with differences that may lead to conflict. It might appear to be a great way to get through the day, but those issues will be back tomorrow. Not tackling what is wrong between you and your partner isn't the sign of a healthy relationship because if you don't get past these speedbumps, how can you grow together and flourish? Very often, what happens is that the issues get ignored and during a highly triggering moment, they are brought up, but in a disrespectful way because emotions are so heightened. That can lead to a lot of hurt.

One of the best things you can do with your partner is to pick apart an argument that happens often. Really take the time to get to the core of it. Once you've dug your way through the trivial bickering, you'll see the vulnerable parts of one another waiting to be seen and accepted.

Being verbally aggressive

I think most of us dislike those who raise their voice, blame/criticize, or try to dominate the conversation. It can be a real turn-off and an indication of a very harmful, unhealthy relationship. But you see this kind of behaviour often, with the person on the receiving end of the hostility usually suffering the humiliation in silence. Coercive relationships frequently play out with this dynamic, and I'll get into those a bit later, in Chapter 8.

SOME COMMUNICATION PITFALLS

If you want to create more space in your heart for a loving, compassionate relationship, adopting any of the above tactics won't work. It will lead to greater problems and a lot of pain on both sides. This is a good time for you to consider whether you have found yourself doing any of the following:

- Giving the silent treatment

- Bringing up past mistakes

- Shouting or screaming

- Storming off or ghosting

- Stonewalling, bringing up only your side then walking away

- Being sarcastic or making fun of someone

- Behaving disrespectfully

- Dismissing multiple realities of what happened (everyone has their own version of the story)

People do argue and have differences, no matter what the relationship, but if you are exhibiting so many negative behaviours with someone you supposedly love, what kind of love is that? If you want to build an authentic relationship based on mutual respect, trust and honesty, you have to be prepared to let go of the emotions that are blocking that.

Despite how it may feel at that moment, arguments can be a positive sign when it comes to your relationship. It means two people still care intensely about the connection and are usually seeking a resolution and to be loved by the other. But productive disagreements can only happen through good communication habits.

A good sign of maturity is when you review your actions after every single disagreement that you have, so you can grow as a person.

The embryonic stages of my own relationship were challenging. I often became frustrated and defensive when my wife had emotional outbursts over issues that I perceived to be small. Telling her what she was doing wrong wasn't helpful – it only seemed to invalidate her feelings. After every disagreement, we began to understand we both had room for growth, and setting a safe space for healing together was essential.

On one particular day many years ago, when Kaushal and I were still dating, she broke down and told me how she felt about herself. She also said that she believed I didn't care about her and, admittedly, I felt like a bad boyfriend. My initial reaction was to defend myself, although I knew she was right to some extent. While I couldn't control how she felt, I could listen to her, acknowledge her feelings, and review my actions. So much of my behaviour was self-focused and I always assumed (conveniently, perhaps) that she would eventually get over whatever was troubling her.

When she was angry, the first thing I thought about was myself, and how it was unfair on me. I often didn't even consider how she may have been defending her pain or that I might have aggravated a wound. My actions would trigger her, and her actions would trigger me. The cycle was vicious and screamed for healing, both individually and as a couple.

Eventually, we realized that both of us needed to be committed to our self-love journeys – the fault wasn't on one person. We both had to look at ourselves in the mirror and see what was hindering our outward expression of love. It felt like we were filling voids using each other – and that was a formula for deep suffering.

Perhaps, when we entered our relationship, the focus on receiving love outweighed the ability to share it. But as we've evolved individually, so too has our relationship. To love ourselves has meant that we've been able to love each other to a greater capacity. We've been able to share with fewer expectations and continue to love and pray for each other during the most challenging disagreements.

Self-love has benefited us both and I honestly believe that throughout the years, even though it's been beautiful to nurture my own needs and witness selfless behaviours from my wife, the most remarkable part of the journey has been seeing her rise. Whether it's her self-esteem expanding, the success and purpose behind her work, or the warmth in her words, it's been an honour to see. But nothing has moved me more than the way she's accepted and celebrated the parts of herself that I've always deeply admired.

WHAT MATTERS THE MOST TO YOU?

Your capacity to love is boundless once it's given the chance. You can make space for that after considering what is important to you. What would you like to give your whole heart to? What would you be prepared to sacrifice? I'm not talking here about grand romantic gestures, but about prioritizing the things you value in life, such as sincerity, honesty, compassion, sharing, trust, respect, and so on. Which of these do you crave and how much attention have you been paying to them in your relationships?

You might truly yearn for stability, yet keep rocking the boat with your volatile outbursts or inconsistent behaviour.

If you feel unworthy of love, you may unconsciously reject it by forcing the relationship to break down.

If you can't put your past traumas and pain behind you, you could end up self-sabotaging your chances of happiness.

You have to look ahead to the future, not back to the past.

Easier said than done, you might say. Releasing yourself from those well-learned constraints, habits, patterns, and templates is a tough one, but it is possible.

Similar to addressing love blockages mentioned in Chapter 1, destructive behavioural patterns can be replaced with good ones. To start, identify and acknowledge them, be accountable for the damage they cause, and create alternatives for how you'll behave the next time the pattern surfaces. This requires exceptional self-awareness and responsibility but it's how the mind and body change.

Example: You know that every time you come home and your partner has left a mess, you end up causing a mindless argument with them. The argument goes too far, you apologize, and wind up admitting the anger was mostly due to a stressful day at work.

It doesn't have to be dishes in the sink. If you are on edge emotionally, anything could tip you over. Unfortunately, we tend to let that be our partner because we know they will still be there once we've dumped our emotional baggage onto them. The key to change in this scenario is to acknowledge the stress you feel from work, cope with it in ways that are rejuvenating (journal, gym time, cry it out), and be compassionate with yourself and your partner when you are emotionally heightened. You know that, today, a dirty dish could set you off. You also know it's not worth fighting with the one you love over it. Now, when you see the dishes on walking in after a long day, let it trigger a warm embrace with your partner. Their love is a powerful antidote to cumulative negative emotions you may have experienced throughout the day.

We have the ability to rewire destructive patterns within a relationship, and that can completely change how we experience love.

In Eastern thought, you'll find the notion of *samskaras*, which are like psychological or emotional imprints left by everything that has ever happened to us in the past. It's these imprints that go towards forming our behaviour, although we aren't usually aware of them. *Samskaras* are said to be at the root of our character traits, impulses, and ways of viewing the world.

The word *samskara* comes from the Sanskrit *sam* ('complete' or 'joined together') and *kara* ('action', 'cause', or 'doing'). Each individual impression, or *samskara*, is made up of ideas, beliefs, and actions that condition us to behave in a particular way. The more often we repeat that conditioning, the deeper these impressions become. The *samskaras* might be helpful or harmful, and while carrying out helpful acts leads us to a sense of fulfilment, harmful ones block our journey. It's like repeating the same mistakes over and over again, without stopping to really look at where you are going wrong.

> **Instead of wondering, 'Why does this keep happening to me?', reflect on repeated thoughts and behavioural patterns that are giving you the same unwanted results.**

The idea of *samskaras* helps to explain why we remember certain things and cling on to specific memories or emotions linked to those memories, which can affect whether we feel happy, content, or miserable. You could say that *samskaras* ripple through our whole being like a thought wave, which then settles into our subconscious or unconscious mind, serving as a kind of store for past experiences.

Think of it as the basement of your house, with your conscious mind being your living room. Anything that triggers a particular memory also triggers the *samskara*, which rises to your conscious mind, accompanied by all of the emotions associated with that particular memory. At the same time, you might block feelings that are too intense for you to deal with, preventing them from entering into your living area.

It's often the combination of those embedded experiences that make us act or feel the way we do, which is why self-awareness is so important. When you understand what triggers you, you can act more mindfully, instead of allowing deeply rooted emotions and behaviours to control you. Whatever is stored in your deeper consciousness can be changed when you bring it out into the open and acknowledge it, because your present experiences are always changing.

> **Wondering what trauma still needs healing? Pay attention to your triggers, notice what's hard to talk about, and shed light on things you avoid. There you will find where pain still lies.**

It's up to us to modify what we don't like. **When we embrace how we are feeling, the energy of hate can be weakened and transformed into the energy of love.** Each time we confront those emotions in our conscious mind, we are disarming them and making them less potent. There's no set way for us to be and the only thing that prevents us from changing is our belief that we are stuck with what we have.

If you want to transform from within (is there any other way?) it is possible to do so once you break down all of those elements that are coming together to form who you think you are.

In a way, that vast storeroom where we keep all of our thoughts and emotions is also linked to attachment. It could manifest itself as being attracted to something or repulsed by it, making you clingy or distant. As a young child, your attachments are basic survival ones related to having parents or caregivers, milk or food, warmth and comfort. As you grow older, those attachments multiply exponentially with your experiences. You might just see them as habits, likes and dislikes, belief systems, and preferences, which are the external manifestations of something much more complex. If we could all take away those attachments, I think we would discover very different people underneath.

If you want to find happiness in your life, what attachments do you need to cast off?

You don't need to be religious, believe in karma, or anything like that to identify your attachments. You can see them playing out in your life and watch how they limit your ability to live happily and respond to situations spontaneously. When you feel vulnerable in certain situations or relationships, you don't usually make the best choices. On any one day, you can go through a multitude of emotional states, all of which can disturb, upset, or influence your actions.

FACING YOUR EMOTIONS

When your partner makes a hurtful remark about you, for example, the hurt you feel can last for a long time, even if you try to forget it. Often, those words will play on your mind and create a sense of anxiety and discomfort.

This is the best moment to raise your self-awareness and reconnect with your inner self.

The minute you feel the pain is the opportunity to release its hold on you.

Hurtful remarks touch something deep within you . . . something that you value. That could be your idea of (or attachment to) who you are, your abilities, self-esteem or self-worth. It can reflect your deep desire to be admired, valued, respected, wanted, or appreciated. When someone attacks that, they are usually tapping into the ingrained beliefs you have about yourself and past memories.

If Mark comments that his boyfriend, Diego, is a terrible driver, it doesn't matter whether that is really true or not. What matters is that Diego takes the comment very badly. Maybe he was criticized for something insignificant when he was younger, which left him with a dread of not being good enough. Although a successful and outwardly confident person now, the pain he felt when spoken to harshly years ago has never been resolved inside him. His reaction to Mark's comments will therefore leave him recalling that pain, but not dealing with it.

This is exactly the right time for Diego to work through it.

By observing those emotions as they come up, he can take away their hold over him. Acknowledging how he feels is a very important step on the way to self-discovery. It can be the difference between lashing out/self-hatred and balanced responses coming from a strong sense of who he is now, not the person he was years ago.

Think about why it is so important for you to be respected or admired and look at how that need is affecting your emotional state when it isn't satisfied. Once you can acknowledge the cause of your triggers and the feelings they generate, you can put them into more perspective and reduce their influence.

Relationships magnify emotional wounds. Are you controlling? You may lack a sense of emotional safety. Do you people-please? You may feel you have to overperform to be loved. Do you over-explain? You may have repeatedly had your reality shut down and your feelings dismissed. Lean in to the lessons love will give you to deepen your connection to yourself and others.

If you value honesty in a relationship, you must make room for it by opening up to your own truths.

If you want to experience compassion, you need to be compassionate with yourself by removing the power that past attachments have over you.

By overcoming habitual thought patterns, you can create space for spontaneity, flexibility, objectivity, independence – all things that help to build beautiful relationships.

When you remove fear, you are free to enjoy life more and to reach your full potential with a partner.

Knowing what matters to you is a crucial piece of the puzzle to help you join the dots.

Relationships are made up of a large number of components: experiences, beliefs, expectations, preferences, learned behaviour patterns, and external influences. No relationship is dependent on one person to make it work – it takes two.

Just imagine how many millions, billions, and trillions of moments need to come together to create something fruitful and worth striving for. It's a wonder couples ever meet and stay together at all, if you think about it. But those who manage to do so and sustain a healthy relationship are in a constant state of give and take, push and pull, expansion and contraction, as they learn how to create more and more space in their hearts for positive energy. That's what love is all about.

The late Buddhist monk Thich Nhat Hanh described it beautifully in his book *Buddha Mind, Buddha Body: Walking Toward Enlightenment*[11] when he said:

> When we look at a flower, we can recognize many of the elements that have come together to make the flower manifest in that form. We know that without the rain there can be no water and the flower cannot manifest. And we see that sunshine is also there. The earth, the compost, the gardener, time, space and many elements came together to help this flower manifest. The flower doesn't have a separate existence; it's a formation.
>
> Using the word 'formation' reminds us that there is no separate core of existence in them. There is only a coming together of many, many conditions for something to manifest.

EMOTIONAL PATHWAYS

Just as a Buddhist might talk about *samskaras*, neurologists talk about neural pathways in our brains that are created depending on our habits. We now know that our brain is being constantly shaped and moulded by our experiences via something referred to as neural plasticity. If a brain can be shaped, then we can help to rewire it through our thoughts, actions, and habits. We all know how the brain is responsible for producing different chemicals that affect how we feel, from the happiness serotonin and dopamine give us to the stress and anxiety of cortisol and adrenaline.

In his ground-breaking book, *The Brain That Changes Itself*,[12] psychiatrist and academic Norman Doidge was one of the first to talk about how, by practising a new habit under the right conditions, we can change millions and billions of the connections between each nerve cell. This can alter how we feel, behave, think, and even help us to overcome physical pain and disabilities. How does this relate to our feelings of happiness?

Well, when you pursue anything that increases your feelings of happiness, activity in your brain's left prefrontal cortex also increases. The happier you feel, the more you will strengthen this neural pathway, making happiness easier to replicate. It sounds simple – and it is. The more desirable the emotions you experience, the easier it will be for you to create new neural pathways that reinforce the feeling. The more undesirable the emotions, the more your synapses will replicate the feeling of negativity. I think you know that positive thinking is one of my mantras, and there's plenty of evidence out there now to prove that it really can improve your levels of happiness and fulfilment.

In life, we're often told never to stray from the beaten path. The reason for this is so that we don't get lost. By treading the well-worn path, we'll stay on the straight and narrow – on familiar territory. Each one of us follows his or her own path and the more often we walk it, the clearer it becomes. Straying away from that path can be scary, because we don't know what's 'out there'. We are, after all, creatures of habit and don't usually choose change for fear of getting lost in the 'unknown'. That makes sense, but when the path you have created for yourself is taking you round and round in circles, you are lost without even realizing it.

Whether you think the same thoughts, experience the same emotional patterns, or follow the same types of behaviour, you are reinforcing the same neural connections, and reliving the same samskaras. Your heart remains blocked, frozen, and unfulfilled.

Those faint trails you can see to the left and right of you in the forest must lead somewhere, so why not follow one of them to see what else there is? The more you venture off the beaten track, the more new trails you will make, which will themselves become well-worn footpaths one day. By giving yourself options, you are expanding your potential for a fuller, more rewarding life. This can happen when you adopt new habits and ways of being, which will eventually make those old pathways less prominent.

If you practise the self-regulation exercise mentioned at the end of Chapter 1 on page 36 each time your emotions become charged with negative impulses, and reframe your thinking in a more positive way, you will eventually form a new way of being. You will break that habit of being over-critical, judgemental, anxious, frustrated, upset, annoyed, and all of the other negatives that make you react badly. Once this begins to shape your thoughts and feelings, you can bring more stability and wisdom to your relationships. Instead of being triggered by a particular comment, action, or event, you will have greater clarity and act in the best interests of yourself and your partner.

Interestingly enough, when we create healthy connections within ourselves, we are much more able to establish healthy connections with others. If you think about it, we are already connected by our shared humanity and our place in this immense Universe, but we aren't always aware of that. I could go even further and say that it's not about connecting with others, but more about re-connecting: discovering those beautiful, complex pathways that converge in the same place – a place of universal love.

When you meet someone that you feel an affinity for or a sense of alignment with, you are actually reconnecting with your soul's purpose, and that's something very special. When you don't know how to appreciate this affinity or aren't ready for it, you can experience problems within the relationship that seem unsolvable. For many people, knowing how to give and receive love is a learning process, and the lessons can be hard to handle. But we are all capable of getting there if we allow ourselves time for reflection and create space for the heart to really expand.

When you come from a place of emotional wellness, the space in your heart can become the place where a magnificent garden will thrive, filled with wonder and beauty. Each colour and aroma will pervade your senses as the lushness of love spreads throughout. I can't think of a more profound or fulfilling human experience than love, and when it comes to sharing that with another person, it is a sacred connection. But you've got to do the hard graft first of pulling out the weeds, clipping back whatever is overgrown, cutting the tangled-up vines, and unearthing the roots of hate and suffering. Your heart will then be ready to receive the seeds of joy, wonder, and bliss.

PRECONCEIVED IDEAS

You may not have had much luck in the past with relationships and could be bringing a lot of negative preconceptions into the next one. It's a good idea to leave these behind you and approach your new adventure from scratch. Each person is different and if your last partner let you down, it doesn't mean that you have to be on the defensive from the word go with a new one. By all means, be vigilant and watch out for any red flags, but don't assume that they will be treating you the same way as your previous partner. Let's look at another example:

After Amanda's two-year relationship with Kyrie came to an end, she had become accustomed to feeling insecure in the relationship. Kyrie's constant lying to her meant that she was distrustful of him and their rows would consist of her accusing him of something he may or may not have done. If Amanda can put that experience behind her and stop thinking that no one can be trusted, she will be able to embark on a new relationship with an open heart. If she continues to react in the same accusative way with her new partner, whatever he says or does, they aren't going to be able to sustain a healthy relationship.

Sure, being lied to is hurtful and can shape your impressions of everyone. But not everyone is a liar, and that's a fact Amanda needs to accept.

What would you have done?

EXPECTATIONS OF YOURSELF AND OTHERS

When you meet somebody new, there's no way you can predict how it's going to go. That's usually part of the intrigue and excitement of new love. No expectations have crept in yet to cripple the connection. In the beginning it's all sweetness and light as fireworks explode and life is wonderful! When those initial fireworks burn out and the excitement dies down, we start analysing what they could do better, or how they can do more for us.

What expectations do you have for the relationship? Not all couples will stay together for ever and you may meet numerous people before you find someone who you want to settle down with permanently. Having a clear idea of some of the compatible traits that a person possesses is a good thing. But expectations can cause damage when it's obvious that someone you're with isn't exactly who you thought they'd be and you begin to bombard them with your desires and needs. This often leads to shame on their part and resentment on yours.

Do you expect every new romance to be 'the real deal'? If that's the case, how are you going to sustain it, nurture it, and help it to grow? And what do you expect of your partner? Should they fit in with your way of seeing things, bend to your preferences, follow you around like a puppy dog? Will you have the emotional maturity to accept them for who they are, without wanting to change them?

These are just some of the questions we all need to think about when we start seeing someone new, because if we haven't worked it out before that, it can get messy. The antidote to expectations is acceptance. Accepting each individual as their own spiritual and emotional being. Ditch the checklist, open your heart to all possibilities, and allow something authentic to flourish.

People have a funny way of showing up authentically when we don't tell them who we think they should be.

HONOURING NEEDS

When you know what is important to you, you owe it to yourself to honour those needs. If you give in to another person just to please them, there's a chance that you will eventually sacrifice your own emotional wellbeing in favour of theirs. This can lead to a build-up of resentment that comes out as passive-aggressive behaviour, even though you hate yourself for doing it. If you value intimacy and need to experience that with the other person, how will you feel when they are closed down emotionally or come across as cold and distant? What are their needs and can you meet them?

It's important to lay your cards on the table from the outset and talk about what your needs are. You may find that your partner has never engaged in such a candid conversation before and will welcome the opportunity to open up. On the other hand, they may be so shut down that you can't access what they really need or want from you, and that can be confusing. Always stay true to yourself, though, and only compromise as much as you feel comfortable with. Trying to go along with things that you aren't happy with will take its toll eventually.

SELF-BETRAYAL LOOKS LIKE:

- Saying 'Yes' when you want to say 'No'.

- Regularly putting the needs of others before your own.

- Compromising your values to keep others comfortable.

- Performing to feel loved or wanted.

PROTECTING BOUNDARIES

Protecting your boundaries in any relationship is crucial if you want to retain your sense of identity. It's easy to fall into the pattern of becoming 'one' with the other and losing yourself on the way. In all relationships, boundaries help us to stay true to ourselves while respecting the other person's boundaries too.

If you're flexible with your boundaries, people will be flexible with how they treat you.

Getting closer to your new partner shouldn't mean forsaking your beliefs, interests, hobbies, friends, or anything else. It is possible to form a caring, fulfilling relationship without letting go of who you are, although many people find this hard to do.

The best way to explain how you can achieve this is to consider that a relationship should be made up of three distinct parts: you, your partner, and both of you as a couple.

There will be some overlap of each, but it's the 'you as a couple' bit that needs attention. When you cross the boundaries too often, give too much of yourself, or take too much away from your partner, the lines can become blurred as you lose sense of who either of you really are. I'll talk more about this later but, for now, remember that the secret to being a happy couple doesn't mean giving up everything in order to make it work.

When you start your own business, you need to know what product you are offering and how much everything costs. Are you selling at a profit, a loss, or just breaking even? Many people settle for the latter in their relationships, but every business needs to make a profit if it is going to be viable, right? If you want to enter into a collaboration with another partner without having a business plan and a solid product, as well as the know-how and investment to make it work, who would be foolish enough to go along with you?

Emotionally invest in your healing and development before you step out into a new relationship, and lay down the foundations for something that can grow into a productive, rewarding, fulfilling experience. From there you can be as enterprising as you like and begin to thrive in your own life, alongside someone who will hold your hand as you walk down a new path together.

If you are currently fostering a connection with someone, be sure to take an emotional audit of where you're at as an individual. Is old pain causing your current relationships to suffer? What attachments, ideas, and expectations can you release so that this bond deepens? How can you create space so that this relationship has an honest chance at thriving?

**The more space you give to your heart,
the more love it will yield.**

**The more you love yourself,
the greater your capacity to love others.**

**When you have made room for someone new to enter
your heart, who does that special person need to be?**

KEY INSIGHTS

- Recognizing the sanctity of your heart as a precious vessel is the first step to understanding your needs.

- Move from the headspace to the heart space to free yourself of past negativity and disappointments.

- The three spheres of love describe love as a pure energy, personal experience, and practice, and can bring a sense of wholeness.

- Healing the heart takes time and self-wisdom.

- The cycle of grieving is an essential part of the healing process.

- Being able to overcome conflicts in a new relationship requires inner transformation first.

- Creating new neural pathways and establishing boundaries are key to making it work.

Chapter 4

DECODING ATTRACTION

Immature love says: 'I love you because I need you'.
Mature love says: 'I need you because I love you'.
– Erich Fromm[13]

Love nourishes our sense of wellbeing and happiness. It brings great joy and deep satisfaction on several levels. It fuels us to be better, think bigger, and do more. It is the root of inspiration and the end of all means. Love is the reason for everything and the source of all. This book isn't going to preach to you about what an ideal relationship is, because it's simply a matter of whether you are *actively creating happiness* or not with your significant other. Instead, you can learn to use the awareness of love within you to transform every relationship you'll ever have.

Today, most single people have the freedom to choose their partners and to live according to their own rules, without much external pressure to conform to a particular standard or way of being. It's really up to each couple to set their benchmark of what does or doesn't work for them, and I'm going to give you some pointers for how to do that. While older generations used to talk about what makes a good marriage, recent generations are more interested in discussing what makes a good relationship. This seems to be the ultimate goal; marriage or not, children or no children, with or without traditional gender roles. How love is represented in relationships continues to evolve.

We shouldn't forget that although marriage is still meant to be for life for many people, and while we want good relationships, we don't necessarily see these relationships as life-long. That could be one of the reasons that a lot of us often struggle to establish quality connections we are prepared to build on, because we see them as transient and disposable.

This freedom to choose our partners and move from relationship to relationship comes with a price tag. As we try to navigate the dating game in search of 'the one', the plethora of available options can be overwhelming.

With so many choices, how do you make the right decision and not leave empty-handed or broken-hearted? You might be attracted to a lot of people, but is attraction on its own enough to sustain a relationship? You might also be attracted to different people for many different reasons, but who is the right person for you?

If someone asks me what first attracted me to my wife, I might say her bubbly personality or her caring nature. Of course, I also thought she was drop-dead gorgeous, but it was her inner qualities that shone through for me. Maybe you were attracted to your current partner because they are physically fit, competitive, ambitious, kind, intelligent, shy, fun to be with, passionate, confident, nurturing, sexy, or any number of other possibilities, and it's all good. We are all pulled by different things and looking for someone to fulfil our need to love and be loved.

Attraction comes in many shapes and forms and, depending on what is a priority for you, can be the beginning of something beautiful or a brief encounter. If you want to have a close, nurturing, fulfilling relationship with someone else, it's good to know what is attracting you to a particular person and if they are right for you. If you are only interested in fleeting connections, then you probably don't need to look too deeply into it, although you might want to consider why you don't want to commit.

By decoding attraction types, you will get more insight into what you may have been doing wrong so far, and be in a better position to create something more sustainable in the future.

A smiling and cheerful face, appealing body shape or height might be initially attractive, but they have nothing to do with commitment, respect, understanding, compatibility, evolution, and love. They won't even keep attraction in place because someone can easily appear undesirable through their actions.

While dates are easy to arrange due to the availability and comfort of apps, building healthy relationships is a little more complicated because expectations have changed. Social media and dating shows recycle subjective ideas on perfection when it comes to love. They encourage people to prioritize the superficial aspects and look for the unattainable in others while either showing severe neglect to themselves or ignorance of their growth in the process. This can lead to relationships that fulfil the status quo but leave us emotionally unfulfilled and spiritually depleted. After all, Instagram said my relationship would be everlasting if it looked like this. If attraction is driven by external influences, it will lead us directly into a dead end.

When love and evolution appear to come fast and easily, people become impatient. What comes quickly will often also go quickly due to the transient nature of our thoughts and emotions. It's that 'flash in the pan' kind of experience, first coined during the nineteenth-century California Gold Rush. While panning for gold, prospectors would get all excited when they saw something glinting in the pan, only to have their hopes crushed when it turned out not to be gold. When this happens in unsuccessful relationships, we also say that it 'didn't pan out'. The disappointment that follows when you realize you haven't 'struck gold' can often be extremely demoralizing.

People can look in the wrong places, for the wrong things, and recycle the same relationships – perpetuating the same emotional pain. And once we account for trauma, emotional suppression, and unhealthy conditioning, decision-making when approaching relationships can lead you down a dark path and keep you stuck there.

When your focus is on form and appearances, your love will not travel any deeper. People often seek relationships not to try to build a home with someone, but instead to occupy rooms inside of them, hoping they're always nicely furnished and clean. When the approach to finding 'love' is driven by pleasure and desire, the relationship won't move further than those things. Once pleasure is absent and desires (such as physical intimacy) are fulfilled, the person and relationship might seem dull, exhausting, and lifeless.

Most people describe love in its conditional sense – 'I love your actions' – whereas the purest form of love is unconditional: 'I love you, although I don't always agree with your actions'. Getting to this state of awareness requires a commitment to one's expansion. If it's mutual, your relationship will be blissful for the most part.

No relationship will be seamless, but finding someone who aligns to you energetically and is devoted to the evolutionary journey with you is critical. Six-foot-tall guy won't contribute to your happiness if they're abusive, and nor will an hourglass-figure lady if they neglect your mental health. You may share kisses, but no laughs and smiles. Symmetrical faces that dish out hate can quickly lose their appeal, while a kind heart can intensify feelings of attraction on every spectrum. And, as mentioned in earlier chapters, the first step to aligning to another who has the capacity to nurture authentic love begins with you being rooted in who you are and understanding what you need.

FALLING IN LOVE

Nothing can beat that feeling of falling in love, and the word 'falling' definitely seems to fit. When you meet 'the one', you suddenly go spiralling out of control in a whirlwind of emotions, and the pull you feel towards them seems totally irresistible. It's like some mysterious force of nature is at work and all free will goes out of the window. The stars align, destiny has spoken, and it's just meant to be.

This reminds me of Newton's Law of Universal Gravitation, because it seems to describe the phenomenon of falling in love really well. If you are familiar with the Law, you'll know it states that *every particle attracts every other particle with a force that varies inversely as the square of the distance between them.* Put more simply, all objects are attracted to each other, and the closer they are, the greater the attraction.

Obviously, Newton wasn't talking about people and feelings; he was referring to objects like apples and planets. But we are all made of atoms, and I have observed that the closer you get to someone, the more gravitational force will pull you together. If you spend a lot of time with your partner, chances are you will create even stronger bonds, because that's the way it works. If one side loses interest, pulls away, or doesn't want to continue, entropy can set in and energy disperses, which leads to the end of the relationship.

Trying to maintain a long-distance relationship can be much harder, because gravity can't do its thing so easily. While mass might affect the way the planets move around each other, with us it's our appearance, values, beliefs, interests, and lifestyle that create a particular pull. Fortunately, we can manipulate and raise our vibration and frequency, which can help sift and sort what we wish to attract instead of it occurring at random.

The Law of Vibration, which I talked about in *Good Vibes, Good Life*, is something different, but it also refers to the fact that like attracts like because nature abhors a vacuum. It states the energy that courses through you and that you radiate out into the world is, by extension, the same energy that you welcome back. This is why exuding positive vibes is so beneficial. Whichever Law you want to go with, there's a lot of truth in the fact that often, when we meet someone new, there can be such an existential pull that it takes us completely by surprise.

When we begin any new relationship, we'll do whatever it takes to make it work and are often prepared to compromise to achieve that. We'll go out of our way to be nice, do things we wouldn't normally do, try food we might not like, spend more time on our love life than with our friends . . . and so on. You could say that we go into freefall, not caring where we land and without a parachute in a lot of cases.

If the relationship is one-sided or one of you is pulling away from the other, there will be less 'gravitational pull' and it will be hard to stay together. Connection has got to be mutual to work. Depending on your attachment style, the slightest sign of discord may cause you to temporarily hold on tighter or let go completely.

You can never be certain about a potential partner, and that's the beauty of it all. Nowadays, with dating apps and less pressure to get married early, predictability has been replaced with spontaneity, boredom with curiosity, and familiarity with mystery. It's an exciting time, during which anything is possible, and your heart beats faster than ever. We won't all experience these highs and lows, but the beginning of a new relationship can bring some fresh air into your life and even give you a reason to get up in the morning.

So, where does attraction fit in and how do we know we are attracted to someone for the right reasons? What are the effects on your emotional wellbeing of being attracted to someone for all of the wrong reasons? Let's dive into this a bit more.

First off, I want to say that everyone's experience is valid, and there are no rights and wrongs. Whatever has happened to you in the past or what you are going through now is all part of life's infinite possibilities. I'm not here to tell you if your experience is good or bad, because I don't know enough about you. My sole intention is to broaden your perspective a little, if you are open to that, and to share my thoughts with you. I'm certainly not coming from a place of judgement, but believe in my heart that we are all worthy and capable of finding deeper connections within ourselves and with others.

I prefer to call it 'rising in love', rather than 'falling', as we soar to new heights of our potential within a warm, loving relationship.

WHAT IS ATTRACTION FOR YOU?

Different relationships are based on different types of attraction, ranging from the psychological and biological to the social and physical. Each of these helps to mould us into the people we become, for better or worse. Within these broad categories, we find the most common forms of attraction, which are the sexual, physical, romantic, emotional, intellectual, and aesthetic attraction. No doubt you have experienced at least one of these in your life, and possibly more than one simultaneously.

All the attraction types occur in different ways in different people, and some overlap. They also change as we grow older and go through life's ups and downs, so aren't something static and rigid. You may have thought your husband was irresistible when you first met him, but now his physical appearance doesn't do much for you, although you still love him and find his sense of humour more attractive than ever.

Here's a quick summary of each style:

Sexual attraction

When we talk about attraction, it's usually sexual attraction that comes to mind, and that's normal. We are all very receptive to this kind of feeling, which can't always be explained or quantified. Meeting someone you are instantaneously drawn to because of how they look or behave may even be a surprise to you, because you don't normally go for 'that type', so there's obviously a lot more going on here than meets the eye.

Sometimes, it has to do with odourless hormones that are secreted by the other person called pheromones, which can affect other people in the vicinity. They are like the sixth sense of sexual attraction and stimulate arousal, desire, and lust. Pheromones are secreted through bodily fluids like sweat and saliva, but don't really have a 'smell'. Rather, they are detected in areas of our nasal tissue, which then sends messages to the brain.

You can also be sexually attracted to people when it's totally inappropriate, such as with your university lecturer, your sister's boyfriend, or your boss. As it happens, the level of sexual attraction we feel can vary and grow more intense or fade over time, so it's a funny thing that's hard to pin down.

And, for sure, some people consider themselves asexual but might experience romantic attraction, which also falls within normal behaviour. There is a wide spectrum of sexuality that allows room for everyone. Relationships are never easy to navigate, no matter what your sexual orientation or preferences.

Physical attraction

When you want to give and receive love and affection, this is known as physical attraction, and you'll often find it in romantic relationships, although not exclusively. Think of the hugs you enjoy from your parents or friends and you'll get the gist of what I mean. It's more to do with non-sexual physical contact when we seek comfort, support, compassion, or just a hug to start our day off well.

Romantic attraction

Being romantically attracted to someone is more aligned to wanting to have a relationship with them. You probably have the desire to be with them, and even if sex isn't a priority yet, it's about much more than just being friends. You want to hang out with them and share time with them. You might know someone who doesn't experience this kind of attraction and could be termed 'a-romantic', although they may still seek out the companionship of others.

Emotional attraction

Emotional attraction is the desire to be emotionally present with another person and to share your feelings with them. This kind of attachment can be found with friends, family, or romantic partners and might be extremely important to you. Most people will agree that this kind of attraction creates the space for a deeper connection and greater emotional wellbeing.

Aesthetic attraction

This is very common nowadays, and it's the kind of attraction you feel when you look at someone's Instagram feed and admire their style, looks, and appearance, regardless of your gender and sexual preferences. While you may not have a desire to have physical contact with this person, you do find them aesthetically pleasing.

Intellectual attraction

This kind of attraction is also more common than you may think, with many people feeling attracted to another on an intellectual level. Whether it's because you are stimulated by their conversation or challenged to see new perspectives, you may find someone desirable because of the way they think.

Spiritual attraction

Not usually talked about in scientific textbooks, spiritual attraction is pretty hard to come by. On any normal day, we rely on our eyes, preferences, beliefs, habits, and lifestyle when considering new relationships and don't pay much thought to any kind of spiritual interaction. You could be cynical about its existence, or don't relate to this way of thinking, but many people claim to have experienced it.

Spiritual connections can manifest themselves when you meet someone that you immediately feel aligned with, as if an invisible force is pulling you to them. It comes with a strong feeling of connection, often accompanied by the 'Have we met before?' question. When this happens, you feel like you have found your other half or your soulmate, and the feeling is mutual.

Have you ever met someone and you just clicked, despite the fact that they in no way resembled what you're typically attracted to? This is a tell-tale sign of spiritual attraction.

I did have this experience when I met my wife, so, trust me, it can happen to anyone! It was as if we were both moving around the same orbit and felt like we had known each other for years . . . for aeons. I wasn't exactly doubtful about this kind of connection, but as I'd never actually experienced it before, it felt kind of weird when it happened. At the same time, it just seemed absolutely right, as if I was finally in tune with someone else. It wasn't all wine and roses after that, of course, because even if you do feel this infinite connection, it takes more than that to make a relationship work.

I just want to add here that this kind of spiritual attraction doesn't always appear at first sight. It may develop years into a relationship, once both individuals are more open and ready to receive it. You will have heard people talking about it and if you have been lucky enough to experience it, then you'll know what I mean.

Whether you believe in spiritual attraction or not isn't the issue here. Everyone has their own belief system and thoughts on life, and all types of attraction bring something to our shared experience. It's a combination of different attraction styles that glue couples together or eventually make them fall apart.

What's most important is being able to determine what you're attracting and the grounds for many of your connections. This can offer insight into what you unconsciously crave, and you can compare it to what you would rather consciously attract. Maybe what you really lacked in your previous relationships was an intellectual attraction because the premise of the connection was physical attraction. But can we have it all?

WHAT IS AN IDEAL RELATIONSHIP?

There's no such thing as an ideal relationship with a partner – but a healthy, empowering, fulfilling one could include the following:

- Mutual respect

- Aligned values and morals

- Good communication

- Physical attraction (not always necessary)

- Empathy

- Shared relationship goals (financial, emotional, spiritual, or otherwise)

- Honesty and integrity

If you think about this model in relation to attraction styles, which ones would you expect to see in each? For example, perhaps a relationship based on mutual respect will include romantic, emotional, intellectual, and physical attraction but not sexual. Aligned values might include the same but exclude romantic attraction, and so on. Spiritual attraction can cover them all.

As you can see, there are many ways to experience a relationship and the thing that attracted you to the other person in the beginning might fade or strengthen as time goes by. Everything is open to adaptation and transformation, which is the beauty of healthy relationships.

The way in which we build these connections is changing, but the common thread that runs throughout is a desire or need to give and receive love, even if that is short-term.

You may change partners as often as you change your socks, but you are still seeking some kind of experience that satisfies your needs.

The surprising thing about attraction is that it isn't everything. It's simply the catalyst for what is to follow. That might sound odd but, as you've probably learned by now, attraction doesn't always last; it morphs into something else, and can often be superficial (especially if it's based solely on appearance or sexual dynamics).

What's more important is knowing what your heart desires in the long run – what you want from a meaningful and, presumably, lasting relationship. Ask those who have been around the dating circuit and they'll tell you that it can become quite soul-destroying after a while. By all means, you owe it to yourself to get out there and meet new people, but running the dating gauntlet can leave you feeling despondent and disillusioned after a while. This happens for one of two reasons: either individuals don't know what they want or are too tightly bound to what they expect from another person.

Dating has lost its sense of exploration, adventure, and freedom. It's become less about exploring someone for who they are and holding space for a unique connection, and more about finding someone who fits a mould that is based loosely on unrealistic expectations. Hence, the dating paradox. It's better to know what you want but allow space for someone to be exactly as they are.

There must be more to relationships than dating apps and one-night stands. We may be lucky enough to lead liberal lifestyles but, deep down, most people are actually seeking the pieces of the relationship puzzle I listed above: mutual respect, common values, good communication, empathy, shared goals, honesty, and physical attraction, if possible. But when it appears to be hard to find, we settle.

If that weren't the case, we wouldn't see so many people struggling in their relationships and having problems. It's pretty clear that most are trying to find the right formula for them, and this can require a lot of trial and error. The point is, how do you learn from your own trials and errors and move forward?

At what point do we accept that relationships are hard? Relationships require work. A relationship is filled with hard work! The spark of attraction, in its many forms, will draw you closer to someone, but it's the willingness of two people to mould around one another that makes it thrive. Remember, longevity isn't the key; fulfilment through authentic love is the goal. But so often this can get lost in the complexities of the dating dance.

THE TERROR OF TEXTING

It's common for people to validate their entire existence based on other people's opinions, and the attention they get from them. For example, how many of us have been left questioning our worth after receiving someone's silence? You leave a welcome mat out in front of your heart for somebody who doesn't treat you like home, and then conclude that something's wrong with your house.

This feeling of incompleteness may come to the surface from something as small as not receiving a text back. Let's demonstrate this using a scenario. Imagine you meet someone at a bar and identify them as a potential love interest. The next day, you send them a text saying:

'Hey, it's me from the bar last night. Was lovely meeting you. I thought I was staying in but my friends managed to drag me out, lol. Anyway, it was a good night in the end because we had a laugh with you guys. Hope you had fun too x.'

A week goes by, and you still haven't heard back from them. As you wait, your mind might take a stroll through a park full of fears where you only see everything that you think you're not, or what you think they think you are; not everything that you actually are. You may then identify yourself as not good enough, purely because they haven't shown you an immediate interest.

Days later, you get a text back from them and it reads:

'Sorry for the late reply, been really busy. Was good meeting you too. Hope you're good. What have you been up to?'

Although it's brief and they don't tell you why they were busy, it seems like they're still interested in you. So you reply to them within a day, but this time you put more effort into your message so you can get a conversation going.

However, again, you don't hear back from them for another week. Despite writing a lengthier response, with more questions, their reply this time is even briefer than the last one, and it includes no questions back to you:

'That's cool, hope you had fun. Yeah I've just been busy with stuff. Can't wait for the weekend.'

Now, you might approach this in different ways. You may decide to play it cool and reply back a week later because this has become a game, where you're both playing hard to get. Unconsciously, you've accepted that it's OK to toy with each other's emotions, and so you invite yourself to get played some more.

Here, it's essential to identify that although anticipation can create excitement, games include winners and losers. When you're not genuinely busy, but you want to illustrate your value by creating a demand for your time, you take the risk of feeling at a loss at some point down the line through their actions or yours.

You'll often find that the healthiest of relationships may have started with challenges, but they were absent from purpose-led games. The connection and communication were both very natural, not forced or purposely delayed.

You may alternatively approach this situation by replying at the same frequency as before: quickly. But this may introduce feelings of guilt because of the desperation you feel that it shows.

With both approaches, you're not only resisting perfect moments of happiness and creating self-sabotage by lowering your self-esteem, but you're also setting the tone for your future with this person. When it begins with you thinking of yourself as lesser than them, you may find yourself constantly submitting to their ways through people-pleasing tendencies, just to feel worthy of receiving love.

If people are unwilling to show you the respect and attention you deserve, there's no need to beg them for it. It's not your job to fix other people's vision, and you can't force a connection that's only coming from one side.

Also, be cautious of those who are only ready to connect with you when it's convenient for them or when they are lonely. Consistent effort is usually the most significant indicator of genuine interest.

People can feel nullified by someone's lack of love towards them because they're not giving that love to themselves in the first place. It seems to be a common occurrence: people look for love to compensate for a self-love deficit.

Those who genuinely love themselves value their time and energy, and they recognize people who aren't aligned to their level of awareness – such as those who only seek to take advantage. More importantly, they know their value, despite other people's behaviour towards them.

Please also keep other people's wellbeing in mind – some people may want to reply but genuinely can't due to essential commitments and priorities, such as taking care of their mental health. Your intuition (not to be confused with trauma) can help indicate whether or not someone is genuinely interested in you. My book *Healing Is the New High* has further details about this.

You can never know if the person you next meet is going to be right for you, but you do need to take that risk. I'm sure you'll discover that the person who is right for you is the one who loves you the way you are and doesn't ask you to change anything about yourself. Who wouldn't want that? At the same time, you are only the right person for them if you don't expect them to be someone else either. **If you want your new partner to change, then you aren't with the person that you wanted to be with in the first place, and nor are they.**

With that in mind, how can we know what kind of relationship we are looking for and how can we improve an existing one?

DIGGING INTO DYNAMICS

Within each relationship, certain dynamics come into play. These are the behaviours by which we interact with each other that then repeat to become a predictable cycle. I wonder if you see yourself in any of the most common dynamics mentioned below when thinking about your past or current relationships.

1. The COMPETE versus CONTROL dynamic

'I can't stand it when Dashane thinks he's always right. I'm not going to let him get one over on me.'

Each participant in this kind of dynamic is trying to win the latest argument, prove the other wrong, and be right about everything. Getting the last word in is one example of how this plays out, and usually there's no giving in on either side. This creates a lot of stress in a relationship as both sides try to exert their will over the other. The thinking is: *If I can undermine the other person and take control, I can feel better about myself.* When this goes on for too long, either one side gives in or the relationship comes to an end.

2. The ACTIVE versus PASSIVE dynamic

'It's always me who has to arrange the night out, choose the movie, and make the decisions. I'm sick of it!'

Often, we see couples playing out this kind of role-taking, with one doing all of the heavy lifting and the other going along passively with whatever comes up. You might see fewer arguments here, but there is still an imbalance, and the active player might become resentful because they don't feel they are getting enough support or are fed up with having to make the decisions all the time. Even if they act out, the chances are that they'll continue to go on in the same vein. The passive participant will do anything to keep the peace, which often leads to anxiety and feeling overwhelmed. This kind of relationship has a lot to do with the backstory of each and their learned behaviour and needs.

3. The AGGRESSIVE versus ACCOMMODATING dynamic

'I try not to upset Adele when she's in a bad mood because it only makes her worse.'

Power is the key here, with the person in charge asserting it by instilling fear in the other. You might find a lot of emotional abuse in a relationship of this nature, and even physical abuse, with frequent blow-ups, bullying, and intimidation. The accommodating person lives in a constant state of fear yet has a higher tolerance for being abused. At the same time, they are always trying to manoeuvre in a way that is less threatening to their welfare but never quite manage it. If the relationship dissolves, the abuser will carry their behaviour on to the next partner if they don't resolve their inner issues.

4. The DISCONNECTED or PARALLEL LIVES dynamic

'I often feel like we've become flatmates rather than husband and wife and it feels very lonely sometimes.'

Many couples drift into this kind of dynamic, especially after a long period of being together. Although they might not argue much, there's really little connection, and indifference seems to be the most obvious trait. Rather than sharing their lives together, they simply share a house, with boredom and staleness setting in. Any chemistry they might have had has long gone and differences they had are ignored by creating distance. Conversations are courteously kept to a minimum as each player withdraws from the relationship and expects it to run on autopilot.

Do you recognize yourself in any of the above scenarios? Can you think of any more you have experienced? If you do, it's a good opportunity to reflect on whether that is what you want. Do you really enjoy conflict in your relationship or being pushed around? Is it worth staying with someone who isn't fully present in your relationship or who has shut down emotionally? Only you can answer these questions and decide on how to go about changing things around. It's important to remember that you can only focus your energy on whatever is within your control.

No doubt, a lot of people are so used to the way things are working that they don't see anything wrong with their relationship. Having said that, the damage to self-esteem that comes from being in a one-sided or abusive relationship is a serious issue. Staying stagnant may also seem OK, but what is your heart telling you? Are your needs really being met, or are you happy to settle for less?

If you are wondering what a healthy dynamic looks like, it will be something like this:

The ACCEPTING and BALANCED dynamic

Teamwork is key here, with both players looking out for each other's back. The couple complement each other while recognizing the other's strengths and accepting their weaknesses. Both are heavily invested in helping the other to fulfil their goals and dreams and will come together to solve problems. They are aware of any failings in their relationship and will constantly do the work to revitalize it in a caring, compassionate way. This kind of dynamic may evolve over time and can build lasting relationships that both participants enjoy and treasure.

> **Relationships are complex, and there is no one way to a happy one. But two people willing to discover the intricacies of problem-solving, forgiveness, and honesty have the best shot at something magical.**

Many couples have this kind of supportive relationship, so it is perfectly achievable. When you come from a place of self-love, you will find it much easier to give love unconditionally to your partner, and this is one of the secrets of success.

THE WEIGHT OF EXPECTATION

When we shift from wanting our partners to be a certain way to enjoying them for who they are, we invite growth from both sides. That being said, expectations aren't all bad and certainly do not indicate that your relationship is weak.

Some healthy expectations to have in a relationship

- My partner will consider how their behaviour affects me.

- My partner will be affectionate physically and verbally.

- There will be a balance of quality time and alone time within the relationship.

- My partner will be interested in who I am, the things I care about, and my major life choices.

- My partner offers comfort, compassion, and care when I am sad or hurting.

- My partner is faithful once we agree to be exclusive.

- It is safe to disagree with my partner without fear of ridicule.

- My partner will encourage what is best for me.

Some unhealthy expectations in a relationship

- My partner will put me above everyone and everything.

- My partner will make me happy.

- My partner will bend to my will.

- My partner will always align with me mentally, emotionally, and spiritually.

- We will never fight or disagree.

- My partner will never complain about me or the relationship.

- I own my partner's body and they own mine.

It's hard to pinpoint the unhealthy expectations we put on our partners, because we usually don't know we have them until they manifest. Every relationship could benefit from asking your partner, 'What expectations have I put on you that seem unfair, unhealthy, or excessive?' You also have to be willing to accept the answer.

LIQUID LIFE

I suspect that the problem is that too often we don't try enough, maybe because we're living in a world where relationships seem disposable. Instead of facing our fears, insecurities, and glitches, we find it easier to give up and move on to the next person. In the swipe-and-date market, why settle for one person when you can try more? The opposite can also happen, too, where we feel that so many options are overwhelming and choose to stay in a familiar yet not-so-good setting instead.

Zygmunt Bauman, the Polish philosopher and sociologist, wrote an interesting book about this kind of behaviour called Liquid Love.[14] In it, he talked about how our desire for quantity has overruled our desire for quality, and this is no coincidence. Past generations got married and had to put up with whatever that meant – divorce was rarely an option. Nowadays, we can flit from flower to flower like a drunken butterfly, getting hit after hit but still being alone at the end of the day.

Bauman mentions that due to our desire for both freedom and security, or 'liquid modernity' as he puts it, we form bonds that offer some sense of security but are kept loose enough to stop us from choking. It's like we want to have our cake and eat it. This is why we find it so difficult to maintain a relationship long enough to make it work. In a way, according to Bauman, it's as if we see love and sex as commodities that we can add to our online shopping cart, and we want novelty, variety, and disposability.

This kind of emotional consumerism is fine if that's what you are into, but I believe that it really reveals the difficulty we have in forming quality relationships that require self-work.

It goes without saying that many of us feel under a lot of pressure to be more popular, more successful, and more attractive – and spend an awful lot of time and energy on those activities. Any insecurity we have about ourselves then becomes magnified, as we try to keep up with people we see on our social media feed, and that can lead to extra stress and anxiety. Instead of doing some kind of internal revamping, we worry about external stuff like what we wear, what kind of tea we drink, how many followers we have on Instagram, and if we have a date arranged for tonight. Social media is often like an arena full of stages that invite performances from people who are trying to feel worthy using metrics such as likes from their audiences. We often mistake acts for reality and, without self-awareness, we attach ourselves to illusions, becoming obsessed with performers and their shows. This can invite comparison and push us to set expectations and follow external pursuits, even though what's on a show doesn't reflect reality.

Never use social media to validate your existence. People can like you without liking your posts, and vice versa. Love is not digital, and you must not wait for likes to like yourself.

I'm not knocking anyone's lifestyle, but I know from the people who contact me on my channels that there's a massive level of disillusionment, loneliness, depression, and anxiety going on behind the scenes. Being relationship-less may seem outwardly OK, but if you can't stand being alone, you have a problem.

Not tending to all of your past traumas and insecurities in order to find a renewed sense of healthy self may seem a tolerable way of handling things, but you won't experience any growth if that happens. It will explain why you can't manage conflict, be open with a partner, handle your emotions, and express your needs. This book can hopefully help you in that respect.

EMOTIONAL INTELLIGENCE

How do we make meaningful connections in a disposable culture? And how do we deal with things like boundaries, rejection, or heartache before, during, and after a relationship? These are issues that can be managed a lot better if we use some kind of emotional intelligence, or EQ (emotional quotient).

While intellectual intelligence reflects your cognitive abilities – your skill with numbers, solving problems and puzzles, analysing words or data – emotional intelligence is your ability to respond to your emotions and handle interactions with maturity and an understanding of the emotions of others. This is an empowering skill to have and it helps both you and your partner.

When you walk into a relationship with a better grip of your emotional make-up, it's a lot easier to create a caring, more meaningful connection with the other person. Many studies, such as that carried out by Professor Brian Ogolsky et al., have found that there are certain patterns and strategies that couples use to make relationships work.[15] A lot of these observations have to do with emotional intelligence, both within ourselves and in the context of the relationship.

After the first flames of passion die down and you settle into a rhythm, what happens when you are tempted to have an affair, don't find your partner sexually attractive any more, or are feeling unattractive yourself? How about arguments over whose turn it is to take out the trash? When the mind and body lead us astray, emotional intelligence can serve as a reliable toolkit, not only in making wise decisions within a relationship, but in life, too.

Emotional intelligence begins with self-love – that ability to honour yourself, understand your needs and desires, and feel good about who you are. When this is your baseline, it's easier to give love to others, as well as receive it. So, in that sense, emotional intelligence is very much tied up with high self-esteem and self-worth. It's about coming from a place of genuine love for yourself and being open to change, as well as navigating the needs of your partner with empathy and compassion.

Using EQ to create stronger connections

Conflict

If you truly want to stay with someone, find a way to resolve conflicts without sacrificing your values or self-worth. It may involve compromise, agreeing to your partner's perspectives or even apologizing. You have to have a heart that is capable of doing that – one that isn't filled with ego, pride, or an over-inflated sense of self. If, for example, you are a vegan and your partner isn't, you can work around that and choose meals to suit both of you. You don't need to shame your partner for liking meat or try to force your preferences on them, which will just lead to unnecessary arguments.

You are bound to go toe-to-toe with your partner. Conflict can arise out of nowhere and, instead of it being a chance to prove your point, emotional intelligence teaches us to make conflict an opportunity to understand our differences, get to know each other, and create unique solutions together. Remember, in conflict, it's you two against the problem, not against each other.

Sometimes, we refuse to say 'I'm sorry' because we think we're admitting defeat. But, when we genuinely say it, it often means, 'I acknowledge your feelings and recognize I can do better.'

Forgiveness

Learning to forgive can reduce feelings of guilt, anger, and hurt and be done by putting any wrongdoings into perspective. When you weigh them up against the value of the relationship as a whole, forgiveness helps you move past these without bitterness or long-term damage. If it's you who is doing all of the forgiving, though, and you are beginning to feel like a doormat, that could be a sign that something about the relationship is off balance and you need to take a good look at that.

It's OK to forgive your partner for forgetting to put petrol in the car – it's no big deal. If they keep doing things like that, maybe something else is going on with them that you need to talk about. Are they preoccupied, absent-minded, or just irresponsible? Talk about it. Open up about what you need and find out if you've also been cutting corners in the relationship, according to them. But be willing to move past the mistakes so that resentment doesn't creep in.

Sacrifice

You can't always have what you want and will have to be prepared to put the needs of your partner before your own at certain points. As long as it is within your comfort zone and you know your partner would do the same for you, sacrifice shouldn't cause feelings of resentment or unfairness. Let's say that they get the chance of a promotion at work, which involves having to move to another city. Are you prepared to uproot and move with them for their benefit or do you refuse because the change seems like too much of a sacrifice? It's something you need to weigh up. Maybe it will be good for both of you, and that's also something to consider.

Relationships aren't viable without sacrifices from both parties. Often, doing the big things for your partner feels good, feels right. You're able to account for all they've done for you and it feels natural to consider these gestures as acts of investment in the foundation and longevity of the relationship. Here again, if you are continuously going out of your way to accommodate them, it's wise to consider if this is going above and beyond your limitations and self-interest.

Encouragement

When you genuinely care about someone, you want the best for them and will be there to support them as they pursue their goals. When you facilitate your partner in their endeavours, it's a truly wonderful feeling to see them flourish. Cheer them on when they go for their dreams and celebrate their wins because it means something to them. Hopefully, they will do the same for you too. It's amazing what even a tiny amount of encouragement can do to uplift the human spirit. Sometimes, the right words of encouragement at the right time can move mountains within your lover's heart.

Respect

Just in the same way that you respect yourself, showing respect for others is paramount. This may seem obvious, but we are challenged when we tussle with our beloved. In any relationship, there may be times when you have disagreements, different opinions or preferences, and these aren't usually game-changers. They are often small things that can easily be sorted out with a bit of give and take.

If your partner likes to go out for a drink with his friends every Wednesday evening, why not respect that? If it just so happens on Wednesday night you begin to pine for their attention and demonstrate resistance to their social life, these passive-aggressive acts show a lack of respect for his need to go out and maintain a sense of closeness with others. Would it make any difference to your relationship if he didn't go? What would be the result if you complained and moaned about it, until he finally stopped going?

The result of a seemingly small situation can have catastrophic results on the respect shared within the relationship. Eventually, both would push the boundaries of the other until trust deteriorated.

Don't let small things get in the way of the bigger picture, unless you genuinely feel it is inconsiderate. When you respect your own space, you can respect the space of others equally well.

There's a lot more that goes into building a successful relationship, and I'll get to that in Part 2 of this book. For now, the key message I want to get across is that self-reflection is the first step to understanding what you want from a relationship, and self-love opens your heart up to so many beautiful possibilities. Expressing how you feel is essential, as is learning how to listen to the other person with empathy. A bit of humour always comes in handy too, and not every conversation has to be deeply philosophical – for many, that can be a big turn-off. It's more about keeping it real and authentic, having fun, and enjoying intimacy.

Romance isn't always the deep talks, extended efforts, lavish gifts and idyllic settings. Sometimes, it's laughing at the cheesy joke, playing their favourite song, and an impromptu slow dance in a grocery aisle.

KEY INSIGHTS

- You may not find the perfect relationship, but you can still achieve balance and fulfilment.

- Freedom is a double-edged sword if you don't know how to use it correctly in any relationship.

- By learning more about the different kinds of attraction, you can better understand what your relationship is based on.

- Instead of succumbing to the law of gravity and falling in love, you can rise in love.

- A spiritual connection can be stronger than any other kind of attraction.

- Decide which expectations are healthy and which are causing you to suffer.

- Emotional intelligence will allow you to connect on a deeper, more meaningful level.

You deserve to find someone who will roam your mind, body, and soul but never reach their destination. May that special somebody crave and conquer the deepest regions of your being, instead of trying to invade and tear apart other lands. And, when they enter your life, I hope their presence is a catalyst for appreciating your own. I pray that they recognize your light during the gloomiest moments of your healing. When you lose your way amid the chaos, may they be the compass that leads you down the road to self-discovery.

PART 2

Together: How to foster meaningful and mindful relationships with others

But let there be spaces in your togetherness and let the winds of the heavens dance between you. Love one another but make not a bond of love: let it rather be a moving sea between the shores of your souls.
– Khalil Gibran

Healthy relationships aren't always glamorous. No matter how much you think you're in love, you are bound to experience conflict, resistance, hurt and destabilizing moments. Precious relationships allow you to see the worst side of yourself and your partner but still choose love.

Chapter 5

TEN RELATIONSHIP RULES

Relationship goals:
Two people who love each other unconditionally not
only share a vision for the future, but also support one
another's dreams in the hope that they both shine.

Far, far away, in the not-too-distant galaxy, stars are in a perpetual state of movement. This is called 'proper motion' and each star moves independently of whatever else is going on in the Universe.

About eighty per cent of the stars in the sky are part of *binary systems*. This means that two stars orbit around each other, often so closely that they begin to form a kind of peanut shape. Most are stable and maintain their own stellar mass and velocity indefinitely.

Sometimes, though, a star can gradually get closer and closer to another star and they begin sharing each other's atmosphere. Eventually, they will slowly merge into a bigger, more brilliant star, known as a 'blue straggler'. These stars burn hotter and brighter than any other stars in their cluster. When two such low-mass stars merge, an 'excretion disc' is often formed by the mass being thrown off in the orbital plane, potentially leading to the creation of new planets. It's an epic event!

If the two stars are moving towards each other too quickly, the astral impact will be bigger and more destructive. As they race into a head-on collision, the crash results in 'star bits' being shattered out all over the galaxy. The impact causes some parts of the star's material to be blown away, but the rest is consumed within.

Astrophysics has a lot to teach us about relationships because, in a way, we are like those stars. We all shine brightly on our own inertia yet are driven to seek out other stars in the darkness and to connect with them at every level. Connections that happen at the speed of light have a tendency to burst and fragment. Some are so destructive it feels as if pieces of ourselves are left floating in space. But with others, the unions that merged with stable momentum, each person shines brighter. While we may not become one being, we are able to bring out the best in our partners and they help illuminate the most positive aspects of ourselves.

If we follow the examples of the stars above, you could say that the most stable one is the binary system, where two people meet, become emotionally involved and intimately connected, but retain their own space and independence. It's as if they are cocooned in their very own peanut shell and if you cracked it open, you'd find two separate nuts!

Then there's the 'blue straggler' style: two people merging to become one and having such an intensely close relationship that they can't tell where they end and the other person begins. You could say it's a passionate connection in the 'I can't live without you' style that burns extremely brightly.

You have probably also witnessed the 'fast love' kind of relationships, in which two people impact each other so dramatically that the relationship inevitably collapses, leaving a lot of emotional damage and debris behind.

A harmful relationship in which one person wants to control, intimidate, or abuse the other is like the black hole scenario, and this can be the most damaging connection of all. No one wants to be swallowed up by a dark chasm of infinite nothingness, but emotionally draining relationships feel like just that.

I believe we can form a healthy 'union' and realize we are one and the same in a relationship. For me, that's where personal evolution takes us – we see ourselves in each other, as well as something far greater than ourselves. Call it God, the Universe, or whatever you are comfortable with, but it is truly a divine experience when you are able to identify the infinite capacity to love and be loved within every being.

At the same time, we don't merge completely, and forget our unique personality as a result. We can experience oneness while also remembering that despite our differences, we are always connected.

The truth is that we can determine the kind of relationships we form: we aren't really astral bodies hurtling through space at an unknown velocity. We have the ability to consider, communicate, choose, and create. It's in our hands how we want to live our lives and the kind of relationships we will accept. If we can merge with another while holding on to our deep sense of autonomy, we can indeed enjoy a stellar relationship.

Perhaps you have gone through, or are still experiencing, problems in your relationships, and it's not easy at all to make the right decisions or to do what's best. I totally get it, and I think a lot of the problems tend to arise when we either jump in head-first, or become so fully immersed that we can't see the bigger picture.

In the beginning of the connection, you are exploring a whole new person with their own stories, interests, ideas, hobbies, style, and pursuits. When you're infatuated, it's easy to get wrapped up in who they are and who they are becoming. But if this goes on for too long, you'll begin to unwittingly lose pieces of yourself. Then, when this person inevitably disappoints or lets you down, you snap back into who you were: back to the parts of you that you're not meant to lose sight of when in a relationship.

Often, we discover that the person we are with now isn't the same person we signed up for. We also change within a relationship, and it's the perfect environment for our insecurities and past traumas to come out. To a large extent, it's a case of not having the emotional skills to know what's best and, before we know it, we're left wondering where we went wrong.

The process of falling in love can be very destabilizing. Everything from your emotional baseline to real-life schedule gets interrupted as you try to find footing for your new 'normal'. This is why it's important to set your intentions when pursuing a partnership. You can avoid idealizing people, remain spiritually grounded in who you are, and navigate love using a few helpful rules.

THE RULES OF CLOSER CONNECTION

Stars operate on natural laws or rules of the Universe that keep them moving through the galaxy and colliding beautifully into one another, creating an even brighter star. Similarly, our relationships could do with a few rules. Yes, rules are important because they keep us on the straight and narrow. We know where we stand when we have rules, and are less at risk of losing ourselves or causing our partner to get lost too. After all, love is supposed to be a positive experience, not a ticking time bomb.

If you were setting out on an expedition to the Antarctic or planning to cross the Atlantic with someone else, you would definitely chart your course before you set off into the unknown. Otherwise, how could you successfully navigate those turbulent seas? You would need to have a clearly outlined route and know the dos and don'ts, as well as have all the life-saving equipment you require.

Relationships are no different – we need to have a direction, the tools to make it work, and an idea of what we should and shouldn't do if we want to enjoy all of the sharing, growth, and positivity possible. Our destination is a loving relationship with someone who truly loves us too. While love may know no limits, it's good to be conscious of our own limitations as humans. We all make mistakes and mess up now and again, which is why the following rules can be so, so useful.

I want you to imagine a couple of scenarios. I'm going to call the protagonists Stella and George. They are both in their late twenties, have been around the block with dating sites and short-term relationships, and are both ready to form something more meaningful.

What should they be aware of if they want to build a meaningful relationship together and what rules would be good to follow?

Stella and George are like the majority of singles out there, or couples who have just embarked on their romantic adventure together. I hear the same story from a lot of people who reach out to me: most of them want to know how to make it work this time around. But it's not just my take on that: all of the recent research also shows that more and more singles (over sixty per cent) are looking for some kind of long-term commitment with a partner who shares similar values, emotional compatibility, and life goals.

A study by Match in the US[16] found that eighty-four per cent of singles want someone they can trust and confide in, communicate their needs with, and who makes them laugh. The figures are roughly the same in the UK, and dating apps like Hinge have done surveys that reveal most singles are looking for quality over quantity, with emotional maturity being a big factor in their search.[17] Even people who have been together for a while can face problems when the honeymoon phase is over, and there's no rulebook out there on how to keep the momentum going in a healthy, balanced way.

That's why I wanted to mention some ground rules – ways of behaving – that will give you a better chance of sustaining a loving partnership. I'm also going to give a few examples of what George and Stella are experiencing as their relationship progresses, which might shed some light on your own situation. Hopefully, it will also help you to find some wisdom.

Rule One: Keep doing the little things

I know how it goes when you hook up with someone that ticks all of your boxes. The early days of a romantic relationship are full of intense energy highs and the desire to please. We shower our new mate with gifts, cute texts, treat them to foot massages, and whisper sweet nothings in their ear. It's like we are driven to make them happy and will do whatever it takes. They have our undivided attention and we will even sacrifice our own needs to show how much we care.

After a while, this kind of heightened activity can fade away as we move on to the next stage of our relationship. Instead of doing our utmost to thrill our partner or even pay them the attention they seek, we slowly settle into a kind of domestic intimacy that ignores their needs. They can also fall into the same kind of inertia, not responding to our desire for greater emotional connection, which weakens the relationship that we were once both so excited about.

> In George and Stella's case, George has noticed that Stella doesn't pay much attention to him when he's talking to her. She's either scrolling through her mobile phone or watching TV. It's like she isn't even listening to what he's saying half the time and George feels hurt by it. But instead of bringing up the subject with her to share his feelings, he grabs his phone instead and starts going through his own social media feed.

We all have a need for emotional connection, and this can be satisfied in the simplest of ways if we remain present in the relationship. You've probably all seen the couples in bars or restaurants who are glued to their phone instead of having a conversation together. What happened to their desire to be fully attentive to the other person, to look into their eyes, and hang on to their every word? As they say, two's company and three's a crowd, so don't make your relationship a threesome (or foursome) with your mobiles!

When such drastic characteristics of the relationship change, the person experiencing less effort often feels like they've been baited and switched. But where love is mutual, effort will be matched. It's no wonder one of the most common phrases for a marriage counsellor to hear is, 'This isn't the person I married,' from a couple on the verge of collapse. **Granted, we will all change, but the way in which you prioritize your relationship isn't meant to.**

It's good to know that relationships have cycles you can loop back to if you want to keep the magic happening. Sure, in that honeymoon phase there's a lot going on that you aren't always consciously aware of, such as spiking hormones and love chemicals, but that doesn't mean you can't recapture that further down the line.

It's a good idea to keep shaking up the routine, trying out new things together, and keeping novelty in the equation.

Complacency can breed apathy and eventually discontent, so be more involved on a daily basis. I'm not saying start base-jumping together or splurge on expensive gifts. These are all great if you can pull them off, but it's more about the multiple nuances that show you care – what you say, how you say it, your gestures, and your ability to stay open. Think about what pleases your partner and if you are nurturing those needs or ignoring them.

You can keep the romance alive too, with a little thought and planning. Maybe George and Stella could start sending each other those cute little text messages again like they used to do in the beginning. Things like, 'I can't wait to see you,' and, 'I miss you so much,' are much more effective than, 'I'll be home at 6,' or 'Do we need any milk from the supermarket?' They could arrange a weekly 'date night', cook a special dinner together, spend an evening recounting how they first met with some chilled music and no interruptions. That would be a great move to make!

It's the simple things that make all the difference if you want to keep the magic in a relationship.

Rule Two: Disagree fairly

You are bound to have disagreements with your partner, and these bumps in the road aren't all bad. Not seeing eye to eye on everything is a sign of two unique individuals who are challenging each other's perspective and will. This can be a healthy dynamic which helps you to learn and grow: not everything has to be a battle of wills about who's right and who's wrong.

While you might say that you are constantly arguing over nothing, the truth is that there's a lot going on under the surface. As you get to know the other person better, power struggles may increase – who needs to be right all of the time and who backs down first? It can become irritating when your partner doesn't agree with you and is always contradicting or opposing you. That may be upsetting or make you angry, with thoughts turning to things like, 'Perhaps they're not so perfect after all,' creeping in. Arguments and intense differences of opinion can be stressful and, depending on your personality type, might make you want to fight head on or withdraw to a corner.

George and Stella have been together for eight months now. Coming from very different backgrounds, Stella doesn't like some of George's opinions about politics and they have a lot of disagreements over that. She feels like he's always shoving his opinion down her throat without listening to her side and that he doesn't respect her views. Stella now tries to avoid sharing her opinions with George so she can have a quieter life, but is resentful about being made to feel as if her views don't count for anything.

What starts out as a casual comment from one side might end up in nit-picking, screaming, and even tears, as both get into a cycle of 'who said what' over and over again. That can feel like reaching a dead end where you never see eye to eye on anything any more. If you begin from a place of genuine care and respect for your partner, you have to accept that there will be differences of opinion. Rather than becoming too overbearing or passive, there are ways to de-escalate conflict and solve the problem.

How about being your own referee, stopping the game when you see a foul? Or agree to disagree before it even gets there. No one likes dirty players, and even if you score a goal, what price does that come at? Follow the rules of fair play – whether you think you are right or not. Take a time-out to calm things down and regroup – that's a lot better than letting things get out of control.

- There are ways to disagree without it ending in a big row or fight.

- There are ways to resolve differences without resorting to manipulation or abuse.

- There are ways to respect the other's opinion without gaslighting them.

Gaslighting is where someone is led to question their perception of reality by another person, who purposefully manipulates the victim to make them believe that their judgement is completely wrong. Gaslighting allows an individual to carry out harm while manipulating the situation and the emotions of their prey so they can look innocent. Furthermore, they can often position themselves as the victim, and have the real victim questioning their own perceptions and behaviours.

Instead of trying to control who is right and who is wrong, take control of the way you argue by de-escalating things. When your partner storms off, banging the door behind them, or the conversation descends into spiteful comments, just STOP!

START listening instead of talking. But listen with your heart, not only your ears. Create a safe space for your partner to express themselves without fear of judgement or criticism. Allow them to talk – it's often as simple as that. There's no need to negate their opinions or belittle what they believe, even if you don't agree with it.

Keep an open mind and allow the other person to state their case. You aren't judge and jury in your relationship and you don't need to reach a verdict! Maybe you are both right, or both wrong, and who cares? What's more important is that you provide room for dialogue to take place as you move towards a place of mutual respect and understanding.

Just because you can shout louder than your partner, it doesn't make you right! If anything, you can come across as intimidating, aggressive, and manipulating, so where's the harmony in that? Instead of verbal bullying, take a moment to breathe and count to ten. Give yourself time to think more clearly before you say something that you might regret later and avoid getting into slanging matches to prove your point. Relationships shouldn't be about one-upmanship, and if that's you, maybe you need to ask yourself why you feel the need to be right all of the time.

Just because you don't have the same views on politics, religion, or anything else with your partner, doesn't mean that the relationship isn't working or that love has come to an end. It's OK to say, 'I disagree, but I respect your opinion'. Healthy differences are welcome, but unhealthy ones are not, and you need to know which is which.

Here are some tips for having a productive disagreement and resolving conflict:

- Mirror the complaint: 'So, what you're saying is . . .'

- Take responsibility for what you did or said that is upsetting your partner.

- Focus on the topic and resist the urge to bring up past events.

- With your body language, avoid:

  Rolling your eyes: This is blatant disrespect and hurtful. It says, 'What you're feeling doesn't matter to me.'

  Crossing your arms: This action closes you off emotionally. If you find you need to self-soothe, it's best to table the talk for another time.

  Looking around the room or at distractions: It's hard to really hear and feel what someone's saying if you're not looking at them.

If you reach the point where you feel that the trust between you has been broken or have noticed a change in intimacy on any level, it will require a deeper, more honest look at what is happening between the two of you.

Another thing to note is that when a small disagreement snowballs into an unhinged battlefield in the living room, there are clearly underlying issues with one or both partners. These issues can be within the relationship or completely separate.

The more attuned you are to your emotions, the more you'll be able to understand your reactions and why a conversation triggers an outburst. In any case, you always have the power to be compassionate and diffuse any situation.

Rule Three: Honour intimacy

There are multiple layers of intimacy within any relationship. Some are physical and others emotional. Some levels of intimacy can feel almost spiritual. When you feel intimate with someone, you are able to share your true self with them, no mask attached. This non-judgemental safe space is where relationships are deeply nurtured. You experience closeness and connection in all its forms. Whether it's sex or communication, intimacy is the silver thread that holds together the beautiful patchwork of coupledom that you are creating.

Even intellectual intimacy is a thing, in which you can share your thoughts and ideas with another person without censorship. Spiritual intimacy can also be enjoyed when you share your beliefs about a higher power, the cosmos, or the connection you feel to the world and the Universe.

Our couple, George and Stella, have been having some issues in bed. Stella finds it difficult to make the first move and it's always George who has to initiate sex. Naturally, this is leading to painful arguments and a lot of misunderstanding. He asks her, 'Don't you fancy me any more? What am I doing wrong?' Instead of discussing the issue, Stella replies that nothing is wrong. She's just tired, not in the mood . . . and so on.

Believe me when I say that many, many people have some kind of intimacy issue, for a whole lot of reasons. While the physical one may seem like the most obvious, problems with emotional intimacy are just as common, and often even more catastrophic for a couple. These problems might become more apparent as the couple move towards a place of greater closeness. We don't know what is making Stella unable to initiate sex, but we can see that it needs to be addressed.

It could be a fear of abandonment or engulfment, usually stemming from past experiences that are triggered in the present. She might be afraid of judgement or criticism, have phobias or suffer from anxiety, which prevents her from navigating a close relationship, even though she desperately craves one. Not everyone understands their own intimacy issues if they have been buried deep within the psyche until now.

When you can't handle intimacy, it's often easier to avoid it than to face it. You've managed so far, right? But it can seriously affect your ability to commit, give, express, and enjoy physical contact. Intimacy comes from the Latin word *intimus* ('inmost', 'deepest'), so real intimacy comes from both partners listening deeply to themselves first: to explore their hidden depths of emotions, desires, and vulnerability. When they are able to do so, they can reveal what they've discovered in an atmosphere of acceptance and intimacy which can be a catalyst for deep healing.

By talking through any concerns or fears, you will help your partner to understand where you are coming from. And when you listen to them, you will gain insights into their behaviour. In reality, intimacy does take time because it requires that an individual is brave enough to get to the bottom of their issues and then to open up about them, but it can be done in a nurturing, loving relationship.

My suggestion to George and Stella, or anyone out there who wants to spark or encourage intimacy in their relationship, would be this:

- Make a point of showing you care. Tell your partner how much you appreciate them and express your gratitude for having them in your life. Even a simple 'thank you' can be very powerful.

- Be curious about each other without being pushy. Ask about their past, their present, their future dreams and goals. As we all change over time, there's always something new to be learned.

- Share stories and experiences. Be open and honest, without feeling ashamed of past mistakes or embarrassing incidents.

- Make it playful with board games for adults like Taboo or 20 Questions to keep the mood relaxed and stress-free.

- Spend time with each other. There's nothing more conducive to building a strong relationship than doing things together and focusing on your one and only.

- Show physical affection, even without sex. Learn to be affectionate and touch your partner with endearment. If you want to liven things up in the bedroom, agree how, with role-playing, toys, fantasies – whatever works for you both.

- Discuss intimacy. Whatever intimacy means to you, be open about it and share your thoughts. After all, sharing is caring. Tell your partner what you like to do together, and what helps you to feel closer to them. Give them the space to also express their inner thoughts about what intimacy means to them.

By being open about intimacy and talking through it, you will be helping your partner to express their innermost feelings in a loving environment, which is all they really need at this point.

Rule Four: Do the dishes

Honestly, never underestimate the impact clean dishes can have on a relationship.

This is more about establishing balance in a relationship and doing your bit to keep things on an even keel. You'd be amazed at how many couples squabble over such mundane tasks as whose turn it is to wash the dishes, take out the trash, cook, clean the car, pay the bills, and so on. These rows usually raise their ugly head after couples have been together for a while and are settled in a daily routine, although the arguments might go on for years and years without resolution.

George is a bit of a stickler for tidiness. He likes everything in its place and can't stand mess lying around. Stella is more laid-back and doesn't mind a few dishes in the sink or books scattered across the coffee table. After being together for two years now, they are still having daily run-ins about domestic chores and haven't been able to agree on priorities. It's driving George mad!

Believe me, it's not the dishes that are causing the problem most of the time. They are simply the tip of the iceberg. When you don't take your turn, pull your weight, or fail to carry out something you said you were going to do, it can be interpreted by your partner as not caring about them. They may believe that if they can't rely on you to do a simple task, they won't be able to depend on you when something more serious comes up.

It might start off with George asking Stella to be tidier, but end up with him thinking she doesn't see his wants as important. Maybe, underneath it all, he feels like she doesn't care enough about him, respect his wishes, or accept his pet hates. From Stella's point of view, it's not that she doesn't care, it's more like she finds his constant nagging tiresome and annoying. A few dishes in the sink are no big deal, after all!

Nothing is going to change until they can both understand what they are really arguing about and get it out in the open. They'll soon see that emotions such as feeling minimized, unappreciated, unloved, disrespected, and so on are the real key factors in the argument and not the dishes, the trash, the car wash, or the untidy house.

Everything in life is about balance, and that means giving as well as taking. While you shouldn't overextend in order to please your partner, it is possible to compromise and to reassure them that you really do respect their desires. Deal with the underlying issues rather than the surface reactions and gain a greater understanding of what your partner is experiencing. Instead of dismissing them as bothersome, try to read between the lines.

If you worry that you can't depend on your partner, sit down with them and use the right words to convey that. Beginning sentences with, 'I feel like you don't respect me . . .' can be much more constructive than accusations of, 'You never do anything I ask . . .' You can see the difference, right?

To make life easier, you can simply agree on a chore list and stick to it!

Rule Five: Have the hard talks

> Think of all the imagined issues we create simply because we choose to ruminate instead of communicating. Problems delayed are problems multiplied. Have the hard conversations now and fewer regrets later.

If you want to deepen your relationship with your partner, you have to be prepared to hang out the dirty linen. How else can you really get to know each other? You can only dance around each other's flaws and/or incompatibilities for so long. It's best to get real with one another right away, although it can be a painful process. Nevertheless, through it, you will both learn more about yourselves and come out of it with a stronger sense of love and understanding, and discover the processes required to meet each other in the middle.

Often, we over-analyse things and let them fester. You'd be surprised how much frequent conversations around your relationship concerns can impact the quality and longevity of the connection. It's not only important how often you have these talks, but how you approach them. This isn't a time to shame or fight with one another. Respect, love, compassion, willingness, and understanding are necessary for making these talks productive. If you must, schedule them, pick a day of the week or month where you two are committed to setting aside thirty minutes to an hour where you create a safe space for both parties to open up about a challenging subject.

Happy couples aren't just the ones posting kissing selfies. They're the ones having uncomfortable conversations, helping each other overcome trauma, and ugly-crying to save their relationship. Happy couples prioritize growth and are a source of inspiration for each other.

George wanted to broach the subject of Stella's apparent lack of desire for him but didn't know how to go about it. The constant rows and late-night bickering were wearing him down, while she seemed to be getting more and more distant. He finally decided to open up the conversation one day and a lot came out of it. He learned that her deep-seated fear of being rejected was blocking her from making the first move. It was all news to him and she hadn't admitted it to anyone else before because it wasn't all that clear in her mind. They managed to end their talk with a much clearer understanding of what was going on and a stronger sense of connection. Things still aren't perfect, but a lot of tension has been released and Stella is coming to realize that she can really trust George to listen to her fears and insecurities.

You've got to do the hard work if you want to grow, and although it can be painful, there's no other way around it. And you know, we often keep things inside for such a long time that the thought of actually uttering them out loud can be terrifying. The thing is, it's often only when we manage to say what's bothering us that we fully understand it.

When you engage in hard talk, you might be challenged by the other person to explain what you mean. This can be a very healing process, and although it sounds scary, you won't regret it. As long as you feel that you will be heard with compassion and love, I think you should go for it!

Rule Six: Never compare

When you start off on a new relationship, you could be tempted to compare the person in front of you now with someone from your past: an old flame, ex-wife/husband/partner. Although it's kind of natural to do so, it isn't in your best interests. First of all, no two people are alike, so setting your past experience with someone as a yardstick by which everyone else will be judged is just wrong. Secondly, whatever went on with you in the past should stay in the past. You might have learned some lessons, but if these prevent you from moving forward, it's going to be hard to make any new relationship work.

> George was very much in love with his last girlfriend, but she two-timed him and they ended their relationship in a big blow-out. Ever since then, he has been quite mistrustful and often wonders if Stella will do the same thing to him. He double-checks all the time to see where she is, doesn't like it when other guys look at her, and often criticizes the way she dresses if he feels it's too revealing. Stella has no idea that this is all coming from a place of past trauma and mistrust.

I'm sure it's obvious to you that George hasn't got over the hurt of his ex's infidelity, and is still unable to fully trust Stella because of that. This is an issue that he has to overcome himself with some hard thinking, but Stella can also help him by showing that she will be there for him. Broken trust is really difficult to rebuild, but remember that Stella isn't George's ex – she's a completely different person. Also, their relationship is unique and it's unreasonable of him to expect it to turn out the same way. If George can work through his pain, he will be able to move on. Being in a loving, supportive relationship will help him to stop comparing his past with his present and have more faith in the process.

In the same way, try to avoid comparing your relationship to someone else's. You might envy friends who always seem to be more lovey-dovey with each other, but this robs you of the joy you could be having with your own partner. If you start having thoughts like, 'I wish my partner was more like x, y, or z,' it's not going to end well. You are making yourself unhappy and discontent with this kind of thinking, and it shows a lot of disrespect for your partner. Apart from that, you will be setting unrealistic expectations that can never be fulfilled because everyone is different and we rarely see the full picture.

Comparisons are also a bit selfish because you are thinking about what your partner should do for you, rather than what you should be doing for them. Instead of dwelling on what's missing, focus on all the great aspects of your relationship and work on expanding those. Otherwise, you need to consider why you are in the relationship at all.

Comparing your relationship and your partner to the previous version of them? We all change as we unlearn old patterns and are exposed to new experiences and information.

A long-term relationship will die and be reborn a thousand times. It doesn't matter how long you are with someone, but how willing you are to stay open to the new versions of them (and yourself) that are certain to arise.

If you've just come from a break-up with a gaping broken heart, it is going to be extremely difficult for you to find ANYONE who can replace your lost love. You will be setting yourself up for failure if you go into a new relationship with that mindset. You probably need some time to go through the healing process before moving on to someone else – you owe it to yourself and to them.

Rule Seven: Have a plan

Most people walk, stumble, or fall into a relationship without any kind of plan or strategy. That might sound OK to you, because we're not talking about a business adventure or military operation, right? Actually, we kind of are, if you think about it. Knowing what possible obstacles you might come up against and how to avoid them isn't a bad thing – it gives you greater ability to handle them when they arise. You wouldn't walk blindly into a minefield, so why would you do that in a relationship?

It's a good idea to agree on some very important ground rules before you let destiny take its unpredictable course, such as:

- What do you both want from the relationship? Are you after a casual, friends-with-benefits kind of thing, or looking for a serious commitment?

- Do you like the idea of a one-on-one connection, or have other preferences such as polyamory?

- What is non-negotiable for you? Are honesty, respect, and communication a must or are you OK with your partner lacking these qualities?

- What couple goals can you agree on? Do you both agree on the idea of marriage or is your partner totally against it? It's good to know if you don't want to be left standing at the altar!

- Does your partner have a lifelong dream of going to live off-grid in Alaska? Are you prepared to go with them if that's the case?

- How are you going to manage differences of opinions, conflicts, and disparities? Are you ready to handle any of these or do you expect your partner to agree with you all the time?

- How flexible are you when it comes to lifestyles, opinions, preferences? Can you overlook anything that you don't agree with?

- What does your heart want?

George wants to quit his job and go backpacking around Asia. Stella is unwilling to give up her great career and follow him, although she truly wants to be with him. The couple have come to a bridge in their relationship they are unable to cross, and neither wants to compromise their dreams and ambitions. What should they do?

Many couples will reach a point where they face such dilemmas and it doesn't have to be about backpacking around Asia. It could be anything that tests the limits of your desire to be together as opposed to your need to fulfil your own dreams. That's where it gets tricky. As couples merge into this cosy oneness, it's all too easy to fall into the trap of seeing themselves as an entity, which might require that one or both have to sacrifice some things in their lives. You might be OK with that, and it depends on every individual and each case. The danger is, though, that you give up too much and lose your autonomy.

Being together in a close, emotionally strong relationship means being able to be apart. That might sound crazy, but hear me out. If you love each other unconditionally, seeing your partner pursue their dreams won't kill your relationship – mistrust and doubt will.

Rule Eight: Hold space

This is very much a continuation of the previous point. When I talk about holding space, I mean allowing for multiple realities and perspectives to be present. I mean honouring your needs and those of your partner while building trust and reliability.

Imagine that you are decorating the interior of your dream home together. You might have differences of opinion when it comes to colours, fabrics, design, and so on. How can you create something that you are both happy with while maintaining your own sense of aesthetics and style? What if you hate the wallpaper your partner has chosen or can't stand the old-fashioned furniture they want to buy? How can you both live in a house that doesn't entirely go with your taste in interior decor?

Now, replace that concept of a house with the concept of your relationship: how present can you be without judgement? How can you accept someone's truths, no matter what they are, and simply allow them to be? As long as your relationship works, how important is it to agree on everything? Can you overcome your differences for the sake of love?

When you hold space for your partner, you can be fully present without feeling the need to enforce your opinion or impose your will. Instead, practise compassion and empathy when they talk about their feelings. Allow them to grow from your connection and expand their experience of who they are instead of trying to fit them into your box, your likes and dislikes, your opinions.

Some of the ways in which you can practise holding space include:

- **Listening deeply.** This is not just about hearing what someone says but listening to understand. Instead of listening with your ears, listen with your heart. There's no need to agree or disagree and it's all about allowing them to express themselves without fear of criticism or judgement.

- **Practising loving kindness.** When you cultivate love and compassion for yourself and others, it creates a warm energy that emanates out to those around you. It's the kind of feeling you get when you do a good deed or a simple act of kindness. There's nothing to be gained from it other than a wonderful feeling of happiness and contentment. If you can approach your relationship in the same way, you will create a place of authentic love.

- **Making room for your partner.** Most people feel like they have nowhere to go when they want to cry. Bathrooms are usually the only refuge, and that's really sad. You can be that place and allow your partner to unload anything they feel: their sorrows, worries, doubts, fears, pain. Sometimes, all it takes is for you to listen to their outpouring and acknowledge what they are experiencing.

- **Freeing yourself from the urge to fix everything.** Giving advice or making helpful suggestions might come naturally to you, but not everyone is ready for that. They might just need a safe space to vent their emotions without getting feedback on what to do. Often, we need to work things out for ourselves, and being told, 'You should do this or that,' really isn't helpful. It can make us feel like our problems are being swept under the carpet or that we aren't being heard at all. Simply listen and sit through the pain with your partner if you want to be truly supportive.

And when it comes to decorating that house, keep two separate corners for each other, which you can both do up in any funky, weird style you like!

Rule Nine: Friendship first

The philosopher Friedrich Nietzsche said that it's not a lack of love that makes unhappy marriages, but lack of friendship.[18] There's definitely a lot of evidence out there to prove he was right, with friendship being seen as one of the key factors to a successful long-term commitment. Even if the marriage or relationship ends, you can still continue to be friends, and many couples were actually friends before they hooked up and it's possible to remain friends after a break-up.

Friendship means being connected to someone emotionally and psychologically and can definitely bring a lot of benefits to your health and wellbeing. Just knowing you have a trusted friend to rely on, someone you enjoy being with, who you get along with really well, is invaluable. If you are fortunate enough to have a partner who is also your best friend, then all the better. But that needs to grow over time if you weren't already friends beforehand.

Stella and George have a lot of friends in common, most of them couples, and often get together with them for a night out. Stella also has a lot of single girlfriends she would like to see more often, but George isn't too happy with that. He often tells her, 'Why do you have to go out with them when you have me? Aren't I enough for you, babe?' Stella wishes that George had more single friends of his own so he could get out more often.

Your partner doesn't have to be your best friend, but most people nowadays look for that. They want their partner to meet all of their needs, from teaching them how to do yoga to introducing them to new artists on Spotify. They want to share everything with their partner-bestie and also expect them to be their shopping buddy, therapist, mentor, guru, and fashion expert. I think that friendship within a relationship is very important, but your partner doesn't need to be your ONLY best friend. It's good to also have other best friends outside of the relationship if you want to create space for self-expansion and independence.

On the other hand, not nurturing friendship in a romantic relationship can make it harder for you to grow closer – you'll be one of those couples who go through the motions of being together without really sharing in real time. So, it's about balance and having a desire to cultivate closeness without getting lost on the way.

When the spark of the romantic infatuation is over and you start to get to know each other on a deeper level, nurturing a solid relationship just as you would if you made a new friend is important. With friends, you are usually positively engaged and interact with enthusiasm and a willingness to communicate. You certainly wouldn't take them for granted or let them down intentionally. Why not bring this same attitude to your partnership and work towards solidifying a lifelong connection!

Communication is obviously the number-one priority here; being present and listening attentively. Lack of communication means lack of intimacy, so if that's what you are after, you have to be invested. The way you treat your partner is also telling: do you show that you respect them the same way that you do your friends? Do you comment on their weight while you would never mention that to a friend? Are you constantly criticizing their taste in music or trying to belittle them in front of others? How about if they do the same to you – would you tolerate that from your bestie?

You can encourage and support your partner, just in the same way that you would with friends. Bringing them down or showing indifference isn't going to make them like you, and that's a fact. Nobody wants to be undermined and a true friend would offer support no matter what the circumstances are. Can you do that with your partner? They say that time spent with friends is never time wasted, but do you often feel like that's the case with your partner? If so, there are plenty of fun things you can do together. Try to get involved in some of their hobbies or interests and show genuine curiosity for that. If you want to be involved with someone, you need to get involved!

If you treat your romantic relationship like you treat your friendships, you can cultivate a closeness based on mutual respect and unconditional love. This can long outlive sexual desire and heightened romance, which might fade or fluctuate as the relationship progresses.

Rule Ten: Prioritize personal growth

One major step along any path of personal evolution, emotional healing, and spiritual growth is the realization that we cannot control the external world. Our power lies in our ability to respond to it. We can interrupt and overwrite any existing patterns that are triggered by external stimuli simply by moving from a place of reactiveness to one of responsiveness.

However, without self-awareness, we usually spend most of our time and energy reacting to situations instead of responding from a place of understanding and loving kindness. The truth is that, although apologies and hearing the words, 'You are right' might satisfy our ego, they won't always be forthcoming. After all, we can't control how someone chooses to behave or what they say, even if they are in the wrong.

> You may never get that apology. And the healing begins when you can accept that.

Nevertheless, the good news is that if we take the time to witness our thoughts, emotions, and judgements, we can find a sense of freedom and empowerment in our ability to sit with discomfort. This is because we always have access to an inherent sense of ease and balance, regardless of whether we're in the right or not.

While the concepts of forgiveness and letting go are hard to practise, they're essential to our healing journey. We begin to 'move on' in the direction that's best for our growth when we:

- Let go of anger and resentment towards others and ourselves.

- Accept that challenges in life can be valuable lessons.

- Acknowledge that everyone is doing their best based on their own belief systems.

George was upset with Stella because during a fight over money, she called him tight-fisted. Instead of lashing out at her and prolonging the argument, he took a step back to think about what she had said. He knew she probably didn't mean it, but he needed to consider if there was any truth in the comment. He did like to control their spending because he

was always worried about paying the bills, but maybe he had
overdone it. George decided not to react to her accusations
and, instead, worked on his own attitude to money and the
way he came across. They were then able to discuss the subject
later on with less hurt and more constructive dialogue.

The way I see it, you either allow someone to dictate your reality by placing the power in their hands, or regain control by focusing on how you can move forward with your life. The way you respond to any given situation is up to you, and never the other person, no matter how provoking they are.

When you are healthy and happy, it is easier to deal with your relationship. If your partner is healthy and happy too, you can build a loving and thriving relationship together.

FORGIVE AND LET GO

I want to finish here by asking you a small question: can you forgive your partner for their mistakes, failures, weaknesses, and weirdness? One way to do this is by creating a Forgiveness Ritual that will help you to foster forgiveness and move on in your relationship. It's really easy to do. Whenever you feel like it, simply fill in the blanks for these two statements, either in your head or with pen and paper:

- The negative thoughts, feelings, and memories I've been holding on to about _____ are blocking me from being able to love unconditionally.

- Holding on to all this is hurting our relationship. It makes me:
  1. _____
  2. _____
  3. _____

Be prepared to accept, forgive, let go, and move on with compassion and love. When you do, you create space for something wonderful to happen.

You have to hold on to your separate identities if you want to allow space for the relationship to grow. Being tied to each other won't encourage growth – it will stunt you instead. Think about who you are and what you are prepared to lose on the way. It is possible to respect your own boundaries and also to respect your partner's. In fact, it's crucial!

KEY INSIGHTS

- We are all like stars in the galaxy, although some of us will merge and burn even brighter.

- When we can establish balance in our relationship, we experience more fulfilment.

- The ten rules of a relationship can be a framework for success with your loved one.

- Each little thing you do creates more love.

- Learning how to disagree fairly helps to resolve conflict easier.

- By honouring intimacy, you can forge stronger bonds.

- Most arguments aren't about the dishes – they have to do with underlying concerns and fears.

- Having the hard talks will ease any future conflicts.

- Comparing your partner to anyone else doesn't bring satisfaction or contentment.

- Holding heart space and being able to forgive lead to inner growth.

Chapter 6

YOUR DEMONS
VERSUS THEIR DEMONS

**Never judge someone's story by the page you landed
on. Take time to learn about their previous chapters.**

Relationships are the perfect breeding ground for pain and
suffering. Although it shouldn't be that way, it often is,
especially if one or both parties haven't done the work
suggested in previous chapters. The demons I refer to here
are the by-products of entering or maintaining a relationship
where unhealthy thought and behaviour patterns persist. They
are when love becomes an addiction and relationships become
entanglements.

Making hurtful comments, being short-tempered, forcing
our opinions, and not considering the other person are just some
examples of how we can sometimes behave in a relationship. It
doesn't matter how spiritually enlightened or emotionally
intelligent you are, we all slip up with those we love most. We
also react badly when our partners say or do something that
triggers our insecurities and any unresolved issues. Their words
remind us of painful past experiences, touch a raw nerve, or
make us go on the defensive. Anything can get under our skin
and set off trigger points without warning. And partners are
especially good at finding out what those are.

When that happens, emotional meltdowns, arguments,
shouting or screaming, attacking one another verbally or

physically, and even distancing become the norm. Before you know it, your relationship resembles a battlefield where you place your partner in the position of an enemy.

It's not always easy to kiss and make up afterwards, and even if you do, the cause of the triggers often goes unresolved. You might bury the hurt but stop seeing your partner in the same positive light. Subtle shifts in the relationship can go unnoticed until the next flare-up, with no one fully aware of the harm they are doing to themselves, and to each other. The cold war sets in, with neither side sure of what the other is thinking.

In many ways, we treat intimate relationships as if they are the perfect place to showcase the worst side of ourselves. While you probably behave differently at work, with friends, and even among strangers, all of your social etiquette goes out the window when you get into that cosy couple situation. I mean, you would never snap at your colleague, sulk in a corner when out with friends, or be abusive to someone you hardly know. By the same token, you wouldn't expect that kind of behaviour from anyone else in a social setting. So why do you act like that or put up with it from your partner?

When I first met Kaushal over ten years ago, it wasn't always smooth sailing. Both of us were coming into the relationship a little bit emotionally immature, which didn't begin to become obvious until we spent more time together. It felt easier to blame and judge each other than to understand where we were both coming from. Often, our disagreements were more to do with who would have the last word, invalidating each other's feelings so we could have control. Looking back, I can see that the early stages of our relationship were more like a power struggle than a loving union.

It's not uncommon for this kind of dynamic to present itself as couples strive to get closer, and I think that, for us, it served a purpose. It forced us both to face our demons and to begin working together instead of being on opposite sides. Rather than seeing each other as enemies, we realized that we both had to let go of our egos and try to undo the conditioning that was preventing us from experiencing something truly wonderful.

To better understand what's happening within when we fight miserably with the one we love most, there are a few things to consider. Your ego wants to protect you. When that rise of emotions swells inside of you as a result of something they did or didn't say or do, you have a choice. You can fly off the handle, embarrass yourself with uncontrolled behaviour, and weaken the foundation of your relationship as well as set the tone for what your norm will be when you fight. Or, you can let some time pass before you respond. Allow the emotional charge to subside, and talk to your partner with respect and love while also honouring your feelings. You don't want to hurt them and you simply don't want to be hurt by them because hurt challenges the love you share.

Anger, the root of fights, is a secondary emotion. There is always something you feel before you're angry – such as that of being forgotten, unwanted, rejected, neglected, not good enough, or lonely. Your partner may unintentionally make you feel some or all of these things. Those are the emotions to bring to the table if you wish to have a conscious discussion and positive outcome.

> **Every relationship consists of two individuals at different stages of consciousness. To evolve together, you must be willing to resolve together – that includes anything that is unhealed within. This is how a relationship matures. Acceptance and openness are essential.**

When you establish a conscious relationship and are mindful of your own demons and those of your partner, it is possible to form a deeper connection. If you can act from the heart instead of from the ego, you stop caring about being right all the time, or 'winning' the next round of arguments. You become more focused on experiencing the true joy of love, and there is no greater challenge or reward.

What is it exactly that makes us act like a five-year-old when our partner says something that touches a nerve or acts in a way that we don't like? And how do we process our response and do better next time?

I think it's a question worth asking because there are so many couples out there trying to grapple with the emotional reactions they experience when they feel triggered by their partner – emotions that don't usually surface in their everyday contact with other people. You wouldn't throw a wobbly with a mate because he called you a lazy so-and-so . . . he's not likely to say that in the first place anyway. If he does, it might be as a joke, and the comment could bounce off you like water off a duck's back. But if your girlfriend says the same thing, that's a real blow below the belt. You are most likely going to feel hurt, disappointed, angry – or any number of negative emotions. Before you know it, you are returning the insult, getting into a slanging match, or walking off feeling annoyed.

FROM HAPPILY SINGLE TO DOUBLE TROUBLE

The truth is that when we get into relationships, we are entering an intimate space where who we are is laid bare before another person – both our good and bad sides. It's not like anyone knows how to move within this space at first because we are used to being just us – an individual. We never had to consider how to be with someone else in such a close-knit way, how to respond to their issues, how to deal with our issues, how to work together to create something healthy and fulfilling.

When we become emotionally involved with another person, conflict, misunderstandings and unmet emotional needs are very likely to appear early on, which can create a lot of hurt for both parties. It's not easy to see that kind of dynamic creeping up on us, unless we have a level of self-awareness and emotional maturity. We can grow and learn within the relationship, though, if we build a supportive environment with our partner that allows us to work through our issues.

Emotional maturity is to have a disagreement without shaming, blaming, name-calling, or projecting your trauma onto someone else.

From being an individual, living according to your needs and desires, to forming a close partnership with someone else is a big step. You have to go from, 'I'll do what I want' to 'I need to consider my partner's wants'. Singlehood can be great, but if you want to enter into a loving relationship, you will have to leave your ego at the door if it's going to be a success.

For all you singles out there, I'm not knocking your status – there aren't any rules in life about how you should live and I'd be the last person to say there are. I'm really addressing couples here who want their relationship to work but keep coming up against the same stumbling blocks and can't seem to get past them.

What might have worked for you when you were single, won't play out in the couple scenario. It's a whole different ball game that requires compromise, understanding, and sacrifices.

There's no room for selfishness, self-centeredness, or narcissism. Sharing your life with your partner and enjoying intimacy, happiness and growth can be achieved, even if you do have to go through some disagreements, negotiations, and compromises. In fact, that's a very healthy way to get even closer and it's often through such differences that we come out stronger on the other side.

The problems occur when you fail to address your inner demons or are unable to handle the inner demons of your partner. There has to be a willingness to confront your own emotional issues and consider how they are affecting your relationship. You also need to understand what your partner is going through and find the right way to handle that, even if it means walking away.

The one thing I want to stress is that it's nobody's fault if the relationship doesn't work out because of this. There's no blaming and shaming to be had. Each one of us is on a road we've never travelled down before and there are very few signposts to point us in the right direction. We are all learning as we go and not everything will work out as we would have wished. The point is to use each experience as a lesson and take stock of where we went wrong, which turn we shouldn't have taken, and how to get our bearings again. We might need to change direction frequently until we get to where we want to be.

OUR DISPOSABLE MINDSET

I think a lot of people in their twenties and thirties have grown up in a kind of throwaway culture, just like me, where we want instant gratification. If something doesn't suit us, we just throw it out or reject it and move on to the next best thing. I know that social media plays a large part in that and, for all its good points, it also has a lot to answer for. We are used to everything being available at the swipe of a screen and if we can't have it, we'll look for a substitute.

In the olden days (I guess I'm talking about the era when divorce still had a bit of stigma attached to, up to the 1950s and 60s), people would meet, get engaged, then marry, and that was it.

Whatever problems they were facing were rarely talked about and it wasn't easy to give up and move on, especially for women. Of course, couples separated, had affairs, and even hated each other, and I'm definitely not saying it was a bed of roses for anyone suffering within a marriage. In my grandparents' day, it was often a case of putting up with everything without the option of bailing out.

Even today, I often see elderly couples out together, bickering about which apples to buy in the supermarket, complaining about the other person's bad parking, and often nagging one another over nothing important at all. It's as if they truly despise each other, but are so used to being together that they don't even notice their bickering any more. I know it wouldn't be easy or even feasible for a couple like this to separate, as their life is probably completely defined by their long-term partner. It does happen but, as I say, it's a life-changing decision to make, and not to be taken lightly.

For us younger generations, we are more used to gratifying our needs and looking after number one. If Kelly is being a pain in the neck, there are plenty more Kellys out there. When Rashid gets on your nerves, you can easily ghost him and move on to the next one. Forget sustainability – we want disposability, or at least that's how it looks from the outside.

Growing up in that kind of culture, a lot of us will be looking for the nearest escape route when we get involved with someone, just in case it doesn't work out. It's a lot easier to walk away than to stay and make the effort to resolve any issues. I get that. But when you meet someone you truly want to share your life with yet don't know how to deal with the negative emotions and reactions that come up, it can be a huge problem. Instead of experiencing the fullness of love, it can leave you feeling totally empty and emotionally exhausted.

OVERCOMING RELATIONSHIP INSECURITIES

In a loving, harmonious relationship, positive emotions and high self-esteem are at their foundations, with each partner looking out for the other person's happiness. You will see disagreements take place within the context of calmness, communication, and caring. Both are coming from a place of secure attachment, which means that they both feel secure enough in themselves to take responsibility for their mistakes and feelings. This kind of maturity helps the relationship to thrive but not everyone is at the stage where they can achieve that. It takes time and means being able to overcome past failures or ways of reacting.

Which of the bullet points below do you wish you could bring to your relationship?

- Appreciating your own self-worth and comfortably expressing your feelings and needs.

- Enjoying being with others, without getting stressed when you're away from your partner.

- Being able to maintain your emotional balance and seek healthy solutions to any conflicts that arise.

- Being resilient enough to bounce back from disappointments and setbacks in the relationship.

It's clear that couples who achieve this kind of togetherness are happier and more likely to stay together. They allow space for each other to grow and feel enabled by their partner to pursue their own dreams and goals. They are able to deal with deep-rooted issues and allow for healing to take place without guilt or shame. Relationships can be truly therapeutic if both individuals can open up to new ways of being, regardless of their fears and insecurities.

AVOIDING BREAK-UPS

Many of you will be looking for ways to prolong your relationship by using the wrong strategies.

You want to avoid breaking up at all costs and will do whatever it takes to maintain your relationship, even if it's damaging you. There are many reasons for this, and one of them has to do with low self-esteem. You might think that you don't deserve any better or have become used to compromise in order to keep the peace. This could stem from early childhood experiences, or be connected to a recent relationship. It's not always easy to find the cause, but you can bring your awareness to how you are behaving now and learn to respond in a way that is better for your emotional wellbeing.

I wonder if you recognize any of these behaviours in your current or past relationships:

- **Discounting any alternatives.** You don't consider other possible romantic partners, even if you find someone attractive. The truth is there are probably at least five people within a five-mile radius that you'd be somewhat compatible with. This is just a mindset to convince yourself to stay with the wrong person. If you've already reached the point where you've considered leaving but this was the reason you stayed, then the connection is in trouble.

- **Idealizing your partner.** You believe your partner is the best thing since sliced bread and that your relationship is more special than other people's. But what happens when your hero falls? Which they will. Idealizing your partner sets them up for failure and puts unnecessary pressure on the relationship to remain picture-perfect. The best thing about your partner is that they are human, just like you, filled with subjective flaws, and they still choose every day to love you and build a life with you. It is unfair to flood your mind with who you believe they must always be. This could lead to them performing for your love and approval.

- **Ignoring your partner's bad behaviour.** Instead of being upset with something your partner does that jeopardizes the relationship, such as disrespecting you, you make excuses for them and carry on as normal. This is complete self-betrayal and can never lead to an authentic, loving, and fulfilling relationship unless they take responsibility for their behaviour and you maintain non-negotiables.

These are just some of the things we might do to avoid splitting up and, if you think about it, it's obvious that we are sacrificing our sense of self-worth to do so. Some may put it down to 'unconditional love', when, in reality, they are scared of being alone or not knowing who they are beyond the relationship.

If you want to nurture an authentic relationship within a loving space, you have to be authentic with yourself first. Otherwise, you are sending the wrong messages about who you are and what you will put up with. That's not conducive to a balanced partnership and I hope you can see that.

The couples who do manage to avoid breaking up without sacrificing their self-esteem will usually:

- **Be good at conflict management.** They'll find ways to settle their differences amicably without stonewalling, sulking, or exploding. They hold space for both people's realities to coexist. They compromise and disagree fairly.

- **Maintain and honour boundaries.** There is no greater guidebook you can offer your partner than a well-managed list of boundaries. Maybe don't create a PowerPoint presentation, but when a behaviour, conversation, tone, or physical interaction occurs that is unacceptable to you or them, clearly state the boundary and the repercussions if it's crossed. For example, 'If you raise your voice at me, I will disengage with this conversation until you've calmed down.'

- **A willingness to forego self-interest.** They will be prepared to make sacrifices if it's of benefit to their partner but know how to keep it balanced and not over-extend this to the point where it's all one-sided.

- **Facilitate their partner.** They will help each other to make plans and reach their goals without sacrificing their own needs and desires.

- **Don't keep tabs.** The love of your life is still a human that makes mistakes. It's your responsibility to forgive daily and never keep score.

- **Soothe each other's stress.** Couples who are in tune with each other's responses know how to calm them in a way that is supportive yet doesn't weaken their ability to self-soothe.

You don't have to fix everything all at once to save your relationship. The most important factor is that you have two people who are both ready and willing to work together. This isn't something that you can do by yourself.

BRINGING MORE INTELLIGENCE TO YOUR RELATIONSHIPS

I mentioned emotional intelligence in Chapter 4 and talked about how to recognize, interpret, and express your emotions and those of others, as well as be able to communicate them effectively.

Esther Perel, a leading psychotherapist and couples' counsellor, has taken the subject of intelligence one step further and talks about the notion of *relational intelligence*, which is our ability as humans to connect with others and establish trust. You can check out her website and TED Talks on YouTube, where you'll find a lot of insights on the subject. She's raising new questions about how couples interact and her suggestions for finding ways to resolve differences through relational intelligence really resonate with my own take on this subject.

A lot of the time, we seem to lose any ounce of clarity in our relationships. Instead, we react to emotional triggers and even push the other person's buttons on purpose. It's like we have turned into a troublesome teen having a tantrum. But, here's the thing: it's not intentional. We just haven't stopped to look at what we are doing or paid any thought to the harm we are causing ourselves and our partner. Unconscious behaviour patterns can include emotional blackmailing, manipulation, gaslighting, or playing hurtful mind games to make a point. For this reason, mindfulness will come up a lot. It is in the awareness of our faults that solutions are found.

You know how it goes: he reaches for his phone again as soon as you both go to bed, she keeps making plans that don't include you . . . and so on. Being talked to as if you are an idiot, making sarcastic digs, muttering something insulting under your breath, coming home to a pile of dirty dishes again, past indiscretions that you can't forget . . . All of these and more are just some of the ways that couples interact badly.

In such cases, we really aren't seeing the big picture but get sucked into a vortex of hurt and anger. We focus on what is or isn't being said and feel so emotionally triggered that it's like living in a permanent state of insanity. Our reactions are completely controlled by our primitive fight-or-flight responses, leaving no room for relational intelligence. Instead of connecting, we are merely disconnecting and growing further and further apart.

If we want our relationships to succeed, we have to learn how to connect again. This means dealing head on with reactive behaviour instead of withdrawing when we don't like what we see.

To do this, it's important to take a few steps back and consider what is really eating at you. I mentioned in the last chapter that the things we fight about on a daily basis, such as who does the dishes, are more about our needs and vulnerabilities. We get triggered every time the same subjects come up, because we haven't delved into the issues that are buried deep within us.

Being triggered means reacting to words or actions that hit a nerve in our inner psyche. When that happens, it's like a seismic vibration that works from the ground up, although we only feel its tremor and don't understand the root cause. As we get closer to another person, all of our inner emotions become raw and exposed, forcing us to rely on instinct as if we were in real danger.

In countries like Japan, where they have a history of catastrophic earthquakes, they now build skyscrapers and high-rise apartments that are capable of absorbing all the energy from a large quake without collapsing. Engineers have spent years perfecting a system called *seismic isolation*, in which the buildings are erected on a kind of rubber shock absorber to resist the motions of any shaky activity. We aren't like those buildings, although we can put similar kinds of shock absorbers in place to help us deal with anything that threatens our wellbeing.

The way I see it, we have to have some understanding of what's causing the tremors in the first place and be prepared to tolerate certain waves of emotion. If we can find ways to maintain balance while acknowledging our weaknesses, we are on the path to building a very resilient relationship.

When you feel triggered to react because your partner isn't paying you enough attention, it could be that your deepest fear is that of being rejected. Your insecurities lead you to believe that he's ignoring you because he doesn't find you interesting or that you aren't good enough. These overwhelming sensations of insecurity can build up over time, leaving you constantly wondering if he really loves you or not. You might even start to look for clues that confirm your fears, doubt what he says, challenge him over his actions, and basically ruin the relationship.

Petty reactions to petty things usually lead to big disasters. I've seen couples arguing among themselves and, honestly, by the time it's all over, none of them can remember what started it all in the first place. You see things getting dragged up that happened weeks or months ago, and there's never any resolution. Just a lot of perpetuating hurt.

NAVIGATING HELL WHEN YOUR DEMONS CROSS

It's at moments like this that you need to step back, take a deep breath, and see the bigger picture.

Sometimes, the dynamic of the relationship is dysfunctional, with one person or both fighting for control and power. You'll hear things like, 'You always talk down to me as if I'm useless,' or 'We never do anything I suggest. It's always you who decides.'

In other cases, one person might not feel cared for or doesn't get the closeness they crave from the other person. Arguments about not feeling supported, not receiving enough attention, or being rejected when they try to initiate sex are common examples of this. There's also the scenario where one or both feel taken for granted and arguments start about money, who isn't pulling their weight around the house, and so on.

When these dialogues play out over and over again, it's easy to see how they begin to frame the way each person reacts within the relationship. It's as if the couple have learned the steps to a torturous tango that they keep dancing, unable to learn any other way to interact.

I want to tell you that you can avoid this vicious circle, and even break it if you are ready to do so. It will mean approaching your relationship from a different standpoint and seeing it through a new lens.

Strong emotions that flare up in the heat of the moment are not a bad thing. On the contrary – they are opportunities to dig down within ourselves and see where it's all coming from. A couple who doesn't argue and have differences is not the ideal here – it is very, very normal to find yourself emotionally challenged in a relationship. It's through such tensions that we learn more about ourselves and can grow from them. Just as relationships can be an arena for pain, they can also be a garden waiting to bloom.

RECOGNIZE YOUR PRIMARY EMOTIONS

The knee-jerk reaction that you have to something your partner says or does is just the outer skin, or secondary emotion, of something much deeper – our primary emotion. As Leslie Greenberg and Rhonda Goldman put it in their book *Emotion-Focused Couples Therapy: The Dynamics of Emotion, Love and Power* and also in Leslie Greenberg and Jeanne Watson's later book *Emotion-Focused Therapy for Depression*,[19] we need to do three things if we want to understand our triggers:

1. Increase our awareness of the emotion we feel

2. Enhance our emotion regulation

3. Transform the emotion into deeper self-understanding

If, say, your partner forgets to pick you up from the train station, the anger you probably feel is a cover-up for the more vulnerable emotion of being hurt. If you can tap into what you really feel, you can address it at the root instead of getting carried away by the anger bubbling away on the surface. It's definitely more painful to inspect our primary emotions, which is why we react based on that secondary emotion instead. We all know that anger is not a helpful way to express how we feel, but we get carried away by it anyway and end up causing shame, anxiety, and hurt.

Although our primary emotions are triggered by something happening now, they're often connected to how we felt about ourselves at an earlier age. For example, if we felt neglected by our family growing up, being ignored by a partner can feel like a punch in the stomach and spark off those terrible feelings of being unloved. This pattern of feeling might be totally unwarranted because our partner isn't really ignoring us – they are just busy or preoccupied.

When presented with a trigger, practise regulating before reacting. Challenge your emotions with rational questions.

Is this being done to me intentionally? Give your partner the benefit of the doubt. Before accusing them, ask if they are aware of how this can be hurtful to you because of your experiences.

Can I create a boundary around this behaviour? Some things are off-limits. Speak up if this behaviour violates your boundaries.

Is this something I have to heal on my own because it doesn't have to do with anyone else? Most of the time, our triggers have little to do with our partners and a lot to do with unhealed parts of us. The world will never dance around your triggers, so use them as indicators of where to focus your inner work. When you can acknowledge that deeper emotion of hurt, sadness, insecurity, or whatever it is, you will learn more about yourself and be left feeling liberated, lighter, and more ready to share love.

The solution isn't always to change partners when you feel triggered. More often than not, it has more to do with changing your own reactions by taking a closer look at yourself. Once you begin to see the attachment patterns playing out, you can change perspective and get more in touch with your real needs and emotions. When you see through those secondary emotions and look at the primary ones instead, it can become easier to get closer to the one you love.

If you are in a situation where an abusive partner is harming your physical or mental wellbeing, then I'm not saying you should stay. If that is the case, you need to remove yourself from that relationship as quickly as possible. **Being triggered and being abused are completely different. Abuse is intentional and intolerable.**

WHAT IS IME?

There's something called romantic competence, which psychologist Joanne Davilla and colleagues talked about in a research paper published in 2017.[20] This is a skill that can help you to work on creating healthy relationships and avoid unhealthy ones using: **insight**, **mutuality**, and **emotion regulation** (IME).

When you figure out what you need from a relationship and find the right person for you, it is possible to build something nurturing and positive for both, using these three skills.

When you develop **insight**, you can reflect on your romantic experiences and consider the impact of your behaviour based on that. When you've had a hard day at work, for example, and come home feeling snappy and bad-tempered with your partner, insight will help you to realize that it's not something your partner is doing. That's the time you need to relax and chill out, so you don't carry your bad attitude over into the relationship.

Insight also helps you to understand that your partner may also be snappy, for similar reasons, and that it's nothing to do with you personally. Insight gives you time to press pause and to consider your next step before you do something damaging to the relationship, like sending a mean text or taking your negative day out on them.

When you practise **mutuality**, you get that a relationship is based on meeting both your needs, which may not always be the same but are both still valid. Your partner might ask you to accompany them to a stressful event such as a hospital appointment and it is a good opportunity for you to meet their need to have someone with them. They should also be willing to do the same for you. When you exercise mutuality, it can help you to consider the needs of both parties when making any decisions about the relationship and how it's going to go from here.

When you can regulate your **emotions,** you are aware of how you are feeling and able to channel them for the benefit of both people in the relationship. Instead of overreacting when something goes wrong, being able to face the challenge with optimism and positivity can seriously reduce any tension that might spill over into the relationship. Instead of acting on impulse, you can think more clearly about what decisions to take.

Going back to the example of waiting for your partner to pick you up and they are late, instead of going into meltdown as you check the time every ten seconds, tell yourself, 'They are on their way. They must be late for a reason and they'll get here when they can.' This definitely avoids a big argument when your partner does show up, especially if their reason for being late was out of their control. In a worst-case scenario, they did forget and have no legitimate excuse. Maintaining an argument in their defence and offering the benefit of the doubt while you wait still massively defuses the situation. If the case is that they are repeat offenders and continue to do the same things over and over, despite multiple conversations, there may be a serious lack of consideration that demands a brutally honest conversation.

In this sense, romantic competence means being aware of both your emotional needs and the actions you need to take to meet those needs in a relationship.

HOW DO YOU RECONNECT?

Whether it's you being triggered or your partner, you both have a responsibility to deal with the issue. Relationships aren't one-sided but are supposed to be based on both of you rooting for the same team. When your partner is reacting unconsciously to a certain trigger, they may genuinely not understand what's causing it deep down. If you approach from a place of love and openness, you can be the space for them to talk about their emotions. Instead of shutting them down or getting into a futile argument, how about creating a safe environment where they can follow that tremor and see where it's coming from? The key is communication.

Love talks

Sometimes, it all comes down to knowing how to communicate, and that includes when to be silent. When someone is ill with the flu or has a migraine, they really need a quiet, peaceful place to recuperate and get their strength back. It's exactly the same with emotional pain – we all need the chance to heal without tension and further friction. Think of it in small steps – you aren't going to build Rome in a day. If it's you that needs to face your demons, explain that to your partner and ask them to help you.

Very often, we send out completely mixed signals instead of just saying how we feel. This is a sure-fire way to confuse anyone and doesn't help you at all. Signalling how you feel instead of speaking your truth is like using sign language to someone who doesn't understand it. They will be totally lost, confused, and frustrated because they can't grasp what you want to say. On top of that, your partner isn't a mind reader, no matter how much they love you, and can't be expected to know what you are thinking all the time.

The great escape

A lot of couples never get to the bottom of their issues because one or both are avoiding the problem. They often do it so well because it's a kind of coping strategy they have learned, and might take the form of going quiet, working too much, or an excessive use of alcohol to numb the pain. In this sense, they are ignoring their own needs and the needs of their partner.

Although any of the above can seem like the easy way out at the time, none of them will improve the relationship, and you should know that. Instead of running away from your fears, be bold and reconnect with your needs. I'm sure that you want to experience all that love can offer, but in order to make that happen, you have to stop repeating those habits.

If your partner is receptive to you, they will be more than happy to listen to your pain, and this can only bring you closer together. If it's your partner who is avoiding the realities, let them know that you are there for them, without judgement.

Attention seeking

When the lines of communication are down, people often try to get the attention of their partners in different ways. Your girlfriend/boyfriend might openly flirt with others in front of you or demand that you go everywhere together and come across as clingy. Here, your partner is trying to tell you that they feel insecure and even worried about being abandoned. It can also be an emotional cue that they don't feel desired by you or that the relationship lacks quality time.

Explain to them that you will be there for them, and show that in your actions, giving them the reassurance they need so they can change the way they act. If it's you that seeks attention, look into yourself and try to find out where that deep sense of insecurity is coming from. Who rejected you or didn't give you enough care in the past? Is your behaviour now fair on your present partner, who probably hasn't given you reason to doubt them? When you get to the source of this need, you can properly delegate where the work needs to go. Does the relationship need strengthening or do you?

Emotional blackmail

There's nothing worse than feeling that your partner is trying to emotionally manipulate you, and it's not a healthy sign within a relationship. When your partner threatens to do something drastic or self-destructive if you leave them, it's obvious that they need a lot of help to change this kind of behaviour. But emotional blackmail may be much more subtle than this, and it's not always easy to pick up on. It might include being told things like, 'I don't think you should see that friend any more. They're a bad influence on you,' or 'I'm only thinking of what's best for you, babe. I'm saying this because I love you.'

When either or both people in the relationship are manipulative, it's always going to be a game of cat and mouse, with each one trying to get the other to bend to their will. You might even hear direct threats, such as, 'If you go out with your mates tonight, don't expect to find me here when you get back.' This is actually a kind of abuse, especially if you concede to your partner's demands, or they give in to yours all the time. It's a death wish for any healthy relationship and you have to nip it in the bud before it goes too far. Open up the discussion with your partner and explain how they are making you feel. Talk about why you are acting this way, even if you aren't sure where it's coming from.

When you aren't fully aware of how your words or behaviour are affecting others, it means that you aren't practising relational intelligence. And you can't respond correctly to the unconscious and repressed parts of your partner if you aren't in touch with your own history.

Usually, it's not the conflict itself that is the issue, but the way it plays out. Learning *how* to enter into a dialogue instead of arguing is the key to fostering better communication, although it takes a conscious effort to make that happen. Like I said earlier, it's normal to have tiffs and go through some emotional upheavals as a relationship progresses. There'll always be moments of intensity, tears, and raised voices, but are these all about what just happened, or remnants of past experiences?

What you need to remember is that when things get emotionally heated, it's often a sign that you care about each other. This is exactly the time for you to come clean, get things off your chest and let the other person know where you are coming from. It doesn't have to be a shouting match, though, and is much better for both of you and your relationship if high emotions are lowered with compassion and understanding.

Relationships aren't a game of tug-of-war, with each one pulling the rope to try to beat the other. If the situation flares up about something that you said or did, instead of going on the defensive, listen to your partner and feel their pain. Help them to find their calmness instead of dismissing or attacking them. Neither tactic can forge a healthy oneness with the person you claim to love.

Create a new dance

Instead of the terrible tango, create a caring waltz or any dance that suits your style. As long as it's a duet, you'll be OK. When you learn new steps together, the result will be much more harmonious and graceful. It will take time, but you can begin by saying things like, 'I feel upset with you, even though it might not be because of anything you've done. Can I just share it with you, anyway?' You can also provide a safety net for your partner by telling them, 'You seem annoyed with me and I'd like to talk it through. Can we do that when you feel able to?'

As long as you are establishing room for dialogue, issues that were once deeply buried can begin to come out into the sunlight, and that's truly beautiful. It can be the beginning of a deep connection on an emotional and spiritual level as you help each other to find peace and harmony together.

As you go through the process of talking and listening, you'll soon discover that, often, it's just a case of you or your partner wanting to have feelings acknowledged. It doesn't mean that the other person will have all the answers or has to come up with solutions. They will come in time, just as you will perfect your dance steps together, building a stronger bond as each day goes by.

LEARNING NEW HABITS

I wonder how many of you witnessed your parents arguing while growing up and, if so, how they reacted to each other. It's a good idea to consider what you learned from them about how adults interact and communicate. What did they do when they were upset? What about if you grew up without a parental presence or belonged to a one-parent family? What role models did you look to and how did they communicate with each other? And, even more importantly, how were you treated when you were upset? Were you allowed to show your feelings or did you have to keep them hidden?

When Zadie was a kid, she witnessed a lot of hostility between her parents, which affected the way she dealt with her own emotions of anger and frustration. Because she didn't want to be the cause of any further upset or even get pulled into conflict herself, she kept her feelings bottled up. Instead of crying, like most kids would, she learned to swallow her tears when she was upset so no one would notice how she felt. This way of behaving continued into her adult relationships and whenever disagreements arose, she would push back her feelings and pretty much concede to anything.

She didn't feel that she was allowed to cry or be upset, and found it extremely difficult to express her emotions. Her partners all thought she was giving them the silent treatment when, in reality, she had become emotionally mute. In cases like this, there will always be secrets in the relationship, because if you can't be your true self, the other person will never really know you. It took a long time for Zadie to change this pattern, and she only managed to do so when she met Hakeem.

He had grown up in a very stable, loving family, and even though his parents had their disagreements, he never saw any real hostility or felt traumatized by it. It was easy for him to articulate how he felt as he had been brought up to show his emotions. As soon as he met Zadie, he realized that she was suffering, and slowly began to help her understand the connection between her past and present. It only took a few months with Hakeem for Zadie to start believing that she was allowed to express what she felt without fear and that she owed it to herself to do exactly that. It was Hakeem's patience and love that allowed her to find a safe space to explore her innermost emotions – and this is a happy-ever-after story, for a change!

WHAT DO YOU NEED?

Someone recently asked me, 'How do I know which needs are my responsibility and which ones I can entrust to my partner?' I think the best response to that is NOBODY else is responsible for your needs. If you are expecting someone else to fill a void in you, you are likely to be disappointed.

The reality of what you want may be very different from what you will get. When you meet 'the one', in your mind, they are going to fulfil all of your dreams. This is a lovely thought, but the cracks soon start to appear when you realize that they aren't living up to your expectations.

A lot of people begin to feel disappointed with their relationship when their needs aren't being met. Sure, your partner can give you emotional satisfaction and make you feel contented, excited, and blissful. But what happens when they don't? Do you feel frustrated, hurt, confused, unloved?

We all have different emotional needs and also show our emotions in a multitude of ways. Your partner might give you the companionship, communication, trust, affection, and sex you want but may not be capable of more. What if you crave mental stimulation, financial security, tenderness, respect, a confidant?

As Esther Perel pointed out in her book *Mating in Captivity*,[21] 'You're asking one person to give you what an entire village used to provide.' Back in the days when we lived in a close-knit community, we grouped according to gender and platonic bonds, getting support from many different people. Nowadays, we expect one person to give us everything we need. It's a relatively recent phenomenon and one that has become totally ingrained in our culture.

Everyone is looking for their soulmate; that one person to connect with who truly gets them. Their one and only love. I love the idea myself, although it's clear that it's one of the reasons that relationships are failing. It's impossible for anyone to meet all of our needs, and we can't load them onto one individual.

It's a lot healthier to have an outlet with other people who can give you what you want, be that friends, family, or colleagues. That doesn't make your relationship with your partner any less meaningful. The opposite is the case – it makes it more durable and rewarding.

You can't be everything for your partner and should avoid trying to make them your absolute everything. They aren't meant to be your best friend, therapist, and shopping buddy all the time.

Although love has no bounds, you do have limits as a person. It's impossible for you to provide your love interest with everything they need to feel truly fulfilled. It's also not your job to do so. When I spoke to one of my single friends recently, she told me she was tired of having to be everything for each new man that came along. She felt weighed down in the relationships when they expected her to be their shrink, chef, girlfriend, and even dermatologist! She was looking for someone who didn't depend on her to meet their every need, and I get why she is finding that challenging.

The modern love story wants to have it all: romance, sex, friendship, security, companionship, domesticity, respectability, and material benefits. That's a lot to hope for, especially if you also expect your partner to share the same weird interests as you, be a dab hand at home decorating, a philosophical savant, passionate in bed, and have a wicked sense of humour to boot. I'm not saying you can't have it all, but be realistic in your approach and consider you're looking for true love, and thus must offer true love. And true love isn't bound by extraneous details.

Here's how you could overwhelm your relationship in the name of finding the perfect 'one':

- When you bring all of the challenges you face in life to the couples table instead of sharing some of them with friends, you could be overloading the relationship.

- When you think your partner should be interested in every twist and turn that happens at work, you might be unfairly asking for too much.

- When you are expected to be an expert on plumbing or ironing, you may feel these are unfair demands being placed on you.

- When you need the solace of a friend to discuss something very personal, you might feel as if you are going behind your partner's back by not confiding in them first.

They should be a space where you can enjoy variety, diversity, and the freedom to be yourself without having to take on too many roles.

When someone wants you to be 'their everything', that's going to create a lot of pressure to conform, which often means forsaking your own needs. You can let them know that it's exactly because you love them that you cannot be 'their everything'. If you can orchestrate the dynamic so that your partner relies on you less, it doesn't mean that your love for each other will weaken. It's all about giving space to each other to grow together.

It is possible to become a vibrational match to the relationship you desire. Once you delve into the depths of yourself and realize how much capacity you have to love yourself, without the need for your partner to fill a void, you can attract someone who is coming from the same level of awareness. Your relationship will be about thriving together, not a survival course.

DO YOU LOVE ME?

We all have different emotional needs that we express in a number of ways. If you want affection, physical intimacy, and loving words, all of which bring you closer to your partner, what if they find it difficult to give you any of these in the way that you want? Does it have to be your way or the highway?

What happens when you tell your partner, 'I love you,' and they don't reply, 'I love you too'?

Does that mean they don't love you?

How will you know if they love you or not?

Do you need to hear them say it?

The expectation you have of hearing your sentiments echoed might seem reasonable to you, but what if your partner doesn't want to express themself in that way and would rather show you by their actions? Is that good enough for you, or should they act the way you want them to?

What if they find it hard to show affection, yet are giving and loving? Can you handle that?

Many of us need to experience validation within a relationship and think our partner has to agree with us on everything. What happens when they don't? Does that cause you to doubt your self-worth because your need for validation is so closely linked to it?

I think we tend to look for a partner who mirrors our likes, dislikes, preferences, and opinions, although that shouldn't be a condition of a successful relationship. Being on the same wavelength is great, but there can be room for differences and respecting each other's views in a secure relationship.

When author Gary Chapman defined 'the five love languages' in his book of the same name,[22] he described the five different ways that people give and receive love, based loosely on attachment styles. They are words of affirmation (compliments), quality time, the giving of gifts, acts of service, and physical touch. We all express love differently and may do so in more than one way. They can also reflect what is missing in your inner void, such as giving affection in order to receive affection back.

I've come up with some additional love languages that come from a place of co-healing. Co-healing is the expressed interest in what your partner needs on a day-to-day basis, rather than any attempt to fill a void that they can only fill themselves through self-healing. There is no wrong way to express love, but it's important to understand where it's coming from and if it is enabling or disabling your partner – or yourself, for that matter.

- There's the language of patience . . . allowing time for things to work out.

- There's also the language of expressing not guessing . . . telling your partner how you feel, rather than leaving them guessing.

- The language of curiosity . . . how about asking them what you can do for them and being curious about how loved they feel by you?

- And, there's the language of boundaries, which offer stability and security.

How many of these can you incorporate into your relationship?

Is your love language coming from a place of deep longing and unresolved neglect, or from a healed centre that is capable of holding space for a partnership? Is it about remaining present for the needs that arise within the dynamic? Love language in a healing context is usually mutual and shows a healthy connection with the other. It's not about what you can gain in order to make yourself feel better about who you are. If that touches something inside you, dwell on it for a while and fold back those layers to see what is underneath. You can only nurture more self-awareness by doing so.

LOSING YOUR AUTONOMY

The closer we get to someone, the more we merge into a unit, and here is where we are at risk of losing our autonomy. When you meet someone and start hanging out as a couple, that doesn't mean you have to forget about your friends, interests, hobbies, and personal opinions. It's much healthier to keep some aspects of your life separate from the relationships so that you don't lose your sense of self.

As I mentioned earlier on, there are three parts to a successful relationship:

1. You

2. Your partner

3. Both of you as a couple

It's a wonderful experience to be so close to someone else that you feel as one, but it can also be a recipe for disaster. That's why maintaining your autonomy is so important – for you, your partner, and for the sake of your relationship.

A healthy relationship is when you and your partner maintain a strong sense of self, even though you still share many things in common. You can and should retain your individuality because the alternative is sacrificing what you need in order to keep your partner happy. This is a type of codependency that can lead you to feel validated only within the confines of the relationship.

This kind of experience is very, very common when couples break up, with one or both feeling that something is suddenly missing. It's a cause of heartbreak, deep suffering, and grief. Rather than going through that, keep some aspects of your independence within your relationship and put aside time to reconnect with friends, family, and your own interests.

If your partner loves you, they will respect your desire to satisfy your own needs, and as long as you trust each other, it doesn't have to be a threat to your relationship. You should also exercise the same understanding with your partner and give them the space they need to indulge in their passions, spend time with their friends, and keep something for themselves. When there is genuine trust, individual needs can even bring excitement, curiosity, and novelty to the relationship and make it stronger, not weaker.

FEELING SECURE

Although security can mean many things to different people, we all feel secure in a relationship when it fulfils certain criteria. Generally speaking, all of us want to know our boundaries are respected and that we feel safe enough to share our feelings. We want to feel physically safe too and believe that we are supported and cherished.

If you come from a place of insecurity, it might be difficult for you to know how to define your boundaries and be able to express yourself without fear. I definitely suggest that you look into your own deep-seated insecurities, because if you feel emotionally unstable, it will be extremely difficult to build a stable relationship with someone else. You need to be able to listen to your inner voice and have the courage to speak your feelings.

It's a fundamental human need to seek security, and nobody wants to feel unsafe, whether physically or psychologically. It is possible to nurture a secure bond with another person if you can practise accessibility, responsiveness, and emotional engagement.

By accessibility, I mean being there for your partner when they reach out to you. You could, after an argument, for example, show them you still care for them. Rather than locking yourself in your bedroom, stay with them and tell them how you're still willing to listen to their side of things, even if you don't agree with them. Of course, this doesn't work for everyone and sometimes a cooling-off period is needed first.

It's easy to get engrossed in what you are doing and forget to be responsive to your partner's needs. If you really are busy, a simple reassurance that you'll be with them shortly may be all it takes to create that sense of security you both need. When they call you at an inconvenient time, message them back to tell them you can't speak now but will be free later on. By being responsive, you are generating a place of security and building stronger connections.

You also have to be emotionally engaged, which means showing a genuine interest. It's not only important to care about your partner's emotional experience and be curious about it, but you should also let them know it. The more attention you give to their emotions, the more you can understand them. The same has to be said for your partner, and if you don't feel like they are paying attention to that, you can tell them so in a calm way. It's not about accusing anyone of committing a crime, but more to do with creating a dialogue to raise awareness of how each other feels.

BREADCRUMBING

The very opposite of being secure is accepting breadcrumbs when you deserve the whole damn cake. When you aren't aware and accepting of the love you deserve and don't maintain spiritual and emotional independence, a self-serving partner can prey on these insecurities. By offering you breadcrumbs, just enough to get by, you find yourself staying longer, waiting, wishing, and hoping that someday soon they'll offer more. It may take some time, but eventually you must realize that there is no more that they can offer. And in that moment, my hope is that you will choose yourself and walk away.

EXPECTATIONS AND REALITY

It hurts when people don't do for you what you'd do for them in a heartbeat. Nevertheless, releasing expectations is the surest way to stop people from having the power to hurt you. Just know your worth – so you can identify who's worthy of your time and energy.

Too often, we expect people to have the same capacity to give and share as us. We expect them to perceive the world in the same way and hold the same values. And, just as the second noble truth of Buddhism suggests, when life doesn't match our expectations, we suffer. You could say that expectation is the cause of disappointment, because when you expect and don't receive, disappointment arises.

There will be times when people let you down. You might expect a sales assistant to be more helpful or your parents to feel sorry for you. When things don't go the way you want them to, you may feel disappointed and hurt. We are always expecting the world to adjust to us and meet our needs. However, we can never control other people's actions, only our own. How people act is merely a manifestation of their inner world and we have no control over that.

Our expectations can direct us towards changes we need to make within – for example, a craving for somebody's presence might reveal a void that's shouting for your own care and attention.

It's impractical to drop all of our expectations because they often help us become aware of what we deserve. Therefore, I suggest you:

1.   Realize that expectations can hinder inner peace.

2.   Discover how they might affect you on your inner healing journey.

3.   Identify if you need to make shifts in your relationships.

Reducing expectations and not taking things personally are liberating acts. One way I try to do this is to assume the best in others – by encouraging compassion, you can break the connection to the outcome you craved. For example, if a stranger doesn't hold the door open for you, you can reframe your thinking by telling yourself there's a good reason for it; perhaps they're going through a tough time, or they simply forgot because they're in a rush to get to somewhere important.

As morbid as this sounds, if a loved one disappoints me, I tell myself that it could be the last time I ever see or speak to them. This inspires gratitude and allows me to enjoy their presence, rather than focusing on what expectations of mine they aren't fulfilling. Also, remember that no one's perfect, including your-self. People don't always get it right. On that note, cultivating gratitude is a powerful antidote if disappointment arises from unmet expectations. Gratitude affirms that what we have in our life is worthy of being thankful for despite expectations. Suffering subsides when you're in a state of genuine appreciation.

THE END OF LOVE?

Your great love story might not work out, for many reasons. That doesn't mean love has to end. Relationships mutate and alter as they develop and it's often the case that we don't like where they are going. You could find out that you just aren't compatible, have too many differences, an excess of emotional baggage, or not enough emotional maturity. Most of us take it very badly when any relationship we have put our heart into doesn't work out, as if we have lost money on the stock exchange. All that time and energy invested, and for what?

> Not every relationship will last. But at one point,
> every relationship made you laugh, smile, and love
> in ways you hadn't before. It's not about lasting
> for ever. It's about savouring every moment
> before any potential goodbyes.

When you meet someone, talk to them about your expectations and dreams. As the relationship unfolds, bring the conversation back to the table and keep reassessing things. Do you still have the same common goals? Has anything changed between you? If so, can you resolve your differences or is it best for both of you to stop here?

You can discuss together things like:

- Is your relationship still working?

- What do you need to change in order to make it a success?

- What can you leave behind as you move forward?

- How can you reassure each other you are committed to making it work?

- How do you aim to work through problems in the future?

Many people cling on to damaged relationships because they fear the alternative, and that can be very harmful for self-esteem and self-worth. The end of the relationship doesn't always signify failure, but it can be a useful experience that helps you to understand how to make it work next time around. As long as you stay connected with your inner needs, you can't go wrong.

Self-care means moving on from those relationships that are stunting your growth or causing you continuous harm. It's OK to say that it didn't work out with someone and to accept that not everything will go as planned in life. Change is a natural process, and trying to swim against the tide is futile. Ignoring the signs that your partner has lost interest in you or that you have lost interest in them isn't going to end well, and although it's difficult, it's better for both of you to accept the reality and move on. Some couples make a decision to stay together 'for the kids', but, as I've mentioned earlier, they could be teaching their kids that love looks a certain way. It's a tough call to make and might mean neglecting your own needs just to remain together or deciding it's best to split up for everyone's sake (kids included).

I've tried to put myself as a priority over the last few years – not for selfish reasons – but for my own wellbeing. While I love being with my wife and the company of others, I also like to have moments of solitude. I feel it charges my being and helps me to reconnect with myself. By staying connected with me, I'm better able to reconnect with others around me. Having this kind of clarity enables me to recognize my self-worth *and* share my love with others.

I like to think that the purest form of love can bring happiness to others, and it begins within you. It's not just about receiving it, but also means sharing it whole-heartedly whenever you can.

KEY INSIGHTS

- Leave your inner demons at the door when you embark on a new relationship.

- If you see your relationship as a battleground, there can be no winners, only losers.

- Learning to go from being single to a couple needs a willingness to do the hard work.

- To avoid break-ups, it takes communication, conflict management, and removing bad behaviour.

- Go from a reactive to a responsive mindset by identifying your primary emotions.

- Reconnect and stay connected through love talks and healthy emotional habits.

- Consider your needs and don't expect them all to be met by your partner.

- When love ends, use it as a time to reflect, heal, and learn.

Chapter 7

BEING VULNERABLE

**Vulnerability is allowing yourself to be seen but
trusting the other person not to hurt you.**

Imagine walking around your local high street completely naked. That's a scary thought, isn't it? Most of us don't even like undressing in front of people we know well, never mind being naked in public. It would make us feel extremely exposed and vulnerable.

We often have the same fear when it comes to our deep emotions, and will do whatever it takes to protect ourselves from being shamed, hurt, ridiculed, or taken advantage of. It might not be obvious that you are uncomfortable with being vulnerable or with creating emotional intimacy. Guard yourself long enough, it just becomes second nature. Struggling with vulnerability can look like down-playing your feelings or experiences.

Have you shared a painful part of your past only to follow it with 'but it's no big deal'? Or, on the contrary, when someone else begins to open up, do you find yourself distancing at the sight of their vulnerability? Much of this stems from fear. The fear of being seen because it can lead to rejection, or opening up because it forces you to feel emotions you've been avoiding. But connection is made through authentic emotional expression.

So, how does that work in a relationship? Can you create authentic connections when you are constantly on guard, ready to protect yourself from someone looking deep into your soul?

You might have heard of the visual artist Marina Abramović, who is well known for her unusual and some might say weird performances. One of them really got my attention, though, when thinking about vulnerability. It was a project called 'The Artist Is Present' at the Museum of Modern Art in New York in 2010.

For three months Abramović would sit motionless in a chair all day while people stood for hours in line, waiting to have the chance to sit opposite her for a minute. The idea was to see how we can create deep emotional connections just by being silent, vulnerable, and open. At one point, her ex-lover turned up and that's a really touching moment to see, as they communicate intense emotions, without even speaking to each other. You can check out her videos on YouTube to see what I mean, and notice how she and the people sitting opposite her connect, just by staring into each other's eyes. It's a great example of the power of vulnerability.

It also teaches us that vulnerability is an energetic experience. It doesn't always mean sharing your body, telling deep stories of a past life, or spilling all of your secrets. Vulnerability is the willingness to be in the moment with another and not suppress the feelings that arise.

When you have two people willing to be vulnerable, an extraordinary safety between you occurs. With no words, you are communicating with one another, 'You are safe here. I am safe here. Let's be here together. Completely.'

There's nothing weak about being vulnerable. It actually takes a lot of courage. We have this idea that exposing our inner emotions is a risk; we might be hurt, made fun of, dismissed, or worse. But what's the alternative? Can we live locked up by ourselves and refuse to interact in the real world? Of course not. Just like everyone else, I also want connection, communication, and to enjoy loving relationships. To get them, I have to be vulnerable. You do, too, even if it's a scary thought right now.

Vulnerability is the key to intimacy and healing. It's the secret to selflessness and a deeper love. Through it, you can gain trust, loyalty, and security.

Despite the fears you may have about opening up to your partner, there is no other way to get closer.

Thanks to Brené Brown, the American researcher and author, the subject of vulnerability was put in the spotlight as a way to help people connect. She started the conversation in her book, *Daring Greatly: How the Courage to Be Vulnerable Transforms the Way We Live, Love, Parent, and Lead.*[23] I love the way she explains how ' . . . vulnerability is the birthplace of love, belonging, joy, courage, empathy, and creativity.'

It gives meaning to our lives and helps us to have a sense of belonging, no matter who we are. For many people, the idea of baring all fills them with anxiety and fear. Imagine that first date, asking someone for help, wanting to initiate intimacy . . . all of these are unknowns and take us out of our comfort zone. That's not a position most people like to be in: what if you get rejected or don't receive the response you want?

In reality, being vulnerable is a fact of life because we never know what is going to happen from one day to the next. We're all at the mercy of fate, destiny, or whatever you like to call it. We come into this world physically and emotionally naked, building up those layers as we grow to keep ourselves safe and warm. But I can understand not wanting to open up if you've been hurt in the past or think that you aren't courageous enough to be vulnerable. I hear you.

The thing is, it's often not a choice we can make. There will be times when we feel vulnerable, no matter how much we try to avoid it, and nowhere more so than in relationships. When you meet someone else, the whole dynamic of your life changes because you are pushed to consider new ways of being – ways you might not be prepared for. Rejecting these new options because you are too shut down to even consider them is really going to prevent you from forming a deeper connection with your partner. It's like trying to make an omelette without breaking any eggs – it just can't be done.

Vulnerability does have boundaries: it's not about oversharing and leaving yourself totally exposed. In order for anyone to open up, they need a level of trust that a worthy partner has demonstrated consistently. Nobody should throw themselves recklessly into an emotional situation if the other person hasn't proved that they will be supportive and caring. That would only lead to distrust and a failure to genuinely connect.

When I hear people saying that they prefer to be alone, I kind of get the vibe that some of them are too afraid to trust again after being burned. We are social animals and need connections to survive; we need closeness and intimacy, even if we say that we don't. Sure, you can enjoy all of these in many different ways – with family, friends, and so on. It doesn't have to be with a romantic partner, but past pain shouldn't stop us from experiencing a fulfilling relationship in the future.

I think that's what vulnerability is about: being prepared to take that leap of faith when we find someone who maybe, just maybe, can enrich our lives. Even if letting the walls down doesn't come naturally, it's always worth it. If a relationship doesn't last, at least you can say you showed up. You didn't present only a portion of who you are.

If you've gone through bad relationships in the past, you might be terrified of failure or feel flawed in some way. The pain that is left over is very real and is often even associated with shame. You may tell yourself, *'I'm no good at relationships,*

I just can't seem to get it right. There must be something wrong with me.' That's a pretty harsh way to treat yourself, and it's also stopping you from moving on to something that could be truly wonderful. Imagine daring to be bold, to believe in yourself, and to embrace the unknown? Amazing, right?

Brené Brown also did an eye-to-eye experiment during one of her TED Talks back in 2015, when she asked studio managers to turn on the lights so she could actually see her audience and connect with them. When she asked the audience if they struggled with vulnerability, most said yes, although everyone knows that we need to connect to create bonds with others. You aren't alone in thinking it's too scary to open up – we all feel that way, honestly.

DARING TO LOVE

Relationships require bravery and a willingness to take action. We are all aware of the risk of falling in love – primarily, heartbreak. **Relationships require the courage to lay yourself open, the bravery to deal with your deepest fears, and the desire to make changes.** That's a lot to expect from yourself, and from your partner. Usually, we meet up with someone, click with them, start developing an emotional attachment, and start sharing our life with them. None of that takes much effort if you are both attracted to each other and want to pursue the relationship.

The real challenge comes as you become more emotionally intimate. That's where the courage and bravery is needed most because it's about to get 'serious'. Now, it's dealing with old wounds, past traumas, bad habits, and unrealistic expectations. Vulnerability is required if you're to face what comes up, whether alone or co-healing with your partner. Vulnerability will be necessary for honest apologies when you inevitably let them down. Vulnerability is essential to forgiving them when they fail you too. No true progress, growth, or closeness can occur without it.

The key to understanding vulnerability is realizing you don't have to learn how to be vulnerable. You simply have to remember that we were born fragile and completely dependent on others. We are born vulnerable. Through conditioning, we learned to put up our guards and be wary of those who came close. When you can face major events that caused you to shield your heart, and process them successfully, you remember what ease and peace vulnerability brought you as a child – a time when it was perhaps easier to trust and feel safe. When you didn't overthink and just showed up as yourself because you knew no other way to be.

The Naikan practice, founded by Japanese businessman and Buddhist priest Yoshimito Ishin, is a great way to remove that overwhelming feeling of vulnerability in your relationships. It means 'looking inside' or 'introspection', a concept that was first introduced into mainstream thinking in the 1990s. You could call it self-reflection, and it's a simple exercise for couples who feel stuck in negative cycles of shame, frustration, guilt, disconnection, and pain from past wounds. All you need to do is to ask yourself three simple questions:

1. What have I received from my partner?

2. What have I given to my partner?

3. What trouble or difficulties might I have caused in our relationship?

You could think of it in terms of what you are getting out of your relationship, what you are putting into it, and what obstacles you are setting up along the way.

To answer the first question, all you need to do is sit quietly and ask yourself: *What have I received from my partner?* What comes into your mind? Let your thoughts flow and observe everything that comes up, from admiration and fun times to a reason to get out of bed in the morning.

Next, let your intuition take over and listen to what your gut and your heart are saying. Stay with any feelings that arise and observe them. How do you feel? Joyous, thankful, happy? Stay with those positive emotions before moving on to the next question.

Again, find a quiet moment to ask yourself: *What have I given to my partner?* Allow your thoughts to run freely through your mind's eye, noticing anything that comes up. Have you given them time, money, patience? Why did you give them these things – for support, out of care or concern? What comes into your mind?

After that, you can consider the third, maybe most difficult question. You need to be honest here – it's no good trying to deceive yourself, right? So be brave and bold as you gently ask yourself: *What trouble or difficulties might I have caused in our relationship?* It's nothing to do with guilt or blame, and everything to do with self-discovery and healing.

What discomfort are you feeling? Just observe it without jumping in to justify it or to judge yourself. You can process whatever it is later on. For now, all you need to do is be a fly on the wall to whatever comes up. Through this kind of self-discovery, you will gain clarity and be able to identify what you need to change, if anything.

- Did you break your partner's trust, upset them, cause sadness and feelings of rejection?

- Have you allowed bitterness to take the place of compassion?

- Have you created distance instead of connection?

- Have you encouraged stressful conflict instead of calm?

- Do you feel sorry about that?

And the final question to this revealing kind of mindfulness is: *How can I create change?* If you want to commit to making your relationship better and to create a space of authentic love, what decisions do you need to take about the way you behave? How can you break the old habits of the past that aren't serving you or your partner?

Be kind with yourself and let vulnerability guide you as you move forward with courage and bravery. Allow your partner to be vulnerable too, by giving them the space to work through their demons. You are already connected by much more than you know and must make room for the roots of love to take hold and grow.

After one of my old relationships dissolved and both of us went our separate ways, I began to realize that we had missed out on so many opportunities to connect. Our text messaging was superficial, our real conversations were mundane, and our intimacy was confined to routines. When we disagreed over something, we stonewalled each other, and even though we had good fun together, there didn't seem to be much depth to what we had. I don't blame her because I know that we weren't even connected with ourselves, never mind with each other.

What I did learn through that relationship was that I needed to find someone who was committed to personal growth and development. I know that it was the only way for me to find real fulfilment in a partnership because I really wanted to pursue that in myself too. I wanted to find someone who, just like me, was ready to explore self-awareness and craved emotional intimacy. I wanted someone who was willing to be vulnerable because I knew there was no other way to form that deep connection as a couple.

> **It's OK for you and your partner to be on different wavelengths or be at contrasting stages of healing and self-discovery. You may travel together, but the road you take is your own.**

It definitely isn't about trying to change your partner, or mould them into someone you prefer. **Love them as they are and enable them to grow by giving them space to explore and discover how they can help themselves.** The last thing you want is to find someone who hangs on to your every word and is prepared to sacrifice who they are in order to be with you. That is not the way to a deep and harmonious relationship.

VULNERABILITY IS THE DOORWAY TO INTIMACY

You can't get closer to someone if you keep building a brick wall between yourself and them. Even if they try to scale it a few times, they'll soon get fed up and walk away. You have to help yourself here if you really want to make it with your partner, and that means being vulnerable. If you feel that there is enough trust and respect in the relationship, it's OK to lower the drawbridge.

By discussing your fears and anxieties with them, you are also inviting them to talk about themselves, which helps to foster greater intimacy between the two of you. I'm referring to emotional and physical intimacy here, if that's what you want. While it's a scary thought to consider the idea of getting close to someone, falling in love has never exactly been a sure thing. It has always involved risks and uncertainties, which is what makes it so exciting!

The risk you need to consider when opening up is that you can't control the outcome. There's no guarantee that you will live happily ever after, but should that stop you from experiencing all the wonders of love? None of us know what's going to happen tomorrow, and there is little in life that we can control other than our own personal space and hearts.

Love can be a paradoxical world. As you crave connection, you are afraid of rejection. While you want emotional bonding, you find it difficult to convey your feelings.

In today's modern love scenarios, we also want security and independence, excitement and stability, passion and reliability. Sometimes these variants can seem irreconcilable. It's as if we can't find the happy medium between what we crave, what we fear, and what we need, and that's scary.

How do you become intimate with someone while worried that they might pass you over for the next person in one swipe? How do you experience passion without letting down your guard? It's a bit messy, isn't it? The good news is that life really is more fulfilling when you make room for vulnerability and show who you are within. While shutting down can lead to attacks, accusations, or retreats, opening up can bring greater trust, connection, and intimacy. The way to do that is by engaging with your emotional blocks as they come up, and take the time to notice what you are feeling.

If you wish to develop intimacy, you might have to cross some bridges, and not all of them sturdy ones. There could be differences of opinion or conflicts because your partner doesn't fully know you yet, and it's a good time to iron out these crinkles. Vulnerability doesn't mean they always agree with you. It's an energetic agreement to sit safely with the disagreement, free from judgement, and inviting acceptance.

- When you feel supported and cared for, there is nothing stopping you from expressing all that you think and feel. Your partner will appreciate it and feel able to do the same, bringing you closer together.

- It's OK to let them know that you feel vulnerable. You will help them to understand you easier.

- You can tell them about something you fear: it will be a weight off your shoulders and you will hopefully find the caring support that you need to work through it.

- Share any negative experience and explain how they made you feel. Even by mentioning it to your partner, you will feel relieved, lighter, and free of the past hurt.

- Set goals you can work towards together and be prepared to surpass your fears in order to make them happen, such as spending a weekend together, or planning a small holiday.

- Explain how important privacy is to you and that you don't appreciate anything you say being discussed in public if that idea upsets you. Trust that they will respect your wishes, and respond in kind.

You need to know what is healthy and what is uncomfortable too. Is the other person making you feel awkward or are you self-sabotaging your chances of letting them get to understand you better? If your gut feeling is telling you this person can't be trusted, it's probably right. There's no need for you to lay yourself bare if that's the case, as long as you are sure that you aren't misinterpreting their vibes or being triggered by past trauma.

You might not, for example, be comfortable about sharing your past sexual history with them, based on comments they have made or opinions expressed. Maybe they seem like they have the potential to be jealous or possessive. It's important for you to consider how tolerant you are to this kind of behaviour and what implications it can have for you further down the road.

As your relationship progresses, the issues you were grappling with in the beginning will subside as you and your partner learn to be open and trusting. The fears you once had will have hopefully disappeared, even though vulnerability can raise its head again when new situations come along to challenge you. A lie or an infidelity can make you question everything you thought about your relationship. When this is the case, you still need to talk it through – you can't just pretend it didn't happen.

Even if your relationship can't continue, walk away intact, without feeling that you lost something. Although it's understandable, remember that you have gained much more than you know and shouldn't revert back to being too scared to commit to a new romantic endeavour. Hold on to the good, and put the bad things into perspective so they don't come to dominate your emotional state.

TRUST ME

Heard that before? I'm sure you have, although I would rather begin by saying trust yourself first.

A lot of couples express trust issues, and while it's one of the foundation stones of any strong relationship, a lack or abuse of trust can lead to deep emotional wounds and heartache.

When you have self-trust, you can avoid a lot of the pitfalls that come with putting your trust in someone else. Before you even go down that road, you need to have established what your priorities are. It's about protecting your needs and staying safe, having confidence in your decisions and being true to your values.

When couples talk about trust, they are often talking about whether their partner truly cares about them enough, or not. While they don't practise self-trust, they expect it from another person. That's where things can start to go horribly wrong.

In truth, you can't always expect someone to be there for you 24/7, but you can count on yourself to be there. When you don't rely on others for validation but feel strong enough to handle your emotions and thoughts, you can navigate relationships with a lot more maturity.

You can share love while still living according to your standards, be able to admit to your mistakes, and pursue your dreams. When someone tries to undermine you, they might make a small dent in your armour but they aren't going to knock you over. Building self-trust includes becoming your own best friend and honouring your needs, regardless of whether you are perfect or not. It's about believing in yourself and staying true to your instinct and judgement.

There are really two issues here when it comes to relationships: one is learning how to build trust, and the second is about how to handle the situation when your trust is broken.

Let's look at the first issue of developing trust between yourself and your new partner.

We all want to feel that we can depend on our partner and that they are loyal to us. It's this feeling that helps you to be more open and giving, even forgiving them for their bad habits. It helps to navigate conflict as you feel like your partner is on your side and not against you. You have an ally who has your back and will seek solutions to problems together.

It also helps you to become intimately closer because you feel safe with them and can let down any guard you have been holding up. Your nervous system actually relaxes and you can find great healing as your intimacy grows.

The lack of trust has the opposite effect in a relationship. If you continuously feel that your partner isn't there for you, your expectations of them doing anything for you will drop off. When they don't keep their promises, don't do what they say, or lie about things to cover up the truth, it's hard to have any trust in them.

You'll now be facing a lot of problems that can take their toll on the relationship, as well as on your emotional health. You won't be able to enjoy intimacy with your partner, either physically or emotionally. You might be overcome with negativity and want to withdraw from them or feel insecure within the relationship. You could even become clingy or more controlling, and go through bouts of anxiety and depression as well as loneliness and isolation. It becomes a real mess!

Many people will try to cling on to their relationship despite the lack of trust, and there are many reasons for that, such as low self-esteem, codependency issues, and being disconnected from their own needs. If your partner has done nothing to cause you any of the above, you may have trust issues that you need to deal with.

You can't have a healthy relationship without trust, but if it is you who is creating this atmosphere of doubt, it could be because of a past experience of betrayal. The after-effects of that pain are still being carried around in your heart and you find it difficult to trust anyone after that. It's a natural behaviour to adopt, although it's also likely to sabotage any new romantic possibilities. When you cannot trust, you might come across the following kinds of unhealthy patterns:

- Your partner is always honest but you still disbelieve what they say.

- You continually question their motives and intentions, making intimacy almost impossible.

- You always assume the worst, which impacts how they respond to you.

- You are suspicious about their intentions and give off totally negative vibes.

- You are very likely to self-sabotage your relationship now rather than end up disappointed later on.

- You'll feel unhappy and find it hard to experience a healthy connection.

- You will most likely be plagued by feelings of regret, guilt, shame, and bitterness.

> **Just because someone let you down in the past, it doesn't mean the same thing will happen in the future. Once you have developed trust in your own judgement and value, it is possible to build up trust slowly in your next relationship.**

It's all about balance here – when trust is broken, don't rush into things too quickly, but stay open to meeting someone that you will be happy to have in your life. Take your time and let things flow naturally instead of trying to force anything. Resist the desire to control the situation, as this shows you feel insecure, even though your new partner hasn't given you any reason to feel that way.

It's OK to talk about your trust issues, although you don't need to go into every detail just yet. Explain that you had a bad experience and are trying to work through it, allowing your new partner to understand where you are coming from. Communicate in a calm, authentic way and be vulnerable without going overboard. You can ask your partner their opinion, or if they have had a similar experience. When you are able to put yourself out there without fear, you are showing that you respect yourself, which is a very appealing quality to have.

If you really want to establish trust with someone else, you need to show that you are trustworthy too. It's no good expecting them to be there for you if you won't do the same for them. You will need to be open and honest, otherwise you are setting yourself up for failure.

Vulnerability is the key to creating a strong, trusting relationship. It's when you open up to someone and show your weaknesses that you will discover whether you can trust them or not. If they give you the love and support you need, when they could have hurt you instead, you'll know that you can trust them with your heart.

FEELING INSECURE?

You might be in a relationship where trust is evident, yet you still feel insecure. This is probably because you have attachment wounds from a past relationship that went badly. Self-awareness is really important if you want to make any relationship work, and there are certain signs you can look for and work on to that end.

As with every other aspect of your relationships, it begins with the relationship with yourself.

- How often and how comfortable are you with being vulnerable to yourself?

- Do you self-validate?

- Do you embrace your mistakes?

- Do you accept yourself as enough?

If not, you will try to be everything you think others need you to be. **Vulnerability isn't always about exposing your weaknesses but also standing in your power.** This is another reason that doing the work in Part 1 of this book is critical to understanding your power and what you bring to a relationship. To be vulnerable is to know yourself, accept yourself, and be at peace with what you can and cannot offer someone.

Lack of trust

Keep a journal about when you feel this way. Are your thoughts logical or can you give your partner the benefit of the doubt? Where are your feelings really coming from and how can you process those reactions and thought patterns instead of projecting them on to your partner? Have they demonstrated behaviour that makes you feel unsafe to be yourself or express yourself? Or have they proven the opposite? When someone hasn't demonstrated that they aren't unsafe, you miss out on true intimacy by just assuming they are.

Problems with intimacy

What does intimacy mean to you and your partner? Does it mean the same thing to you both? How can you let your guard down to enjoy being close to your partner without past abuse, insecurities, or expectations getting in the way? Talk to each other about it and be patient – it takes time to synchronize and understand any differences between you.

Panic responses

When did you first start to experience feelings of panic and wanting to run away from a situation? How did you resolve it then and how can you resolve it now? What do you need from your partner now? Allow yourself to work through these thought processes and learn to validate your feelings. This self-soothing technique will really help you to change how you react when you are challenged.

Feeling attacked

Ask yourself why you feel criticized by your partner and consider if you may be making the wrong assumptions. Did they actually say or do something hurtful or is it your interpretation of events, based on previous wounds? Is there any possibility that you are making something up that didn't occur? The more you question your reactions, the greater clarity you will get, and be able to understand what your partner was trying to say without any drama.

Making something out of nothing

What were you fighting about and was it worth it? A lot of couples get caught up in arguments about tiny little things, not stopping to look under the carpet to see what's hiding there. Is this a pattern developing that signifies something is fundamentally wrong, or are you simply making a mountain out of a molehill? When you find it hard to get close to someone, it's often easier to create an atmosphere of disruption as you self-sabotage your chances of a harmonious relationship.

LEARNING TO TRUST AGAIN

You find out your partner has had an affair, been lying to you, deceiving you, and abusing your trust . . . all very hurtful situations to be in. What do you do then, when the trust is broken?

It can take a long time to heal, and there's no denying that. But often, time goes by and we haven't really healed at all. We've just been treading water. If you want to trust again, you are going to have to resolve those broken feelings of pain and disappointment. If you want to continue fighting for your relationship, and don't think your partner's actions are unforgivable, how do you move on?

Whether you stay or you choose to walk away from the relationship, the power to trust has to be restored inside of you. There are aspects of betrayal that damage the individual and the relationship. Even if you decide to leave the relationship, it is important to heal what's been done to you. As a protective mechanism, the brain will develop all sorts of stories to keep your trust from being broken again, and it's up to you to challenge those stories and keep your heart from hardening.

If you want to stay in the relationship, you are going to have to work together to rebuild what you used to have. That means letting go of any doubts, or at least putting them on ice, as you give your partner the opportunity to come back to you from a place of honesty. Infidelity is one of the most painful experiences that couples try to deal with and it's not a new phenomenon. You could say that it's always been around but society has dealt with it in different ways through the ages and across cultures.

Some couples come back stronger when a spouse has had an affair, while others just can't weather that storm. It really depends on how you personally feel about it and whether you can put infidelity to one side.

What I would like to say, though, is that trust is a two-way street. If your partner has been unfaithful, can you trust yourself not to keep bringing it up for the next ten years every time you have an argument? From the moment you accept what happened and decide to move on together, you both have to create a fair playing field where there are no dirty fouls or tactics. Are you prepared to do that?

Loving someone can mean accepting their errors and failures, just in the same way that they accept yours. There doesn't always have to be an either/or ultimatum, and we can exercise compassion after the event. You can build something new, with the transgression actually revealing what was missing in your relationship and allowing you to fix it.

I'm not trying to condone or condemn infidelity here. What I want to focus on is how to re-establish trust if that's what you want. You might need to move boundaries, alter habits, and rearrange the furniture as you work to rebuild from the beginning. But before all of that, I must come back to the most important step you have to take – to trust yourself.

- Can you come to terms with your feelings and move forward?

- Can you sit down and talk things through with your partner without spitting out accusations, criticism and judgement?

- Can you listen without prejudice?

- Can you assume responsibility, if it was you that cheated?

- Can you understand what was behind your actions?

- Can you express your needs and hear the needs of your partner?

- Can those needs be met?

- Can you keep the promises that you make to each other from now on?

If you feel you are being abused, you need to get out, as the situation could seriously harm your emotional wellbeing. You should never stay in a relationship that is stripping away your self-esteem. At the end of the day, only you know what you are prepared to put up with and if it is in alignment with your self-worth.

As Miguel Ruiz said in his book, *The Mastery of Love*,[24] 'Let us trust ourselves completely to make the choices we must make.'

If damaging behaviour by your partner is an ongoing thing, set yourself a deadline, and if those unhealthy patterns persist, make the break. When you commit to a person who isn't committed to themselves, you run the risk of losing sight of your journey towards awareness. But until that point, you will do a disservice to yourself and others by withholding vulnerability and playing it 'safe'. The power of the connection will be determined by how deep you're willing to go.

Trust in yourself, be open to love's great gifts, and dare to be vulnerable – it's the only way to live and love!

KEY INSIGHTS

- Being vulnerable requires strength, not weakness.

- Building trust and support are the building blocks of an authentic relationship.

- The fear of failure can restrict your ability to love, but daring to do so can be a game-changer.

- Reflecting on what you bring to the relationship and what you ask from it can reveal some invaluable truths.

- If you can practise being vulnerable, you open up the possibilities of true intimacy.

- Know your limits and think about the conditions you are putting on the relationship.

- Seek to resolve your own trust issues so you can learn to trust your partner.

Chapter 8

WHEN TO WALK AWAY

The Universe will replace people who do not reciprocate your love. That is why love is never lost, it is only found.

So, you've done the work. Yet you feel as though you are over-extending yourself with no improvement in sight.

You might have spent your whole life looking for the right person, and now that you have found them, it's all going wrong. Your demons can't seem to stop grappling with theirs, the passion is gone, and the natural chemistry is starting to fade. Perhaps you fight often or barely even talk any more.

Things have changed. They have changed. You have changed.

What was once a brilliant love story has become a monotonous soap opera.

The question is: how do you know when to try to make it work and when do you decide to walk away?

If you look at the research,[25] you'll find that the most common reasons that couples break up are disagreements over money, incompatibility, responsibilities, kids, and outside factors such as in-laws. You will also see things like alcohol abuse, a history of childhood trauma, or even mental health disorders coming to the fore. These are obviously important but, as I mentioned earlier, squabbling over money or chores is often a symptom of something much deeper. These types of arguments reflect a lack of connection, or power struggles within a relationship.

Although the title of this chapter is 'When to Walk Away', I could also have called it 'When to Stay'. Both topics are worthy of discussion. It seems to me that it's often more difficult to make the decision to break up than it is to stay with a partner, and this is actually what a lot of people settle for. However, some jump the gun and fail to put in the work that can completely reverse the trajectory of a relationship on its last legs.

When you've invested your time and energy in a long-term relationship (even if that's only been a few months), the thought of losing that can be scary and intimidating. You might tell yourself that it's better to stay than to be alone, that you have built a life together and can't face the alternative. You could even say that you love your partner and can't imagine life without them.

Self-love helps you recognize who's worth being around and who's best to avoid. It doesn't encourage loneliness; it just ensures that you aren't travelling a lonely path even when you have someone around.

I remember someone telling me about her unfaithful ex-boyfriend. It started with something as innocent as him liking lots of random women's pictures on Instagram. He would also follow and message them, despite her requests for him to stop as it made her feel uncomfortable. She also thought that he could be sending the wrong message to these people.

He'd regularly go out clubbing with his friends and turn his phone off so she couldn't contact him. She wouldn't even know when or if he got home on those nights. Then, the next morning, she'd find that he'd taken multiple pictures with different women during the night – some of which seemed inappropriate for a man in a relationship.

When she tried to express how this made her feel, he would label her insecure, and tell her she was paranoid and proving that she didn't trust him. While there was an element of truth to this, he was quick to shut down her feelings, manipulate her emotionally, and continue to disrespect her. It was not reassuring.

Each time they fell out, he would try to woo her again with his words, expressing how much he loved her. Nevertheless, deep down, she knew the behaviour would continue. As it did, she became more self-conscious, less confident, and completely paranoid. She kept asking herself, 'Am I not good enough for him? Doesn't he love me? What am I doing wrong?'

Unfortunately, I am hearing more and more tales of gaslighting within relationships. And it's so easy to judge her and say, 'Leave him already!' But how many of us have allowed ourselves to be manipulated, even on a small scale? It's much more comfortable for us to identify unhealthy dynamics in other relationships than to face our own. We continually make excuses for our partner. They love us after all; there is no way they'd intentionally hurt us.

The woman tolerated his ways because she believed that she loved him, and he also loved her – even though he would always leave her questioning herself. He continued to act inappropriately because he knew he'd get away with it. Sure, she might moan and get angry, but she'd remain by his side, and he didn't want to lose her. However, their relationship eventually came to an end when she caught him in bed with another woman in their home. Her worst fears had come true and it was only at that point that she was able to make the decision to leave him.

More often than not, even though the excitement, passion, and intimacy might disappear in a relationship and be replaced with complacency, contempt, and distance, you may still prefer to stay. You know things aren't how they used to be and can't seem to fix them, so you settle for a lacklustre life together that is missing everything you used to enjoy so much. This isn't what you signed up for, but the thought of leaving? That's too difficult to even contemplate for many.

Infidelity is a massive blow to a relationship and incredibly hard to come back from. With the help of therapy, it's possible for some people to rebuild their relationship in a new way. But many of you aren't likely to be worried about your partner cheating. It's perhaps more an accumulation of many small things that have you questioning the potential longevity of the connection.

In a way, it's easier to go on, following the daily routine you've both become accustomed to, enjoying an intimate moment here or there. You might even make a great team, both working together to raise a family. It's possible that you are best friends, helping and supporting each other when needed. And if you have children, splitting up may never be an option for you as you feel the cost would be too much on their stability. You could stay with your partner because you are financially dependent on them, or because they are the only love you've ever known. You might also stay because you have nowhere else to go or the alternatives just aren't feasible.

A lot of couples struggle with this kind of dilemma. They may consider breaking up because they are experiencing too much conflict, don't feel attracted to each other any more, have differences of opinion, or have outgrown each other. This list is by no means complete – there are so many different reasons and everyone will have their own take on why they want to end a relationship.

When you think about why some couples break up and others don't, even though their relationship is broken, love comes into the dialogue a lot.

'I love him but don't feel happy any more.'

'You don't give up on those you love.'

'I thought she loved me but she was just using me.'

'I can't walk out on him. I love him too much.'

'If she loved me, she wouldn't leave me.'

When we talk about our relationships, love factors highly in the conversation. It's as if it binds us together like superglue, no matter how we are coping with practical issues and which emotions we are trying to deal with. I agree that love is paramount, but does loving someone mean that you'll sacrifice yourself for it?

When I say 'sacrifice', I'm talking about your wellbeing, your mental health, your physical safety, and your ability to access happiness. Does love conquer all? Maybe, but not in the way that you might think.

LOVE AS A GUISE IN BROKEN RELATIONSHIPS

I want to take a step back and talk about what love means to you in the context of a relationship. Is it about giving and receiving, finding your other half, sharing your life with your soulmate? Does it have a beginning and an end? Is there an expiration date or is it infinite? Is it a matter of 'until death us do part' or 'I'll see you in the next life'?

A major reason love gets a bad rap in modern society is because broken and unhealthy relationships use it as a guise. When things have clearly turned sour and all the components of authentic love have expired, what actually remains keeping the two tied are attachments. Attachment to their identity as someone's partner, attachment to the fear of being single, a codependent need to cling when it's clearly time to let go, and/ or a false sense of hope that things will turn around. To be fair, in most of these cases, one or both partners do truly believe they're staying in the name of love.

Everyone has their own idea of what love means to them, depending on their upbringing, character, social and cultural norms, experiences, and opinions. Love is whatever you want it to be and can be expressed in a million and one ways.

Modern love is complicated, though. In the past, we looked to God or a specific religion to bring us completeness, but today, we want that from a person. We turn our attention to finding someone who can fill all of our intellectual, emotional, and spiritual needs, day in, day out. You may even be religious but still expect your partner to fulfil you – to complete you. So, what happens when they don't?

I can't give you definitive answers on when to walk away from a relationship, but I can share with you my ideas about what love is, and what it isn't. It's a conversation that I hope will bring you some insights and cause you to reflect on what you want from a life shared with another. I sincerely hope it can be of benefit to you.

WHAT IS LOVE?

As I searched for words of wisdom in books on philosophy, psychology, spirituality, religion, science, and works of literature, one theme kept cropping up.

I found that love itself exists totally independently of what we do and say. It's like an eternal light that never goes out, an expansive ocean without end, a blue sky that stretches endlessly on the horizon. It's an energy that is always present; an infinite, universal law. Even the lack of love highlights the fact that it exists on the other side of the coin. You might prefer to use another word to refer to love, like 'universal energy', 'God', 'spirit', 'numen', 'totality', or the 'Universe'. I think we all understand what it is as a concept, though, no matter what words we use to describe it.

What happens after that is a complicated series of events and environmental conditions which go into forming our personality and expectations. But from the very start, we all have an infinite capacity for love, no matter how we are treated. Of course, infants and children need to receive love in order to grow into emotionally balanced adults, but it's not like they come with a list of demands: 'love me and I'll love you back'. Even people who have suffered trauma at the hands of their parents or carers often still feel love for them, and it's a very complicated developmental response to work through.

As Rumi said, 'It's not about finding the right person. It's about being the right person.' I think that this is a wonderfully insightful statement because he's basically saying that we have to understand self-love before we can share it with another in the best way possible. To do that, we need to strip away the ego and all those layers of conditioning that we've formed through our experiences. We have to reconnect with our inner potential to love freely and to find fulfilment in the act itself. In that sense, it's not dependent on the other person or the conditions surrounding our relationship. It's about us and how we share that love with others.

With this understanding of love, you know there is a potential within you to love anyone and everyone. Thus, a relationship with that special, chosen person whom you'll share your life with, doesn't consist of only love. It is compatibility, attraction, and shared values that help you thrive. Break-ups often occur because compatibility was never established, just the desire to love and be loved. It is often later when you discover the two of you want very different things but lean on the crutch of love every chance you get.

What is this really saying about how you feel in yourself?

Consider how often you make excuses for your partner. You have always wanted children, but three years into the marriage they tell you parenthood isn't for them. Do you sacrifice this lifelong desire for the sake of love? This is simply sacrificing yourself. Love would say we don't want the same things any more and because I honour you and I honour myself, this is goodbye.

Maybe the differences aren't this extreme. And, to some degree, compromise is necessary. But true love is freedom to be who you are and live a life your heart truly desires. Authentic love within a relationship opens you up to the brightest and fullest expression of yourself. Your heart, body, and mind are exceptionally intuitive and know when it's no longer working. The question is, how long will you stay when you see that it's not?

When they're no longer right for you, it'll feel wrong most of the time. Like an incessant ache in your heart, you'll notice yourself change. Your spirit shrinks, your sparkle dulls, and you find yourself faking a smile. It's often subtle how being with the wrong person makes you feel less like yourself, and may lead you to seek validation from them that you are enough.

If you enter a relationship without understanding the nature of love, you will come across many difficulties, especially if the other person is also out of touch with their love potential. Imagine two newbies trying to teach each other how to communicate, create, and interact. It is possible to cultivate a deeply loving relationship, but it takes time, skill, awareness, and a willingness to learn.

We usually dive head-first into a partnership without considering any of that.

We're on a high, we feel ecstatic – this is 'the one'! We are on cloud nine, we were made for each other – life is wonderful. All of those feelings and emotions are beautiful to experience and truly magical. But there's no denying the fact that they don't last for ever and will gradually change into something less intense.

Couples who have been happily married or lived together for a long time can vouch for this, and have plenty of wisdom to share about how their relationships have remained fulfilling for so long. They usually mention things like being willing to compromise, accepting the other person's quirks and flaws, having mutual respect, making important decisions together, maintaining their own interests or hobbies, agreeing to disagree on certain issues, and enjoying affection and sex.

They may have also found ways to keep their relationship alive with romantic gestures, experimenting in the bedroom, having date nights, and so on. If you want to keep the fire alight, you have to be prepared to fan the flames, right?

Love doesn't need reciprocity to exist, and thus love does not equal a relationship. You can love someone who doesn't love you, or who loves you in a different way. This is what we call 'unconditional love', and I know there's a lot of confusion about that. Perhaps you have heard of the term but aren't exactly sure what it means, or how to apply that to your relationship.

If you consider, as I mentioned above, that love isn't a transaction, that may help. Also, remember that love exists within us and is part of our being. You might ask, 'Don't we need to feel loved?' Of course we do, and that's part of feeling fulfilled within a relationship, but we still have the capacity to love whether we experience love in return or not.

You can love someone even if you never see them again.
You can love someone even if they are not the one for you.
You can love someone even if you walk away from them.
Why?

Because love is an energy you generate and it isn't about the other person. When I think of unconditional love, I see it as giving love for love's sake, not for any other reason. I prefer to say that it is the purest, or deepest form of love that we all have a propensity for. The problem is that, somewhere along the way, it gets mixed up with romantic notions, societal trends, cultural expectations, individual needs, and emotional attachments. Relationships become complicated, but authentic love is very simple.

If you have lost a loved one, does that mean you don't love them any more? I'm sure that any of you who have grieved over the passing of someone very important to you still feel an immense amount of love for them. In that sense, love doesn't disappear just because we no longer experience the love of another person. It remains within us, in our memories, and in our hearts.

If you have children, most of you will know that your love for them knows no bounds. You will give them love selflessly, and no matter what they do, you have an abundance of love for them. It never dries up or runs out.

When it comes to romantic relationships, it is slightly different in the way love plays out, but the main idea of love as a distinct energy remains the same. If you think of love as the big, wide ocean, we are on a tiny boat, trying to navigate our course through the endless expanse without a compass.

The thought leader Eckhart Tolle talks about love in his book *Practising the Power of Now*.[26] He hits the nail right on the head when he says, 'Love is a state of being. Your love is not outside: it is deep within you. You can never lose it, and it can never leave you. It is not dependent on some other body, some external form.' I think that you can also replace the word 'love' here with 'happiness'.

> **They asked,**
> **'How can you love so deeply?'**
> **I replied:**
> **'Because I love myself deeply. I don't give in**
> **order to gain. There are no price tags on the love**
> **that I share. It's an offering – I give it because I**
> **want to, not because I need to.'**

When it comes to romantic love, the relationship becomes a vessel for two people to be in this heightened state or high vibe, together. If, at any point, either feels like their joy is compromised, they become a martyr for their relationship instead of an active participant.

A FISHY TALE

Very often, we share our version of love before understanding what it is someone else really needs within a relationship. Commit to knowing and understanding your partner above all else. Though the capacity to feel love is universal for all humans, the way we express and experience love varies from person to person.

Here's a rewrite of an old story:

I loved my pet fish. I fed it everything I could offer, spent lots of time with it, decorated the inside of its tank, and did whatever one would do to express love. One day, I was so over-whelmed with my love for the fish that I took it out of the tank to hug and kiss it. The fish unfortunately died. I was too busy showing it what I believed to be love instead of understanding what it needed. The tank was overcrowded, it was overfed and, sure enough, couldn't breathe outside of the tank.

Love can be pure, unconditional, maintain the best of intentions, and yet still go wrong. It's not unreasonable for you to want to find someone who loves you the way you need to be loved. It's also important to understand that the kind of love you want to give may not be right for someone else. We might even have to walk away from good people, not because they did us wrong, but because we know ourselves well enough to identify our need for a different experience of love.

FANTASY BONDS

Often, we are misled by the illusion of love and maintain a relationship in which we are 'together' but emotionally disconnected. This is what psychotherapist Dr Robert Firestone has called the 'fantasy bond' in his book *The Fantasy Bond: Structure of Psychological Defenses*.[27] It can start to manifest itself early on in a relationship and become more embedded as time goes by. The term refers to the kind of situation where real love is substituted for going through the motions of being a couple. During this kind of relationship, the reserves of vitality and attraction fade away pretty quickly.

If you have a fear of intimacy, which many people do, you might be self-protective yet don't want to be alone. The solution is to form the illusion of connection and closeness with someone even though you really keep an emotional distance from them. For this reason, it's almost impossible to achieve intimacy, and it's like playing happy couples without any real deep emotional bond to each other.

You might have never realized that you've been going through the motions of seeking a partner simply because you don't want to be alone. When you do find someone who seems compatible, you end up playing out certain styles of interaction that you first learned in childhood. It's like you revert to a kind of defence pattern that might have served you in the past but interferes with your ability to establish secure and satisfying relationships in the present. Once this kind of fantasy bond is formed, it's more likely that you'll maintain a defensive position rather than nurturing trust in each other. If you have been hurt in the past, it's difficult to stop being defensive, which blocks you from enjoying closeness with your partner.

How do you know if this is happening to you? You can take a look at the following behaviours and consider if you have unconsciously fallen into any of these negative patterns:

- **Openness or anger?** Any healthy relationship requires openness and being willing to listen to our partner without angry reactions. When we start to withdraw because we are afraid of any triggers we might set off, it's the beginning of a shutdown in communication. Keeping quiet to keep the peace can only make matters worse. This passive behaviour can be as detrimental as someone who shouts to voice their opinion.

- **Open to the new or closed doors?** In their infancy, relationships are exciting because everything is new and novel. Sparks fly and the fire is hot! When the flames have died down, an unwillingness to try anything new can be a sign that the relationship has run out of oxygen altogether. If you see this happening yet ignore it, you might be entering a cold war.

- **Honesty or deception?** Being honest with your partner allows them to get to know you and increases intimacy.

When that becomes less important than prolonging the relationship, you are forfeiting trust and closeness. Dishonesty can begin with little things, like hiding how much money you have spent, until it becomes a habit you adopt to avoid arguments. When you commit to not doing something, i.e. bringing up a hard topic to avoid confrontation, you commit to doing something you don't want. This is self-betrayal and will lead to resentment. Like a sneeze, better out than in. Bring your concerns to the person you love. Equally, when they come to you, that's your opportunity to hold space and demonstrate that coming to you with the issue instead of bottling it up was the right decision.

- **Maintaining or overstepping boundaries?** Fantasy bonds are based on the notion that we are one with our partner. That incurs overstepping boundaries and losing ourselves in a relationship that may become codependent. Rather than holding on to our autonomy, we begin to see our partners as extensions of ourselves and cling to that dynamic because we believe it's the best way to keep things ticking over. As a result, we gradually begin to despise them more and love them less.

- **Affection and sexuality or non-affection and loss of sexuality?** When affection fades, it causes tiny cracks in the relationship that soon become gaping holes in our sex lives. Going along with routine or uninspiring sex in the hope of maintaining the relationship will only create greater distance. Without authentic affection, it's hard to enjoy authentic physical contact.

- **Non-controlling or manipulating?** Very often, we slip into specific roles in a relationship – parent and child, teacher and pupil, mentor and student, where one is in control and the other is submissive. This encourages shaming, humiliation, and an imbalance in the power dynamic. There is no room for growth or maturity in this kind of role-playing and the show will eventually end in tears.

SHOULD I STAY OR SHOULD I GO?

The love you give isn't always equal to the love you receive. I wish it was, but sometimes that's just not possible. It's easy for differences to arise within a relationship when expectations aren't met or past traumas interfere with our ability to move on. Emotional triggers can stop us from nurturing a more meaningful connection and prevent us from committing fully. I've talked about this earlier on in the book and it's possible that a lot of your problems could be stemming from these unresolved issues.

When this happens, something changes in the dynamic – usually going unnoticed for a while. We stop checking in with our partner to ask how they are, and don't pay as much attention to how the relationship is progressing. It's easy to become complacent and bury problems in order to escape conflict. In reality, we do a great job at keeping the peace without admitting that things aren't how we want them to be. But the problems do resurface.

Marital expert and researcher Dr John Gottman[28] has identified four kinds of relationship conflicts that predict break-ups within couples. He calls them the Four Horsemen (with a reference to the Apocalypse) and has identified them as: Criticism, Stonewalling, Defensiveness and Contempt. Relationships are complicated, and you might experience one or more of these behaviours, plus a lot of other things such as dishonesty, abuse, disrespect, and so on. I can't mention every single one here but we can take a look at the four Gottman examples, based on conversations I've had with some of my followers and friends.

Criticism

Jaz: *I really love Kiera, but it upsets me when she criticizes me all the time for the slightest thing. If I forget to take out the trash, she calls me lazy and selfish. Even when I buy her gifts, she complains that I've bought the wrong colour or size. To be honest, it seems like I can't do anything right.*

Criticism can be very damaging in a relationship. When your partner attacks you for who you are, it's hurtful. They are supposed to support you and, instead, they are pulling you down. For a relationship to work, you have to start from a place of compassion and work through your differences together. At the same time, it could be that you don't feel there is any room for improvement. You need to do some soul-searching here and decide whether this person is right for you or not. There will be things going on with Kiera that are making her behave this way, and Jaz also needs to think about which triggers her behaviour are setting off in him.

When you find yourself in a situation where your partner is complaining, it can touch a nerve with your own feelings of insecurity, but if someone is just plain mean, that's a completely different story. Abuse in a relationship can be both emotional and physical and you should NEVER have to put up with either. You may notice that I mention this is non-negotiable a few times in this book, in the hope that at least one person will step out of a harmful situation.

Love is, by its very nature, never hurtful, but expectations and demands can be.

If you feel your self-worth is being attacked, you can't afford to let that happen. When you are being criticized for who you are and cannot resolve the differences, you may be tempted to ignore them or hope things will change.

Consider: Ignoring your emotional wellbeing is never a good idea as it comes at a high price. Secondly, nothing is going to change within your relationship if only one of you is trying.

Stonewalling

Kelly and Jasmin: *Basically, Jasmin keeps stonewalling me every time we have a disagreement or fight. She'll storm out of the room, refuse to talk to me for days and give me the cold shoulder. When things have calmed down, she always acts as if it was all my fault and expects me to apologize. I've had enough.*

Here again, Jasmin may never have learned how to communicate her emotions or be dealing with something that she can't even understand herself. Her behaviour is hurtful to Kelly, who truly loves her and wants to stay, but she's feeling locked out and rejected. Stonewalling is one of the main reasons that couples break up, and I can understand why. When the walls go up, how can you even begin to communicate?

If your partner shuts you out and isn't prepared to do the work to open up, how long should you wait? Sometimes, this kind of behaviour is manipulative, coercing you into apologizing or making you feel guilty for something you haven't done in order to get back to normal. If, after offering your support, you feel that your integrity is being compromised, you need to think about what the future will look like.

Consider: You must always stay true to your values and be prepared to stand your ground to uphold them, even if that means walking away from someone you love. Not everyone you meet will be ready to embark on a healthy relationship.

Defensiveness

Sharmi: *Did you make the reservation for tomorrow at the restaurant like I asked you to?*

Izaac: *Jeez! Do you know how busy I've been at work today? Why didn't you just do it yourself!*

Attack is the best form of defence, right? After being caught out by your partner, it feels natural to want to strike back and defend yourself. And then you can declare all-out war! When couples engage in this kind of tit-for-tat exchange, things can get way out of control. If your partner acts defensive even though they haven't been attacked by you, it may be the sign of a victim mentality in which they don't have the emotional tools to be accountable for their actions.

To us, it might appear like they aren't invested in the relationship, making out that everything is our fault. If we take on that blame, it's like admitting that we did something wrong. As the conflict escalates, you can't nurture a caring, compassionate partnership and something will have to go.

Consider: Defensive behaviour can occur when your partner has a victim mentality or is unable to assume accountability. If you feel humiliated and unfairly treated when the blame is constantly shifted onto you, you need to avoid this negative cycle at all costs.

Contempt

Jayden: *I used to be a strong, independent person, and now, Max is making me feel like I'm worthless. He laughed when I told him I was thinking of going for a promotion and said, 'What makes you think they'll give you the job? You don't even know how to turn on a computer.' I don't know how much longer I can go on like this.*

When your partner is sarcastic, mean, puts you down, and mocks you, it will eventually eat away at your self-worth. I'm not talking about harmless banter here, which has its boundaries and isn't usually meant to offend. When someone puts themself in a morally superior position to you, it may be out of a desire to cover up their own inadequacies or perhaps from a desire to have control. This kind of behaviour doesn't appear overnight – it's a long process of negativity that has built up over time and can become a common pattern in a relationship.

Contempt between couples is one of the main reasons for break-ups. It expresses disgust, condescension, hostility, and the 'I'm better than you' model. It can get you involved in a slanging match and, even more dangerous, conflict fuelled by anger and loathing.

Consider: If you want a relationship in which you both support each other on the journey to self-love, healing, and organic happiness, there is no room for contempt. The more self-awareness you gain, the less of this kind of behaviour you will tolerate.

RECOGNIZING WHAT YOU HAVE

I remember hearing a story about a woman who thought she was in a healthy and happy marriage until a charming young man came along. She didn't intend for feelings to develop: the new guy was just an attractive colleague from work. Although her mind wandered from time to time about how an intimate encounter would feel with him, it didn't prompt her to cheat on her husband.

After spending some time with this colleague, she began to fall for his personality. He was kind, intelligent, and funny. She also saw traits in him that her husband lacked.

A few months passed by, and her colleague admitted he had fallen for her. While she didn't react to this, the idea played on her mind a lot. Eventually, she found herself sharing a physical encounter with him after a corporate party.

From here, she developed deeper feelings for him. He would surprise her with flowers and gifts. Plus, he always kept her on her toes; she hadn't felt like this for a long time. She found excitement again in a relationship. Mentally, physically, and emotionally, her colleague stimulated her. After a year, she decided to leave her husband for this new love interest and settle down with him.

However, this is when it turned sour. A few weeks into the relationship, she witnessed a different side to him; he was manipulative, controlling, and abusive. He stopped providing the treats she received at the start. She even caught him flirting with other women.

She began to realize that although her husband wasn't perfect, he did more than enough for her – and he never stopped showing her love. It was simple things, like trying to work through disagreements, having a respectful tone when they fell out, or even sharing the cooking, which her new boyfriend didn't do. He relied on her to do everything, even when unwell, and provide sexual favours when she wasn't in the mood.

Great relationships need nurturing, and while people will never be perfect, you should not overlook someone's consistent efforts and commitment.

Anyone can treat you right for a short period of time, but it takes a special person to continue to give to the relationship for the rest of your life. That takes a lot of love and commitment.

WHEN SHOULD I LEAVE?

There's no right or wrong time to walk away from a relationship. You will do it when you are ready. It can take months or even years for you to reach the point where you make the decision to break away, and it's never an easy thing to do.

While you may have had some good times together, you can't go back to the past. All you can do is focus on the present situation. Even though you may share a long history, you might be feeling that the relationship has run its course, for a variety of reasons. I would like to suggest that you tune into your inner needs and see if they are being satisfied before you make any decisions. I'm not talking about how much your partner pampers you or how often they take you out. I'm referring to those deep emotional needs where you feel respected, honoured, and loved for who you are.

You can be so in love with the past, their promises, and their potential, that you forget about what's happening in the present.

The closer you are to yourself, the harder it will be to betray your needs and go against your desire for a stable, healthy, happy relationship. There is only so much convincing and excusing you can do before you finally go. But so much time and so many emotions can be saved when the relationship with yourself is solid enough to look within and concur, 'We are on the right path and continue to strengthen our relationship,' or 'My heart, mind, and body are no longer interested in investing in this connection.'

It's not your job to change your partner, nor for them to change you, although you may have spent some time working towards doing just that. You might have more emotional maturity or be more connected to your spirituality while your partner is in a different place to you. If you really feel that you aren't growing in unison or that the differences are making you suffer, you must accept the reality of that and go from there.

Here are some things to think about:

- Are you able to stay true to your deepest values within the relationship?
- Does your partner honour your principles, even if they don't agree with them?
- Are you able to maintain your independence and autonomy freely?
- Are conflicts and differences remaining unresolved for long periods of time?
- Does your gut feeling or intuition tell you that something is wrong?

> **Never let boredom, loneliness, or temporary suffering be the reason you go back to the people, places, or circumstances that brought you down or drove you away.**

For love to flourish, you must stay true to yourself. There can be no other way. This is a non-negotiable aspect of your happiness and when you forsake that for a partner, it is an act of self-betrayal. It doesn't make you a bad person, selfish, or uncaring to walk away from a relationship. It means that you are being authentic and have the emotional maturity to do what is right for you.

I wish I could tell you that every problem can be resolved. Unfortunately, that's a myth that many people want to buy into. The reality is that we won't necessarily be with our current partner in five, ten, or twenty years from now. Love might still prevail, but life can take us in different directions as we search for greater happiness and enrichment. Just because you break up from your partner, that doesn't have to negate all of the love you experienced together. You can treasure those memories as you both move on to explore different relationships and realize your potential. Nothing is lost in love and all of the experiences you have provide nourishment for growth and fulfilment.

Relationships are in a constant state of flux, changing and morphing from one day to the next. Certain events can come along to challenge the dynamic, such as children, illness, a move, the loss of a family member, more money, less money, an affair, and so on. We also change as we go through life and are never static. Love can also fluctuate in its intensity and go from intense longing to a playing down of emotions. When it starts to wane, that doesn't mean it never existed. It has simply faded for this particular person or circumstance. You still have the capacity to love greatly, even after a relationship has run its course.

Maybe people aren't leaving you. Maybe the Universe is leaving room in your life for people who are worthy of the love you share.

THE ONLY CONSTANT IS LOVE

Seek out someone who will hold your love in their hands like a precious gem; someone who honours your heart space and allows you to be yourself. Find a person who will give you space to grow and expand while you allow them to do the same. Align yourself with someone who responds to your energy and will let it flow; someone who will cherish your individuality and love you for that. Sail on the vast ocean together, bringing a richness to life that comes from great depths.

Become a vibrational match to the relationship you desire. Focus on the good in yourself and you'll find good in others. If someone isn't right for you, the most loving thing to do for them and yourself is to walk away from the relationship.

Unconditional love doesn't mean staying for the sake of it.
Unconditional love means always doing what is true and right from your deepest sense of self-awareness.

I love this quote by the motivational speaker Yasmin Mogahed, from her book *Reclaim Your Heart.*[29] She says:

'Love without attachment is the purest love because it isn't about what others can give you because you're empty. It is about what you can give others because you're already full.'

If you can navigate your relationships with this compass, you will never get lost.

You will always feel anchored, unafraid to give love completely, and ready to receive whatever comes back to you with an open heart.

KEY INSIGHTS

- Sometimes it is easier to be in a bad relationship than to make the decision to leave.

- Couples stay together for many reasons, even when love has faded.

- Knowing why you wish to stay with your partner needs some soul-searching.

- Love isn't always enough to make the relationship work.

- Many couples rely on the guise of love to cover up their differences.

- Knowing what love is can guide you into making the right decisions.

- Unconditional love can be achieved once you recognize love as a state of being.

- The fantasy bonds that keep two people together can mask the lack of genuine emotional connection.

- Knowing when to leave comes through having clarity about what a loving relationship means to you.

Although no one is perfect, you are worthy of finding someone willing to build bridges over mistranslations of your love language – and pave passages to your thoughts so that they can build knowledge of your perception. I hope you meet someone who will journey with you through different dimensions and constellations, to show you that your magnificence stretches beyond this physical plane, and among the other stars. While passion lights up our relationships like wildfires, I hope you connect with someone who would rather entertain you with comedy than drama, and laughter over lies.

PART 3

Love: The fundamentals of authentic, unconditional love

Unconditional love is the outer
expression of inner peace.[30]

– Alaric Hutchinson

Chapter 9

LOVE IS A VERB

**Love is in the doing, not the feeling.
Love doesn't happen as a result of the circumstances;
love happens because of you.**

Idealized romantic love is big business and a commodity that sells. From blockbuster Hollywood movies to chart-topping pop songs and best-selling books, we can't get enough of romance. That feeling of falling in love or being in love is such a powerful concept that we all want to experience it, and our idea of what it means has been highly influenced by great works of literature, art, and entertainment.

Romantic love is the Holy Grail, the elixir of life, the fountain of youth, the secret to everlasting happiness. We crave it, demand it, and pursue it. And once we get it, we feel as if the whole Universe has aligned to fulfil our dreams. It's well and truly embedded in our cultural psyche and most of us are completely sold on the idea of romantic love. We seek out a partner who will give us it and we hope to live happily ever after in a fairy-tale scenario, whether that involves marriage or not.

With the structure of the nuclear family ever evolving, we are among the first few generations to expect to marry or stay together long-term because of romantic notions, rather than practical ones. So, to be fair, this is new territory for our modern culture.

WHEN DID LOVE BECOME IMPORTANT?

It wasn't always this way, and for most of history, romantic love didn't feature all that much within marriage, at least not in the West. That's not to say that love between two people didn't exist across cultures throughout history – of course it did. It simply wasn't always part of the public domain or the prime reason for people to tie the knot.

The concept of romantic love as we recognize it today started to take hold in the 1800s, towards the end of the Age of Enlightenment, when rationality ruled. The Romantic Era that followed was a reaction to all of the rationalist thinking and focused more on inspiration, freedom of expression, and human emotions. The arts, literature, and music flourished through the works of Romantic thinkers like William Wordsworth, Mary Shelley, John Keats, and Victor Hugo. Now, love was seen as an uncontrollable impulse based on sexual or emotional attraction and didn't have to be constrained to marriage.

As modern society started to become more diverse and complex, science opened up new ways of thinking, economies became more money-based during the Industrial Revolution, and mass media grew into a powerful influencer. Along with these changes, women gained greater equality and by the time the twentieth century had arrived, our grandmothers were working and often financially independent. Women could enjoy sex without the fear of getting pregnant due to the introduction of the contraceptive pill, which changed the dynamic of the male–female partnership. People were able to follow their hearts more than ever before and as taboos in Western society decreased, divorce became more accessible and acceptable. We began to experience greater freedom of choice.

It wasn't so long ago that a love-based marriage usually had to be within the confines of your social status, your geographical location, family pressures, societal norms, and a host of other factors. Nowadays, you can find someone to love without even leaving your house, and there are an infinite number of options out there for you to explore. You don't even need to marry someone either, and can live together without any legal bond keeping you tied down.

OUR LOVE LIFE

Once we began to focus more on the idea of romantic love in the twentieth century, we started to see it as the foundation stone of any relationship. Romantic love as we understand it today is now a 'must' and the concept of being in love dominates art, culture, and our own relationship expectations. It's actually taken on a kind of superpower status, seen as the antidote to all our ills. Now, we identify our personal happiness and sense of fulfilment as being almost exclusively dependent on our love life. We also want love in our marriage, which has changed over the decades from being a mostly economic or social transaction to something more personal and intense.[31]

This in turn has stigmatized being single, especially at a certain age. With the romanticizing of relationships came the fear of being alone for too long and the judgements around singlehood.

We also discovered that love-relationships are truly fragile and extremely problematic, mainly because they are based on such a fickle thing as emotions, which can take us from ecstasy to chaos in one split second.

There's also the new-found reality and practice of leaving a relationship and seeking other options – something that was once frowned upon. And yet, we are so enamoured with the notion of romantic love that we still use it as a yardstick for how well our life is going, at least in terms of relationships. We even take it for granted now that break-ups are part of the process, that love hurts, and that real-life relationships are fraught with tensions and expectations.

We think we know what the 'ideal' version of love should be, yet are painfully aware of how elusive it is. Within this new-found freedom to love whoever we want, whatever way we want, comes great responsibility to honour the real meaning of love beyond romance and attraction.

We put so much store on love that when we stop seeing our partner through rose-tinted glasses, we panic and wonder if our relationship is working or if it has a future. As routine sets in, the glow of love is replaced by dull interactions, mundane practical problems, and the realization that our partner might not be 'the one' after all. We may blame them for not living up to our romantic expectations and seek a new partner to fulfil that role. It might be easier to walk out of the relationship rather than stay and try to make it work.

Romantic love is not very reliable. It's a feeling that comes and goes, depending on an infinite number of variables. One minute we are head over heels, and then, before we know it, it seems to have slipped through our fingers. We can fall out of love just as easily as we fall into it.

At first, that feeling of being in love is like the explosive energy of a rocket launch. We are all fuelled up by intensely powerful emotions and are ready to soar sky-high. The take-off is usually spectacular, with the energy being released so explosively that it propels us way up into the clouds and beyond. Who doesn't recognize or long for that feeling of total synergy with another person?

But after we've penetrated Earth's outer atmosphere and started to settle down to life in space, nothing seems as exciting any more. The propulsion slows down and we have to start paying attention to the routine maintenance needed to keep us in orbit. It can become painfully unexciting and bland. That is, if we define love by the inconsistent bouts of excitement and attraction that is common in the beginning phase of a relationship.

Physiologically speaking, humans are not designed to stay in a heightened state. The hormones, including adrenaline, dopamine, and cortisol, that course through our body when falling in love are not sustainable, and if the body wasn't regulating them, it would destabilize multiple bodily functions.

To believe you fell in love with the thrill of the initial attraction is really the addiction to these emotional highs. This is why many people become serial daters. As soon as the real work is required, they are on to the next person, chasing that high again to fulfil the emotional addiction.

The human body and mind function better on stability or homeostasis. It is believed that routine and predictability can make us feel safer and create a healthy environment for expansion. Yes, sometimes things can get boring. But are they boring within the relationships or are you simply lacking things as an individual? Perhaps your social life has been absent, your hobbies need fine-tuning, or you crave personal discovery and adventure. There is no better place to explore all of your options than within a stable relationship rather than a volatile one with a cycle of drama, tension, insecurity, and resolution.

WHY LOVE IS A VERB

Love is a verb because you don't show up to someone's life seeking an emotional hit. You commit to someone because you want to build, you want to traverse life with them. Emotions fuel the active participation within a relationship.

The feelings of love you experience need to make way for actions that help you sustain a relationship. You have to build trust, respect, and loyalty – not through words alone, but through making a commitment to the relationship.

It can't rely solely on feelings, because emotions are not the most reliable signposts for how we should proceed in life. Some days we feel off, and on others we feel blissful. One minute, we have an argument with our partner and get angry, upset, hurt. Next, we are all lovey-dovey again because we want to restore peace to the relationship. A lot of the time, we could be trying to patch up the damage with a Band-Aid without looking at the root cause of our differences.

One thing is for sure, though: if we don't put the time and effort into nurturing a strong, committed bond through our actions, love can't sustain itself. Instead of it growing into something deeper and resilient, it will wither away like an unwatered plant.

Every day you wake up is an opportunity to choose your partner. Put them in the front of your mind instead of on autopilot where they naturally take their place as an after-thought or play an assumed role in your life. When you consciously choose them each day, how you move through the day reflects decisions that align with you as an individual and fortifies your relationship as a unit. Everything you do is either adding or taking away from the quality of your rela-tionship. This isn't pressure; this is a privilege. To have someone, to love someone, is an honour not to be taken lightly. Nothing worth doing or working for is greater than love. It is a pleasure, a state of being, and a consistent demonstration through actions and behaviours.

Love needs actions that replenish the essence of your relationship. It requires you to check in more often, be present, and create a shared story. It's about doing things that cultivate togetherness, not separateness. And it requires a committed practice of being curious about what it means to love and be loved.

THE GEOMETRY OF LOVE

Maybe you are married, thinking of getting married, or have separated/divorced but are still into the idea of married life with the right person. Tying the knot is still a popular way for many to establish a committed relationship, and according to research done in 2019 by the Pew Research Centre,[32] the top three reasons that people still get married are: love (88%), commitment (81%), and companionship (76%).

Obviously, if you aren't in a place to commit, you aren't likely to want to get married, even if you love your partner. A lot of people also want companionship without commitment but many don't want to be alone or keep dating around. Some don't necessarily need to be in love in order to build a committed relationship and are looking more for the stability it promises with another person.

Seeking companionship can also lead to wanting to marry someone, even if you aren't romantically connected to them. In a lot of long-term marriages, romantic, passionate love does fade as it transforms into a kind of companionate love instead.

The leading academic and psychologist Robert J. Sternberg devised a theory about these three factors and called it the *Triangle of Love* in a paper he published in 1986.[33] Basically, imagine a triangle made up of three components: intimacy, passion, and decision/commitment, all of which manifest different aspects of love.

Intimacy is important because it's those feelings of closeness that lead to the experience of being in a loving, warm relationship. You could equate this with companionship, which is something that people seek in a marriage. Passion is the drive that leads to romance, physical attraction, and sexual consummation that we want to experience in a loving relationship. Commitment is the acknowledgement of loving someone else and wanting to maintain that loving relationship with them in the long term.

There are different elements to this geometrical equation and they might look something like this:

Companionship + commitment = friend love
Passion + companionship = romantic love
Commitment + passion = fatuous love (love at first sight)

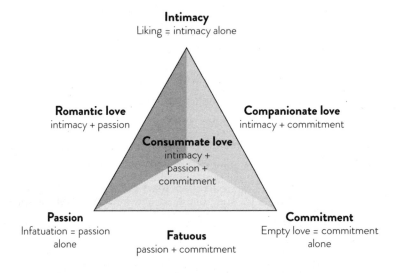

All of the three aspects of the triangle are separate, but when they interact with each other, they can create a truly loving, fulfilling relationship. Their importance may differ from one relationship to the next, or over time within the relationship.

Although it would be great to enjoy all three, it doesn't always work like that. To make a perfect triangle, you need to bring a lot of love to the relationship and a balance of each aspect of love.

For example, if your desire to get married is based on passion alone, that's not going to be enough to form a healthy, resilient relationship. Neither is it likely to work if you only seek companionship, without forging a commitment to the other person.

As the balance shifts through the course of the relationship, we need to adjust if we want to continue to uphold it. Being aware of each aspect of the triangle can help us to avoid the pitfalls that might occur and work on any areas that need improvement. They can also tell us when a relationship has run its course and might have come to a natural end.

I would take this concept of the triangle even further and say that some couples experience a relationship that combines all three elements, even though they might not be able to marry or share a common life with each other, for various reasons. One or both of them may already be married to someone else and have decided not to leave their respective spouses. Maybe they are caring for a sick partner or have children and do not wish to break up their marriage, yet cherish deep feelings for another person who reciprocates and understands their predicament.

They will continue to support and love each other despite not being married or able to enjoy a public, formal relationship. Their bond to one another may be so strong that they can accept the restrictions imposed on them and continue to be devoted to each other in their own way. In such cases, practicalities don't come into the equation yet the couple somehow manage to maintain a close, trusting relationship.

If you are considering the idea of marriage, do it because you see a future with someone, not because you're alone, unhappy, feeling left out, or pressured by parents and aunties. A marriage doesn't take all of your troubles away; it often amplifies internal conflicts. So pick your life partner carefully.

Relationships and marriages require work, patience, and understanding. Sometimes, we pick a partner and rush marriage for the wrong reasons – only to find ourselves stuck, confused, and even dreading our lives. And this burden can feel even heavier when you have kids.

None of these are strong enough reasons to get married:

- All your friends are getting married.
- You want kids or already have a child.
- Family keep telling you that you're getting old.
- You feel like you need someone to be by your side to live your best life.
- You feel like something is wrong with you because you're still single.
- You want to feel complete and heal through someone else.
- You are afraid of being alone for ever.
- You feel like a failure for not being married while other people are.
- Everyone on social media is getting engaged – and they look happy.

- Something seems to be missing in your life and you suspect it's marriage.

- To maintain a premeditated timeline of your life milestones.

- To appease a family member pressuring you to have children.

Yes, you don't need to be fully healed (or perfect in any sense) to enter a relationship/marriage. And, while it's OK to desire a healthy connection, don't expect someone else to solve everything you feel challenged by in your life.

Don't expect someone else to be your source of happiness.

Don't expect to live a fairy tale once you find someone to journey with.

Don't expect to suddenly feel like people will celebrate you, leave you alone, or won't judge you because you're now married.

The truth is, if there are unresolved conflicts within you, a partner will probably bring them to the surface (often unintentionally). And it's here where you'll realize the power of a healthy, devoted partner who wants to work with you rather than against you.

And remember, marriage or kids might not be your end goal, and that's OK. Love is a human instinct and spiritual endeavour and is not confined to the validation of laws, mandates, or certificates.

LET YOUR LOVE FLOW

Fill your relationship with an abundance of loving actions and stay connected to your own vibrancy, creativity, and sexuality. When you yourself feel alive and vibrant, you can bring this into your relationship and create some real magic. There's nothing more rewarding than an authentic, honest connection with both yourself and your partner to keep your love in orbit indefinitely.

Pure, authentic love comes from a place in the heart – a sacred space of abundance and light. It exists for its own sake, without an agenda.

The more you practise love, the greater your capacity to give. To do this, it's important to let go of any unhealthy illusions you might have about romantic love. If you can manage that, you will experience something much calmer: a healthy, sustainable relationship that is more of a rich red claret than a bottle of bubbly without the fizz.

RELATIONSHIPS REQUIRE WORK

This is one of thousands of books on love and relationships. If we require so much advice and direction, clearly relationships don't come easy or are sustainable without significant effort.

You know when the credits come up at the end of that soppy romantic movie and you feel all warm and fuzzy inside? Although I'd like to say that real life is the same, it's not. We can't script a happy ending with any certainty and just have to take each day as it comes. No one said it would be easy so you need to keep going even when you meet obstacles and hurdles in the way. It might seem easier to bail out, but if you keep doing that, it becomes a pattern that will leave you feeling alone as you try on different relationships in the future.

When you accept from the start that difficulties will arise and are prepared to work through them, you will create something much more valuable and durable.

The great Austrian poet Rainer Maria Rilke wrote,

'Once the realization is accepted that even between the closest human beings infinite distances continue, a wonderful living side by side can grow, if they succeed in loving the distance between them which makes it possible for each to see the other whole against the sky.'[34]

When we recognize our separateness, we can appreciate our togetherness and be thankful for each moment that we share: two people coming together to create something beautiful. Our differences are part of that, and with difference comes disagreement, but that doesn't have to lead to decay. It can lead to growth and a closing of the gap.

But love isn't only a verb: bending over backwards to keep your partner happy can easily become a habit if you ignore the emotional side of your relationship.

If you are going through the motions without being present it can begin to feel more like a chore than an enriching experience. Imagine having a car that you drive every day, but you ignore making sure it's kept clean, well-maintained, and looked after. The wear and tear will become obvious after a while. Just like a car, your partnership needs tender loving care as well as a regular service to make sure it's able to perform and meet your needs.

NURTURE MORE LOVE

There's never been an easier time to walk away from a relationship or have so many options to meet someone 'better'. I love that people have a greater choice nowadays, but feel that this digital dating culture is also blocking us from learning how to build a long-lasting, fulfilling relationship.

Instead of exercising patience and understanding, we are tempted to choose convenience and disposability. In search of the 'next best thing', we might be ignoring the potential in front of us. That's why you need to take action in love, because love is action in itself.

We all expect ambivalence in our relationships with others: we might fight with our siblings, have disagreements with friends, our children can get on our nerves, and we all need space sometimes. It's no different with romantic relationships, and having bad days doesn't mean that the love you share isn't worth preserving.

Once you get over this mindset of expecting everything to be perfect between yourself and your partner, you can work on deciphering the arguments and decoding the needs that aren't being met. When you do that, you can move towards more compassionate responses that feed intimacy and mutual appreciation rather than building walls of misunderstanding and contempt.

Think of your relationship in this way:

- The point isn't to meet 'the one . . . your soulmate'. It's about learning how to evolve through love and sharing that with a person of your choosing who values and appreciates it.

- It takes time to know yourself within a relationship, just as it takes time to really get to know the other person. Being unsure is part of the beauty of discovering something new and can help you to grow and mature.

- Love is a choice that you make and a commitment to your partner based on intent. It's not only some uncontrollable feeling that comes in and out of your life like a scale 3 tornado. The more love you practise, the more love you will nurture and the deeper its roots will grow.

- As a whole person, you don't need and shouldn't expect your partner to complete you. You have to cultivate your own aliveness, which you can then bring to the relationship. There will be times when the fireworks don't light up and you can't expect that every day, just in the same way that you can't be wholly reliant on your partner to remember to bring the matches. If they do, great, but it takes three things to keep a fire burning – oxygen and fuel as well as those matches. One is useless without the other two.

- Love is an adventure. You cannot predict entirely what will become of a relationship. Go into your connection with curiosity. Be a safe space for another to fall in love with you and with life. There is no checklist process for discovering love. It is a unique creation that comes to fruition with a compatible being.

When you keep your heart open to love and avoid letting insecurities and past pain shut it down, you will experience more abundance. This requires work on your part, as well as on your partner's side, and as long as you are both willing to do so, love can flow with greater ease.

ACTS OF LOVE

What can you do to instil your relationship with depth and meaning after the initial excitement has died down? As I said earlier, being present and aware is key as each day unfolds before you. But what does that mean in practical terms? It begins with seeing your partner as more than just someone you are attracted to and translates into **building a friendship, cultivating shared bonds**, and **creating a strong heart connection**.

BUILDING YOUR FRIENDSHIP

Friends are people you like to hang out with. They bring added value to your life, act as sounding boards for your cares and worries, and you offer the same in return. They have your back and will overlook your flaws and imperfections because that's what friends are for. They are the ones who will tell you, 'You messed up there. You can do better. I'm here to support you because I want to see you flourish.' They keep you accountable while supporting your aspirations.

Your partner doesn't have to be your best friend

It seems to be a trend I've read a lot about recently. The main thing here isn't if you see them as your bestie, but what you are doing to let them know that, apart from being partners, you can also be friends.

To do this, take an interest in aspects of their life that don't include what you do together as a couple. Ask them regularly how they are doing in their job and what issues they are dealing with. Gain an awareness of their world (one that doesn't necessarily include you) and pay attention to what they say. You are giving them the space to grow in it and can be there to support them on their journey. Not everything has to be about you and them. There can be things going on in their life that you know nothing about but you can still be engaged with them in a spirit of genuine curiosity and interest.

As a friend, you should be happy when things are going well for your partner

Celebrate their successes and let them know that you are happy for them. Say how thrilled you are to hear about their good news and be physically affectionate as you express your happiness and joy. Support them even when they don't succeed, without making soul-destroying statements like, 'You should/ shouldn't have done this or that . . .' or 'Never mind, it's not important . . .'

Tell your partner what your needs are and be prepared to listen to theirs too

Start to store all of that information in a shared pool of love that you can dip in and out of when you need to. This is a reservoir of feelings and emotions that are important to both of you, so keep topping it up as you go through life together and use it as a source of regeneration and growth.

Don't be afraid of your differences

No two people on this earth are alike, and although you may have a lot in common with your partner, that doesn't mean you have to agree on everything. Variety is the spice of life, so just embrace that. Even if you feel challenged by their strongly held opinions on religion, politics, or values that might not align with yours, you can work through that. Create a respectful space for dialogue so you can really understand where they are coming from and remember that by acknowledging their individuality, you are showing how much you care for them.

Manage conflict by keeping calm

You can take breaks when things flare up and practise self-soothing instead of getting all pumped up and ready to cross swords. One useful way to do this in practical terms is to set yourselves half an hour to discuss a major disagreement. Establish from the offset that this is a chance for you both to express your opinion and to hear your partner's. When the half-hour is up, end the discussion and agree to reflect on what the other person has said. Come back to it together later to see what you have both learned and any insights you have gained.

Get out ahead of it

Being a mindful couple who live intentionally, everything you do together, from arguing to intimacy, can have a clear intention. I want to get closer to you. I want to express myself. I want to explore ways of contributing to your happiness. Being able to confidently say and make known your intentions will align your experiences with your highest good. Intention-setting as a couple allows a childlike friendship to flourish because there is no guessing, just pure enjoyment of each other.

CULTIVATING SHARED BONDS

Imagine that the love you feel for your partner can be doubled, even trebled when you cultivate stronger shared bonds. By creating your own story, it's possible to enjoy the richness that being part of a couple can bring to your life.

When someone shares something they're excited about doing, try not to begin by expressing doubt or concern. While your personal opinion might be beneficial, immediately dismissing someone's trust in themselves to pursue their passions can do more lasting damage than good.

Be your partner's cheerleader

Let them know you are there to support them when they strive to achieve their dreams. If that means driving them three hours to a squash tournament or helping them to choose a new outfit for an important interview, be there for them. Participate in their dream-chasing and show them they can spread their wings without fear of losing you. If you feel that you are overextending yourself, check in with your partner about this. Find ways to be flexible in your plans and agree on mutual compromises so that you don't run the risk of sacrificing your own dreams in order to fulfil theirs.

Share meaningful rituals

These can help you both to connect and bond even more. Take long walks with each other at the weekend, cook together, set aside one night a week to talk about personal dreams and plans. Create a joint vision board of what goals you have as a couple and check off each milestone as it's reached. Make plans to do things you both enjoy and generate excitement about them as they approach. Share your time in a meaningful way during which you are focused on each other, not on the TV or your phones.

CREATING A STRONG HEART CONNECTION

As you work on nurturing your relationship, concentrate on speaking from the heart. This means allowing yourself to be vulnerable, honest, and open, even if there's a risk that your partner won't always understand exactly how you feel. In the same way, you need to be ready to witness their emotional pain and triggers, without making hasty judgements about them. While it might not be easy to tell your partner everything you harbour in your heart if you aren't ready, express what you can with a genuine willingness to come closer.

The aim is to create connections that help you align and, sometimes, you will both need to explore emotions that haven't been attended to for a while. Show your partner that your relationship is a refuge for their feelings by letting them know that they will find comfort and safety there.

Shake up the routine before you both get bored with predictability

Instead of telling your partner you love them just before you go to sleep, tell them when they are brushing their teeth or having a shave. It might sound like a simple thing to do, but it's the intention that counts. There doesn't have to be a set time to express love, so keep it coming any time of day and not just at bedtime.

Be close to your partner, not necessarily in a sexual way

Sit next to them at home, offer to give them a relaxing massage, hold their hand in the street – let them know you enjoy physical contact and aren't doing it as a way to initiate sex. Human touch cultivates a great sense of belonging and bonding, as well as having a soothing effect and reducing stress. Touch is the primary language of compassion and you don't need fancy words to show how much you care – a hug can say it all!

Keep your story alive

Talk through the changes it has undergone, including all of the ups and downs. Keep the conversation going about what attracted you to your partner in the first place, why you love them, and how you see your relationship growing in the future. Let them know how important they are to you and show that through your actions.

Be ready to make compromises

There has to be give and take on both sides, otherwise you'll end up arguing about even the simplest of things. You don't have to sacrifice your values, but going along with small requests isn't really a big deal, if it's important to your partner. Hopefully, they'll do the same thing for you, too. I often find myself making small compromises for my wife, just as she does for me, even if the idea doesn't initially thrill me. It usually goes something like this:

Kaushal: *Bubs, let's take a picture together?*
Me: *Do I have to?*
(I do it anyway.)

Kaushal: *Can you come to this event with me?*
Me: *Are there going to be any other guys there?*
Kaushal: *Umm, maybe.*
(I go and end up being the only boy!)

Kaushal: *Bubs, can you take a picture for me?*
[100 photos later]
Kaushal: *Why didn't you tell me there was a strand of hair sticking out? You'll have to take them again!*
(I unwillingly continue to take them.)

When you face these moments with a sense of gratitude and love, the small things can feel less like trivial chores that you resent and more like moments you get to show up for your partner and make them feel seen. Celebrating your relationship in small ways is twice as important as huge romantic gestures. Just be there. Really be there – like you want to be. I sometimes ponder the alternative. Someone else could be behind the lens, enjoying Kaushal's every pose. Or I could be with someone who doesn't value my feedback on the little things. But here I am, fortunate enough to be her photographer. She chose me and I chose her. Suddenly, compromise seems to be the wrong word for everything I'd do for her. Or what any of us does for those we love.

Even so, you never want to bend until you break for the sake of another.

HOW TO WEATHER THE STORMS

When you've been involved with someone for a while, you will likely come across problems that test the limits of your relationship. Most couples who have a genuine desire to be together will do whatever it takes to resolve their differences. They might decide to try couples therapy if they can't work through their issues alone, and if you feel that you and your partner could benefit from that, it's definitely worth looking into.

Love doesn't guarantee that your relationship will be sunny every day. Life is full of challenges and there'll be plenty of dark clouds bringing stormy weather for a thousand and one reasons. These challenges can allow your love to mature and deepen even more, bringing you closer as you face them together.

Although every relationship is unique and you can't compare yours with anyone else's, some common themes do keep popping up among couples. How do you let love shine through when you are constantly arguing about things like money, hurtful comments, lack of intimacy, disrespectful behaviour, or feeling distant? These are just some of the frequently mentioned reasons that couples reach a stalemate. If you genuinely want the best for each other, you can overcome these hurdles and retain the love you have both cultivated.

Clashes about money

- Unsurprisingly, money can make or break a relationship. The cost of living, different spending styles, saving habits, and money management can cause friction between you even if everything else seems OK. How do you handle it when you see your partner as wasteful, and how do you feel when they accuse you of being stingy? What about when you are stressed due to lack of money or can't agree on who pays the bills?

- Because we give so much importance to money as a society, there's a lot of power attached to it, and this can easily spill over into the dynamic of your relationship. The subject can trigger feelings of anger, anxiety, and even envy, all of which manifest themselves in your interactions with your partner.

- The thing is, your relationship with money should have nothing to do with the deep emotional bonds you have nurtured with your partner. If they are bad with money, be supportive and show them ways to handle it better instead of criticizing and scolding them. When you face financial problems, look for ways to work together to solve them instead of blaming each other for the mess you are in.

- It's important to remember that the way you view money is most likely linked to your past experiences and how your family handled their finances. You will have learned to respond to money in a certain way and now might be an opportunity to change that. You could have a 'poverty' mindset, which means that you view money as a scarcity, or be used to wasting money without accountability. It's very likely that you've never really thought about this before, so sit down and consider these preconceptions with your partner. You will find that spending habits are exactly that – learned patterns of behaviour that can be undone. Work as a team to face financial worries rather than taking on the role of bank manager and help each other to deal with them in a responsible way.

The war of words

- Hurtful language is the ugly face of conflict in a relationship. Although arguing and having differences of opinions can be healthy ways to get closer, name-calling and insults are not. Depending on your attachment style, you might deal with confrontation by being defensive, passive-aggressive, or by adopting a victim mentality. Some people even thrive on confrontation as it makes them feel alive and validated, even if the fallout can be catastrophic.

- Most couples get into a pattern of bickering about the same things over and over again, so it's good to be aware of that and try to break the cycle. I've talked earlier on about ways of dealing with conflict, and if you want to nurture love not war, you have to be prepared to sit down and talk things through once the battle is over.

- Use conciliatory language like, 'I want to understand why you feel the way you do,' and hold up an olive branch to your partner. Show empathy and a willingness to listen, which will encourage them to join the conversation without feeling threatened. This is the start to repairing broken fences and finding ways to communicate from a place of deep love and respect.

Infidelity strikes

- Trust is a massive part of any successful relationship, so seeing that being abused is terribly painful to most of us. Infidelity is one of the main reasons that couples break up and it's much more common than you might think. In the UK, figures from an infidelity study carried out by Global Investigations in 2020 showed that the percentage of married women having affairs was 14.7%, while the number of men admitting to extramarital affairs was around 22%. A 2017 study also found that 57% of unmarried males and 54% of unmarried females admitted to committing infidelity in one or more of their relationships.[35] The numbers for the US are similar, all of which go to show that infidelity is something many couples are trying to deal with.

- You don't need to find out that your partner has been sleeping with someone else to feel betrayed by them. Even learning of an emotional relationship they have with someone else that has crossed the line can feel just as bad. If you find yourself in this situation, dialogue is more important than ever. Rather than blaming your partner, or yourself, for this breach of trust, it can be an opportunity to find out what has changed (if anything) in your relationship that has led one of you to go astray.

- If your partner has cheated on you, there is still a possibility of saving your relationship once all of the cards are laid out on the table, if that's what you want. You should bear in mind that even if you do this, the relationship will never be how it was previously. You may find that their indiscretion was more to do with how they were feeling about themselves than the relationship itself. Sometimes, people are looking to rediscover themselves, not find someone else, and all of this needs to be talked about if you want to mend the relationship.

- It could be that you can't repair the damage done by infidelity and decide to break up. If so, instead of leaving full of anger and resentment, try to process your feelings and stop yourself from being overwhelmed by pain. Hold love in your heart instead and walk away feeling informed and empowered. Even better, learn to forgive and move on.

Growing apart

- The seven-year itch used to be a thing: it was said to be the time it takes for major cracks in a relationship to start showing. If you could get through that, the next crisis point was around the twenty-one-year mark, which was when a lot of couples used to finally agree to divorce. In today's world, what is long-term for one person might be too long for someone else. We see a lot of singles dating more partners than ever before and putting off getting married until much later. In the US, the average age for men and women to get married in the 1950s was 22.9 and 20.3 respectively. Now, it's thirty-two years of age in the US and thirty-one in the UK.[36]

- In a way, it's hard to know if you are growing apart or the relationship is simply coming to a natural end. Not everyone you date will be your life partner and there's a big temptation to walk out at the first sign of dissatisfaction or lack of connection.

- If you feel deep love for your partner but have noticed that a distance has replaced the closeness you used to have, take the initiative to open up the conversation about it. Distance comes to fill gaps in a relationship and can take over if you don't pay attention to it. When you are both so busy every day, it's important to create some togetherness. Reinforce the fact that you are a couple by sharing the same space, re-telling your story, and reminding yourselves of why you are still together. Rekindle the love you feel for each other through intimacy and change the routine of daily life to bring back the magic.

- Being with your partner should always be a choice and not an obligation alone. If you have children, you might feel a responsibility to stay together, but you need to invest in your relationship if you want to set a healthy example for your kids. When distance and lack of closeness become the norm, relationships can become more like working partnerships and many couples accept that transition. It's up to you to weigh up what you want and what is compromising your values and preferences.

No love life

- Repetition can be boring, especially in the bedroom. Lovemaking should be a time to connect mind, body, and soul, and if it isn't, you and your partner will soon start to feel like there's something missing. Sex doesn't have to be a deal-breaker, but it very often is, and the longer you stay together, the more work you will need to do.

- Either you or your partner may feel too tired, not in the mood, too busy, replacing with an addiction like pornography, or have medical issues . . . there can be any number of reasons why someone isn't always up for sex and it doesn't always mean they have gone off you. But if you feel you are losing the intimacy that you both had, you can do small things to re-ignite that which don't include sex.

- Spend time showing affection to your partner without initiating sex. Demonstrate small gestures of intimacy, such as caressing their cheek and holding them in a warm embrace. Hold their hand and look into their eyes often to re-establish that bonding ritual you once enjoyed.

- Open up a dialogue about closeness without making accusations like, 'You never want to make love any more.' There could be deeper issues that your partner finds it hard to talk about, so show them understanding and patience rather than exerting pressure or making threats. Tell them how you feel, about them and speak in a language of love that will touch their heart.

What issues are you facing in your current relationship? How can you work through them from a place of love? What is your love story and how can you stay present and active within it?

Ask yourself these questions and let love be your guide: love for yourself, your partner, and your relationship.

When the excitement of your first dates has died down and you become a couple, you are committing to cherishing each other for as long as it lasts. You can't always know how long that will be, but give it one hundred per cent of your time and energy to create something special. Life is way too short to spend it being unhappy, feeling unfulfilled, trapped, or resentful.

Love can bring so much contentment and bliss if you act on it, instead of relying on a simple 'I love you' now and again.

As Dr Iannis, one of the characters in the book and movie *Captain Corelli's Mandolin*, tells his daughter, 'Love itself is what is left over, when being in love has burned away.'[37] Doesn't sound very exciting, does it? But it is! He also says that love isn't breathlessness, excitement, or promises of eternal passion, but is more about growing together and sharing the beauty that intimacy brings. Why not make that your kind of love story!

Love comes from deep within us and we have the potential to share it in abundance with others. What begins as a connection of attraction, chemistry, compatibility, and shared values with someone else can grow into an extremely powerful bond fuelled by a mutual exchange of loving energy.

You have the power to make it happen, so why not start putting your words into action!

KEY INSIGHTS

- The romantic love culture may give you a false impression of what relationships should be like.

- Assuming that your partner will fulfil all of your needs is an unrealistic expectation.

- Love is a human need and a life-giving force.

- Different kinds of love from different people can serve those needs.

- The experience of love knows no limits.

- Marriage is not the only model in which a loving relationship can grow.

- All relationships take hard work and nurturing in order to be successful.

- Acts of love can secure bonds, create friendships, connect hearts, and solve problems.

Chapter 10

LOVE IS A VIBE

Love loves to love love.
– James Joyce[38]

Love, sweet love.

As messy, painful, challenging to navigate, and growth-inducing as it is, love is still the sweetest thing we get to experience in life.

When love is in the air, we are intoxicated, ecstatic, and able to transcend reality in a fusion of intimacy and passion. It's as if we are a flame rising, two souls intertwined, two hearts beating as one. Life becomes wonderful and we want to shout out from the rooftops. There's nothing else to compare love to in human experience and we yearn to find it at least once in our lifetime.

Love allows us to catch a glimpse of the divine, or the spiritual, and we feel complete. Love is the alpha and the omega. It's the endgame of all we do.

But love isn't something we can easily explain. You probably know how it feels, but to talk about it? That's a bit tricky. How do you put into words what you feel for your partner – the adoration you have for them? How do you articulate the sensation of bliss, belonging, and heartfelt happiness that often transcends time and place, reason, or logic? The mind struggles to intellectualize what the heart and spirit experience when in love. Perhaps it's not meant to.

I truly love my wife, but those words alone come nowhere near to expressing how I really feel about her. I just can't sum those emotions up in a few words because they are so much more than syllables. There's something going on deep within me that draws me to her, like an invisible force. It's an energy that seems to expand every day and allows me to feel fulfilled, complete, positive, and at one with myself.

We all get into this kind of love state of mind when we finally meet someone who we feel in tune with – a person we resonate with. But what does it actually mean when we say that we resonate with someone? Is it just a flaky term used by New Age hippies or is there more to it?

GOOD VIBRATIONS

Love is a vibe, literally. It's a vibrational frequency that we all emanate, without even knowing it. It's already present, within every cell of our body, and we can tune into it every single day. When we meet certain people, it becomes even more active and vibrates on a higher frequency. It can also resonate on a lower frequency if you meet someone you aren't in tune with. Learning to live in this love vibration ultimately drives our purpose of being and doing. It is the elixir of life that brings us all the joy we need.

We actually know a lot about resonance, or what is often called synchronized vibrations. It's a physical reality that also pervades our human consciousness and it's the basic mechanism for all of our physical interactions. Life itself is all about vibrations.

Everything in the Universe is in constant motion, even things we assume are stationary. When I say motion, I mean vibrating, or oscillating, at various frequencies. The interesting thing is that when two different vibrating entities come into proximity with each other, they will start to vibrate on the same frequency after a while. It's as if they mysteriously synchronize, which is known as spontaneous self-organisation. By observing this phenomenon in his book *Sync*, mathematician Steven Strogatz gives us some great insights into life itself. His work provides a window into what happens when we meet someone and experience authentic love.[39]

After looking at examples from physics, biology, chemistry, and neuroscience, Strogatz found that everything resonates at certain frequencies. Whether it's fireflies flashing in synchronicity or neurons sparking simultaneously in the human brain, resonance is a universal phenomenon that we are just beginning to understand.

The neurophysiologists Ernst Strüngmann and Pascal Fries measured the electrical patterns of the brain, like gamma, theta, and beta waves, which show the speed of electrical oscillations, or frequencies, going on in our grey matter.[40] They found that gamma waves actively vibrate at approximately 30 to 90 cycles per second (Hz), theta at a 4 to 7 Hz rhythm, and beta at 12.5 to 30 Hz. All three work together to produce electrical brain patterns that might help to explain things such as consciousness.

The interesting thing here is that these gamma waves seem to synchronize naturally, allowing information to be seamlessly passed from one neuron to another. As complex beings, the way information is handled in our brains on a micro level is really astounding and it's not something we are aware of in our daily lives. But when it comes down to it, it's all about vibrations and their shared synchronicity.

OUR LOVE VIBRATIONS

Now that we know we are a living energy field, with each cell of our body in constant motion, it's clear that we are vibrating and creating energy all the time. It's not something spiritual in the grand sense of the word, but much more of a physiological process. Many energy practitioners even offer therapies that involve tapping into these vibrations so you can improve your health and wellbeing.

Apart from your heart beating, your lungs breathing, and your circadian rhythms flowing, there are tiny vibrations going on within each molecule of your body. If you happen to have an atomic microscope handy, you will be able to see vibrations on the nanoscale of less than one thousandth the diameter of a single human hair. All of these vibrations generate electromagnetic energy waves that cause changes in how your body functions.[41] A rise or fall in temperature, for example, can change the speed of a molecule's vibration, either speeding it up or slowing it down.

The way we behave and think can also affect these vibrational changes, with anxiety triggering the release of cortisol, the stress hormone. Your heart begins to beat faster or even slows down as you respond to external situations, and I'm sure you've all experienced that kind of thing at least once. Even music can affect the vibrational frequencies in our body, which is why certain music calms us while other kinds of music pump us up.

Einstein himself said that everything in life is vibration, and we know now that molecules vibrate at different speeds throughout the natural world, even in objects like rocks. When it comes to humans, these vibrations are influenced by everything we do and oscillate on faster or slower frequencies, or higher and lower vibrations.

When you are vibrating at a higher level, you will feel lighter and happier, whereas lower vibrations weigh you down with resistance and sadness. When you raise these tiny vibrations, you can change your mental state and even your physical health. Life can become more harmonious as you send positive energy out into the Universe. Instead of feeling down and pessimistic, emotions which feed off lower vibrational energy, you can experience harmony and good vibes.

Some say that love is one of the highest vibrations in the Universe, resonating at a specific frequency based on calibrations measured in hertz (Hz). In his book *Power vs Force*,[42] Dr David Hawkins created the 'map of consciousness', which explains the seventeen different stages of consciousness and their energy calibrations.

Imagine a multi-coloured funnel which is very narrow at the bottom and gradually widens as you get to the top. Each colour on the spectrum represents different emotions or levels of consciousness, with their 'calibration values' noted on a logarithmic scale from 0 to 1,000.

By measuring muscle responses to stimuli, Dr Hawkins observed over his twenty-year research that our responses can differentiate not only between positive and negative stimuli, but also between truth and falsity. He basically claimed to have captured the weight of emotions, stating that each one resonates on a different frequency, with love being close to the top of his map of consciousness. To reach those levels, we need to transcend low-frequency emotions first, and when we can do that, we will feel lighter, brighter, and even more confident.

At the bottom are undesirable emotions like shame, guilt, fear, anger, frustration, and hate. We are all capable of these reactions and many of us will experience at least one of them on a daily basis. You might feel guilty for not paying enough attention to your partner, or angry because they didn't support you in something that was important to you. You can see how it goes. Further up the spectrum are things like courage, acceptance, reasoning, and other experiences that can be positive influences in our lives. At the highest point of the spectrum, we find more expanded levels of consciousness like enlightenment, peace, joy, and love.

Here is a breakdown of the seventeen different levels, in descending order, with their values:

Enlightenment (700 – 1,000)
Peace (600)
Joy (540)
Unconditional Love (500)
Reason (400)
Acceptance (350)
Willingness (310)
Neutrality (250)
Courage (200)
Pride (175)
Anger (150)
Desire (125)
Fear (100)
Grief (75)
Apathy (50)
Guilt (30)
Shame (1 – 20)

According to Hawkins, these 'higher' energy fields have incredible power, and I'm sure you can think of many examples where love has been a force for great change in your life, or in the world as a whole.

Although Hawkins' work is quite controversial among the scientific community, and you certainly don't have to agree with everything he says, it does give us some interesting insights into our emotions. There's still a lot to learn about what consciousness really is and there are many viewpoints on the subject. Hawkins provided one possible explanation and I'm putting it out there for anyone who wants to look into it further.

In my previous books – *Good Vibes, Good Life* and *Healing Is the New High* – I write about ways to deal with heavy, low-resonating emotions, and to begin transforming your life into positive energy. Negative emotions such as shame, guilt, and apathy can be changed by raising your frequencies to ones of pride, acceptance, and joy. It's a blissful thing to experience and can be achieved if you focus on your inner energy and start practising ways to raise your vibrations. And because energy moves from one medium to another, you can pass it on to others.

When you meet someone resonating at your frequency, it's as if you were made for each other. In this space, you can give and receive love in equal measure, taking each other's vibrations even higher.

KEEPING THE LOVE VIBRATION HIGH

When you raise your love vibrations, you will exhibit more kindness, have more clarity, and feel a real balance between your mind and your emotions. Everything just feels harmonious and you can avoid negative emotions like intolerance and impatience with greater ease. You even lift those around you, helping them to sync with your higher vibrations. Love is actually much more powerful than you might have thought!

Just as healthy relationships lift you up and raise your heart vibrations, unhealthy relationships can bring you way down. You might not be able to synchronize your frequencies with each other. This manifests itself through arguments, low-energy behaviour and emotions, and the feeling that you just can't get on with each other. You might even grow apart from a long-term partner when you stop resonating on the same frequency and it's difficult to re-sync again after that.

SEVEN WAYS TO STAY HIGH ON LOVE

To keep your love vibrations resonating at a high frequency, here are seven unique and easy practices from my own life that you can incorporate in yours.

1. Go for a walk and look for hearts. For example, look for heart-shaped rocks or leaves.

2. Lift weights and repeat a positive affirmation after every rep, such as, 'I am beautiful, strong and resilient.'

3. Find one thing you admire about every person you see throughout the day. It could be the way a stranger's smile radiates warmth.

4. Listen to a playlist of uplifting songs and listen out for the word love. I like to do this during train commutes and keep a tally.

5. Close your eyes in a spare moment and visualize giving your partner a tight hug. Take note of what they're wearing. Notice how it feels; how they feel. What do they smell like? Can you hear them breathing? Are there any thoughts about love and joy going through your head?

6. Create. Art in the form of writing, painting, dancing, singing, and making music can all be expressions of pure love. When you sink into a childlike energy of playful creation, the vibrations are sky high.

7. Consume high vibrational content. You are likely to regurgitate what you consume on the TV, social media, and books. These external influences affect your frequency. You can walk away from fifteen

minutes of scrolling through Twitter or an hour-long reality TV show in a whole different mood. So be discerning about what you're inviting into your heart, your most sacred vessel.

It's OK to unfollow social media accounts that no longer contribute to your algorithm for happiness.

These are just some of the things you can do to keep those vibrations resonating on a high frequency that will also bring positive energy to your relationship. You can try them out and even switch them up to suit you. Even though you might not be aware of it, you are cultivating a deeper, more loving connection that will bring you and your partner even closer.

HABITS THAT INCREASE THE LOVE VIBE

One thing that many people get confused about is thinking that love is somewhere out there – residing in another person or thing. They go around looking for love, expecting to find it in a particular partner. They chase after it as if it's something to grab hold of. Then, they feel all of the disappointment that comes with unrequited love and the disillusionment of rejection.

In reality, love comes from within us and has no limits. Once you realize that, you will begin to invite partners who resonate on the same frequency as yourself and will discover an endless abundance of love together. In Buddhism, the idea of *metta*, or loving kindness, is the heartfelt wish for the wellbeing of yourself and others. It's more of an outlook on life than a feeling and you can cultivate it by practising compassion, good will, and connection for those around you.

As you do so, you will begin to find a greater sense of wellbeing and connection with yourself, and by resonating on a higher vibration, you will welcome the same vibrations from the external world.

Absolute, or unconditional, love isn't dependent on external vibrations, pre-existing conditions, limitations, or the needs of others. You can love everyone unconditionally whatever the circumstances, and this is a powerful internal energy that can transform the world. In relation to unconditional love for your partner, you are talking about two people coming together in a deeply fulfilling way. Your relationship will be based on joy, not pain; meaning, not emptiness; and love, not fear. This is a spiritual union because it nurtures growth, creativity, vibrancy, and purpose.

**You don't have to be spiritual to experience love,
but love can be a spiritual experience**.

Simply choose love

I say simply, but this can be one of the most difficult and most rewarding decisions we make each and every day when with our partner. There is a list of complaints we can hurl their way as soon as they get home from work or when responding to a text. But if you consciously and mindfully shift your positioning and lead with love, the energy will resonate like a ripple effect. Their tone of anticipation and annoyance will become light, your agitation and resentment will ease, and you'll be able to talk calmly about whatever it is you need. Relationships don't have to be so heavy. When you choose love (especially in the moments where it's most challenging), everything can change and you are more likely to get the outcome you desire.

RAISING LOVE FREQUENCIES AND VIBES

In Imago Relationship Therapy, largely pioneered by Dr Harville Hendrix,[43] the theory goes that we fall in love with someone who contains the keys to our past. It's the person who can also incite us in meaningful ways to grow and mature. Although we are born whole and complete, we accumulate both positive and negative experiences in life from our parents or caregivers and form an image of that, the Imago, in our unconscious mind. We then look for someone to match that image in our romantic relationships and want our primary lover to heal us from those early wounds and scars created by our parents.

When we fall in love, it's like looking into a mirror of ourselves, as well as a glimpse of our potential to find wholeness. Sometimes, we choose the wrong partner, who might not be able to help support our healing journey or allow us to grow, and it's up to us to be conscious of that and not carry on in a relationship that is harming us. Instead, we need to connect with someone who is able to give us the space to heal, mature, and grow, and to offer them the same thing.

If you wish to find someone with whom you truly resonate or want to increase those love vibes, there are a few things you can do. It begins with being conscious of your needs, but also realizing that *you are love*. Your aim shouldn't be to go out there desperately seeking love. It will come to you when you resonate that high-frequency energy, allowing you to experience it in all its glory with a loving partner who resonates with you.

When you find yourself analysing a current or potential partner, consider how they make you feel first. Then consider how they treat you and others, what they believe about love and closeness, and how consistent they are in demonstrating their active participation in building an intimate connection with you. This is more of what an appropriate checklist would look like when seeking an authentic love relationship, if there were to be one.

Stay open to the vast spectrum of love in all its forms. Don't focus on the small things that prevent you from experiencing the full power of love, such as thinking, 'He didn't tell me he loves me today,' or 'I don't like the way she's always late.' Create a canvas together that can be coloured with the multiple aspects of your connection with each other and stand back to admire it now and again, instead of getting caught up in the unimportant details. Love is vast and can grow even more so when you see the bigger picture.

TUNE INTO LOVE VIBES

'If music be the food of love, play on . . .'
– Orsino in Twelfth Night by William Shakespeare

We all know what a massive impact music can have on the way we feel and get us into that love mood. What you might not know is that there are certain sounds known as the solfeggio frequencies that can tap into our energy frequencies and either raise or lower them. These sounds, which have been used for centuries by Gregorian monks and in ancient Indian Sanskrit chants, have remarkable effects on our body and mind. The solfeggio frequencies found in sacred music belong to a six-tone scale that resonate on different frequencies, with the love frequency vibrating at 528 Hz. This is the frequency that many say transforms our state of being.

Music resonating on 639 Hz also has the ability to help us reconnect because it allows for introspection on our life and the people we love. When you play music containing a 639 Hz tone, you will receive a significant boost of love and positivity that can help you to deal with conflicts in relationships and bring you both back in sync with each other. You'll find plenty of playlists for solfeggio frequencies on Spotify and YouTube, so take a look and choose one that suits your mood of the day, sit back with your partner, and enjoy!

LISTEN TO YOUR INTUITION

Have you ever had the feeling that something is wrong without being able to fully explain it? When that happens, it could be your intuition trying to tell you something you need to know. From a psychological perspective, intuition is an innate ability to piece together snippets of information and emotional impressions to form a 'gut feeling' about something or someone. It's the process of coming to a conclusion without realizing how you got there.

Some say intuition goes beyond the use of our five senses, tuning into energy vibrations that we don't usually notice. It isn't something that we normally think about, but if you've ever experienced it, you will know that it can be very reliable.

The more connected you are to your intuition, the higher your vibration will be. To do this, you need to quieten the noise in your mind and pay more attention to that calm inner whisper. You need to listen to it and trust its power, without trying to rationalize it or bring logic to the table. It's essential to know if it really is your intuition speaking to you, or if it's your trauma. My book *Healing Is the New High* can help with this distinction. Self-awareness and self-trust are key.

When it comes to your relationship, intuition will help you to evaluate your own needs and those of your partner. This unconscious gut feeling is a great indicator of how happy you really are in a relationship. You can tune into it by asking yourself certain questions on a regular basis. Answer them by saying the first thing that comes into your mind and don't overthink them too much. Your intuition will take over and give you the answers you need to know where to go from here. Ask yourself:

- How healthy is our relationship?

- Does it feel true?

- Is it what we both want?

- What is the most important thing in it?

- Is it working?

- How can we improve it?

- How can we support each other more?

Being on the same wavelength as your partner is important. When you have a niggling feeling that you can't put your finger on or something is unsettling you without knowing why, take some time to quietly reflect. Allow your intuition to guide you. It will never be wrong.

Your intuition is also a great internal compass for navigating the weather of your partner's heart. You never want to guess what is wrong, but it's natural to be able to sense it. With strong intuition, you can help start conversations that need to be had or better support your partner who doesn't know how to ask for help.

Stop doubting your gut feelings and lean into intuition.

Your intuition is threaded throughout your being, and when you're aligned with it, it can give insight in ways nothing and no one else can.

Ultimately, the love frequency depends on how frequently you check in with one another, and with yourself. You can't sustain a romantic relationship unless you have a common goal, are still interested in each other, and want to be together. Emotional distance creates indifference, so you need to keep tuning into one another if you want to make it work. Being there for your partner through thick and thin is what counts, not ignoring their fears, worries, and problems.

A loving partnership needs emotional, physical, mental, and spiritual energy to thrive, and when you synchronize in all of those spheres, you will be recharging the power of love every day of your time spent together.

The more you love, the larger love becomes. If you can open up to the beauty of love in your relationship, it will continue to fill you with an abundance of positive energy. When you understand that you are the source of love, you can begin to change your life for the better. Your relationships will be more expansive, mature, and satisfying, as your actions become attuned to creating more and more love.

Love is a vibe and all you have to do is tune into it and let it resonate freely. Allow it to flow through you and refresh every cell in your body, allowing you to vibrate as high as possible.

You won't regret it!

KEY INSIGHTS

- Love is often hard to describe but easy to experience as it resonates on a vibrational level.

- The science of brain frequencies reveals the impact our emotions have on us.

- Cultivating love through positive vibrations is the secret to happy relationships.

- When you weigh up your emotions, love is amongst the highest frequencies..

- Staying high on love takes healthy relationship habits and focusing on your needs.

- Music is great therapy for distant hearts to merge.

- Your intuition will never let you down as it resonates in tune with your inner self.

- Do a relationship self-check often and ask yourself if you are meeting your needs while honouring your partner's.

Chapter 11

LOVE IS A WAY OF LIFE

**If there was no love in life, there would be no life.
We can't exist without it.**

Love can be found in all that we do, think, and feel, far surpassing just the love shared in romantic relationships.

It all begins with us: how much we love ourselves and then how much love we share with others. It's not about what you can get or how someone else can make you feel. Of course, being loved by others brings special value to our lives, but when we exude love, that's a gift in itself.

**Loving yourself deeply enables you to love others
with more authenticity and fewer judgements.
When you become accepting of yourself, you will
find it easier to accept others for who they are.**

The opposite of love is indifference, which leads to hate. How many times have you hated someone? Hate might be a strong word, so let me ask you this: How often have you felt angry, upset, enraged by someone? Can you remember how that feels? It's like a destructive tsunami overtaking you, isn't it? The negative energy of hate that rises up when we feel disappointed, used, cheated, hurt, is totally self-destructive because it uses up the positive energy we possess. Violence, aggression, toxicity, revenge, envy, spite – these are all symptoms of hate.

You might have an argument with your partner or even a complete stranger and become overtaken by negativity and anger, which aren't great feelings to have. When you calm down, you realize that this isn't how you want to be, but in that rabid moment, you aren't yourself. It's like you've become possessed by something you can't control. Hate, even disguised as anger or bitterness, is not a healthy state to be in or a productive way to live.

Now, think of all the times when you've felt the power of love. You might have experienced that at a football game, a rock concert, during a demonstration for world peace, when you took part in a sponsored run or charity event. It could be when playing on a team, during yoga class, at a family gathering, at Christmas, during Diwali, even at a party. That feeling of overwhelming joy, unity, and shared connection is much more powerful than anything else in this world. It's love.

I've mentioned this a lot in this book and I truly believe that love is an energy that can help us to overcome any difficulty in life and create a better world.

Love knows no boundaries, sees no colour or race, comes with no conditions or expectations, and exists even if you don't feel it all the time. Love is an awareness and when we can accept that we have access to it at all points in our day, love becomes a way of life.

It's up to each one of us to fan those flames of love: to reconnect with our inner potential to embrace love, to be love, and to give love. When we do that, we are spreading the energy of love all over the world in a wonderful ripple effect.

Love isn't a commodity – it's part of being human.
Love isn't a transaction – it's free for all.
Love isn't a privilege – it's a human right.

When love becomes a way of life, the world changes. We can see love between simple interactions among strangers in a grocery store. We'd come to feel love among world leaders making important decisions. But as with the love experienced in a relationship, it starts with yourself.

LOVE IS MUCH BIGGER THAN ANY OF US

It's a life force that you just can't put in a bottle and sell. Even though everywhere we look, there's a brand promising us this. Love is such a powerful unconscious motivator that many of us would do anything for it. Love can bring down walls, unite enemies, create peace and harmony, save the planet, and much, much more. Your initial response to this might be to say that I'm too idealistic, or that I'm having a kumbaya moment. My point is, what's the alternative?

Love is unity and peace.
Hate is division and destruction.

You don't have to be spiritual or religious to recognize that love is a much better alternative to non-love. It can bring us more than any other emotion in life. When you feel love within yourself, the world becomes a beautiful place. When you lack that feeling, the world seems harsh, cold, and cruel. And love isn't just experienced through romantic love, although that's an obvious example of how we express and receive it in an intimate way.

HOW TO CHOOSE LOVE

If you want a deeper appreciation of yourself, a more meaningful and authentic relationship, and to do your part in creating a more peaceful world, you'll have to make choosing love a habit. It's like a muscle that has to be worked on regularly. Here are practical ways you can integrate love into your personality, habits, and entire being.

Validate others

Many people feel unseen, unheard, and unwanted. But it takes so little for us to validate someone's experiences. Listening is a good start. Don't attempt to offer solutions or alternatives, dismiss their feelings, or share how the same thing has happened to you. Be a mirror for them reflecting love and humanity. Confirm for them that how they felt or feel is perfectly fine. See them, hear them, and love them anyway.

Radical acceptance

It's tempting to try to shape others to fit the holes in our heart created by previous lovers, family, or traumatic experiences. But no one is here to fix us. When you stop seeing people for what they offer you and begin to seek who they really are, radical acceptance and genuine curiosity takes hold, creating an environment of pure love. I want nothing from you but to enjoy you as you are.

Find the best in others

Where your focus goes, attention grows. Imagine what a positive impact we'd have on each other if we hyper-fixated on the best in one another. The world is constantly reminding us how imperfect we are or that if we buy into this or that we'd be happy and loveable. I don't even want to think about the number of markets that would fail if we made a habit of total love and acceptance.

Practise genuine interest

In the present-day hustle culture, the focus is always on ourselves. We must be productive and win at all costs. It isn't until those unbearably sad infomercials impede our self-serving feeds that we remember there are so many opportunities to help and support those around us. Embodying love doesn't mean you have to save the world, but getting outside of your own life and circumstance and practising interest in others will result in deeper connections and the expansion of universal, unconditional love.

THE POWER OF LOVE

The greatest sages, writers, and spiritual leaders in history have recognized the power of love, and you only have to do a quick search on Google to find quotes by them on the subject.

Some of my favourites are ones such as: 'Step out of the circle of time and into the circle of love,' by the Persian poet and Sufi master Rumi.[44] If you can stop trying to measure the quality of love you give and remove expectations, it will be a much more fulfilling experience for you.

In *The Alchemist*, Brazilian novelist Paulo Coelho said, 'One is loved because one is loved. No reason is needed for loving.'[45] That is a two-way thing, in that you don't need a reason to love or be loved. You can even love someone that you don't like because love surpasses that.

'Spiritual love is without limits or boundaries. Worldly love is superficial and fluctuating',[46] according to the Indian Hindu spiritual leader Mata Amritanandamayi. She makes a great point: love is a form of spirituality that isn't defined by short-term flings or the feeling of 'being in love'. There is so much more to it than that.

I love the words of the Indian philosopher Jiddu Krishnamurti, who stated,

'Freedom and love go together. Love is not a reaction. If I love you because you love me, that is mere trade, a thing to be bought in the market; it is not love. To love is not to ask anything in return, not even to feel that you are giving something – and it is only such love that can know freedom.'[47]

Buddha said in the Metta Sutta, 'Radiate boundless love towards the entire world – above, below, and across – unhindered, without ill will, without enmity'. I think he hit the nail on the head here because it's true – spreading love should be the purpose, not seeking to find it in a false idea of perfection.

I also love the famous quote by the writer Oscar Wilde, who stated, 'To love oneself is the beginning of a lifelong romance.'[48] He was right, of course, and what a romance!

Don't even get me started on all of the songs about love that have become popular anthems . . . The music industry is pretty obsessed with producing songs to do with love, and we all have our favourites. They are the ones that touch our hearts, give us goosebumps, and make us feel all fudgy inside. We seem to love love songs, and there's a good reason for that. It's like they speak to us, express what we want to say, and describe how we feel. Whether you are into rap, country, rock, EDM, or K-pop, I'm sure you can think of one or two tracks that remind you of someone you love or have loved in the past.

Love means different things to different people and we show it in all kinds of ways, but I think that one thing remains constant: self-love heals us from pain and allows us to love others unconditionally. If we can aim for that, we are on the right path. When we nurture a deep respect for our own needs and cultivate a sense of self-worth and regard for others, the love we give can be life-changing.

LOVE IS A RIGHT

There's an interesting page on Instagram that I follow called @whereloveisillegal and you can check out their website here: https://whereloveisillegal.com.

It documents and shares very touching LGBTQ+ accounts of discrimination and survival from around the world using the stories of different individuals. It's interesting because it shows the pain, struggles, and challenges faced by those who aren't allowed to be themselves and to love in the way that they want to because of cultural, social, and political restrictions.

It's very sad to think that thousands and thousands of people from all kinds of backgrounds in many parts of the world have to hide, flee, or are assaulted, ostracized, and even imprisoned or killed because of their sexual orientation or gender choices. It's like they really aren't allowed to love, which is the only thing they want to do and a human right.

Prejudice and injustice breed hate, not love, and the more we try to dictate to others how they should live their lives, the more damage we are doing to our own society. No one should have to earn the right to love – love is non-negotiable and if you feel suffocated by this type of oppression, stay close to your values and don't let the outside world destroy them. We are all worthy of love and should be free to give love, no matter what.

RIGHTS WITHIN RELATIONSHIPS

And when we find ourselves in a relationship, we also have rights. This goes back to boundaries, which every healthy relationship needs to flourish. You have a right to:

- Say 'no' without feeling guilty.

- Be treated with respect.

- Make your needs as important as others.

- Be accepting of your mistakes and failures.

- Not meet unreasonable expectations of others.

You also have a right to say 'no' in a relationship without having to explain yourself every time. Although you might not know it, a single 'no' is a complete sentence. If you want to assert your boundaries so that your partner gets the message, it really isn't necessary to waffle on about why you don't want to do this or that and allow for the 'no' word to be sufficient. In the same way, respect your partner's boundaries and don't keep asking them to explain themselves when they say no. Be tolerant, not demanding.

You might find this strange, but you are also entitled to your privacy when you are in a relationship, too. It's OK to close the bathroom door when you have a shower – you aren't being impolite. You need your space just as much as anyone and it's important that your partner respects that, just as you respect theirs. Here are some more privacy policies you might want to adopt:

- Use a password on your phone – why not?

- Lock any private items away that you don't want to share. This could be a journal or diary. I'm not talking about hiding photos of your lover, for example. That's a different story altogether.

- When you want some alone time, politely ask your partner not to disturb you.

- Don't feel the need to have to reply instantly to messages if, say, you are out with your friends. Explain to your partner that you want them to respect your time without them.

The above are quite simple requests but can cause so much hassle and arguments between couples.

You can still be a loving person who respects people's needs while setting boundaries to protect yours.

Remember that boundaries are a form of self-care. They don't make you less compassionate but help you keep your relationships healthy without suffocating yourself in the process. The right person will not feel threatened by your boundaries and will respect you for standing your ground. It goes without saying that boundaries aren't meant to be used to hide damaging secrets. This would just be manipulation and flat-out deceit.

LOVE IS A BUZZWORD

Everyone talks about love because it's part of our cultural mindset and probably the only thing we all universally desire, whether conscious of it or not. It's a word that we use often when talking about food, music, art, work, holidays, people, places, experiences . . . it goes on and on. We all get what it feels like to love someone or something and understand that it's the ultimate high.

When we fall out of love, get hurt, feel rejected, abandoned, or abused, we turn away from love, thinking that we did something wrong by loving. What I've mentioned several times in this book is that love is never wrong – it's people who warp it, misinterpret it, or use it to their advantage.

We are the ones who set unrealistic expectations on what we think love is or try to shape what we think love should look like. Everything begins and ends with how we deal with the experience of love. We are in control of our responses to our emotions and thoughts, no one else.

When I hear people talking about the hurt they have gone through in any relationship, I want to tell them that the pain they feel isn't because love is bad or cruel. Love is never bad, but people can exercise hurtful actions. And it's not about blame either – nobody is an expert on how to give and receive love – there's no handbook. Add to that past trauma, insecure attachments, erroneous patterns of behaviour, the inability to communicate, lack of intimacy or emotional connection, and it's no surprise that we can get hurt in relationships. I feel for anyone who has gone through that pain and hope that they can find the wisdom and support they need to heal from it.

If you think that love is a dirty word, you have probably been hurt and are justified in feeling that way. But understand it wasn't love that hurt you. It was a wolf in sheep's clothing: someone who didn't know how to love themselves or you. It was a circumstance that didn't favour or value you. But love is what will heal you. I'm not going to try to 'self-help' you out of your pain, but what I would like to say is that persistent negative feelings are usually rooted in something much deeper. If you can find out where they are coming from, put them into some kind of perspective, and detach them from who you really are, you might find it easier to embrace love again.

LOVE ISN'T BLIND

Despite what you might see on TV, blind dates and blind weddings don't usually work out. The ones that do are exceptions to the rule. I'm not saying don't go on blind dates, but if you do, remember that love can't be built if you are wearing blinkers.

Apart from the sexual chemistry and the pull of attraction you might initially feel for your partner, there's got to be more than that to make a relationship work. You need to be able to communicate, resolve conflict, and pull together to solve problems.

You have to both be prepared to invest in creating something strong, intimate, and resilient. I call these **RICH** relationships because they contain four key elements that make them successful:

Respect · **Intimacy** · **Communication** · **Honesty**

When you are able to see the person opposite you for who they really are, and still love them after the first crazy dating days have died down, you will know that love is not blind: it sees everything.

- Love sees every flaw and annoying habit your partner has and still stays.

- Love sees any problems or issues you face together and works to overcome them.

- Love sees the truth about your partner's past and not just the polished version.

- Love sees the things that aren't being said and can deal with sadness and discomfort.

- Love sees the parts of your partner you didn't notice at first and makes you find them even more beautiful.

THE PUREST LOVE DOESN'T COME WITH CONDITIONS

The purest love is unconditional, which can be confusing to a lot of people. When you fall in love because of how someone treats you, who they are as a person, your common interests, the fond memories you create together, and the physical chemistry, you are falling in love with an idea of how you think love should be. If your partner is kind, sincere, and consistent, you become hooked, based on all of their good points. This is exactly how you imagined love to be with 'the one', right?

But then, when your 'one and only' starts to appear human again, you soon find that they actually have faults, are imperfect, often annoying, and not necessarily your ideal mate.

Once you see them in the cold light of day, what happens to love? You see, you started out with love as a condition of this, that, or the other, and when those filters slip away, you are left with a real person. That's when authentic love can begin to manifest itself. Loving someone despite their flaws and imperfections is what makes relationships work. Adapting, being flexible, and showing compassion can build love up to where it belongs. You might find these flaws too much to accept, and that is also part of love – knowing when to walk away without leaving a trail of hurt behind you.

Unconditional love isn't about being on a constant high but also involves getting through the tough times together. It's when you support your partner in their goals and encourage them to grow. It's about abandoning expectations of how they should act or think and accepting them for who they are.

If you want to change the person you are with, then you are probably with the wrong person.

When you take them as they are, along with all they will ever be, you show the noblest kind of love – one free of conditions. Loving someone unconditionally means wanting what is best for them, without sacrificing your own peace of mind. If they are being abusive, controlling, or dishonest with you, it becomes obvious that they aren't loving you from the same level of awareness, and you may find it is necessary to move on.

Unconditional love means loving with curiosity for your partner and a willingness to see their scars and share their triumphs, as well as being ready to share your own. If you find yourself in a relationship with strings attached, that's not a healthy situation to be in and will lead to a great imbalance.

Loving unconditionally isn't dependent on things like distance, social standing, economic factors, or anything else from the outside. It's completely separate from any of these things because it comes from within you.

You will know your relationship is healthy when you both:

- Show up for each other on the hard days.

- Communicate honestly and respectfully.

- Set boundaries with love.

- Hold space for healing.

- Root for each other.

In all the relationships and connections we experience in our lifetime, the most meaningful ones bring you closer to your life's purpose. This is the kind of love that makes you feel like you are coming home to yourself.

'I love you' means that I've seen your dungeons and I'm still proud to call them home. It means that I will be there to give you a hand with your baggage because you will never travel alone. It means that the only thing I will continue to do behind your back is to pray for your wellbeing. It means that no matter what changes you go through, the way I feel about you will always remain the same.

You can show it every day to your loved ones and don't need to receive anything in return. The giving of love is a gift in itself. That might sound hard to do because we live in a society where everything is a transaction. It's often a case of 'you scratch my back and I'll scratch yours'. But love can't be quantified like money, favours, or commodities, so we have to handle it differently. Love is an action we each choose for ourselves – you aren't doing it for anyone else. It can't be forced, which breeds resentment, and neither can it be demanded from someone without their ability to give it.

One of the hardest things people go through is loving someone who doesn't feel the same way about them. This unreciprocated love strikes deep at the heart of our self-esteem, and our sense of self-worth. But, in reality, it doesn't say anything about your potential to love or your inability to give love. It says more about the other person, who simply does not feel that emotional connection with you in the way that you want them to. I know it's painful to experience that when you think they 'should' love you. But, there's no 'should' in unconditional love.

Heartbreak hurts. But it also shows you how to value yourself and be accountable for your own happiness.

When you choose love as a way of life, you will never lack love. You can love others even if they don't reciprocate it. You can walk away from your partner and still have love for them. They might walk away from you, and you can still hold a healthy love for them. When I say healthy, I mean without bitterness, anger, resentment, or spite. Respecting their wishes and accepting that they aren't going to be a part of your life in the way you would have liked takes strength. But unconditional love is the epitome of strength and acceptance at the same time.

You can live alone, without a partner in your life, and still experience unconditional love. Many people choose this option for their own reasons and can still give a whole lot of love to others in their life, be they friends, family, workmates, neighbours, or the dogs in the local shelter.

Those who are comfortable being alone can often love so deeply and purely, because they are not sharing to receive, but simply giving.

Yet, unconditional love does have boundaries, which we need to set in place to avoid unhappiness and abuse. Letting someone walk all over you isn't a prerequisite of unconditional love.

Remember, if you practise self-love, you won't allow anyone to do this to you. The problem occurs when you haven't developed a strong sense of self-love and rely on harmful attachments and co-dependency to guide you in a relationship. These aren't usually in your best interests, leading you to accept behaviours and conditions that really aren't good for you.

When you practise unconditional love, you won't feel the need to exceed your boundaries or try to maintain dynamics based on unacceptable behaviour. Both people in a relationship are accountable for their actions, and you have a responsibility to yourself to feel safe, free, and content with your partner. If this isn't the case, go back to your centre and recheck where your boundaries lie. Be your own linesman and don't expect someone else to do that job for you.

It's one thing to support your partner through times of hardship, when they lose their job, are sick, suffer some kind of mental breakdown, or are dealing with emotional turmoil. It's quite another to accept harmful, damaging behaviour intentionally aimed at you, which includes things like control, manipulation, jealousy, gaslighting, and being plain mean. For example, you can say, 'I love you and support you no matter what. However, I can no longer support you financially in your spending/drinking habit.'

Again, problems like this arise in most relationships. But if there are cycles and repeated behaviour, understand that despite the amount of love you may have for them, if they don't love themselves enough to be a responsible partner, you'd be hard-pressed to experience emotional fulfilment with them.

If you feel harmed by someone and they aren't willing to repair that damage, you need to draw a line for your own wellbeing. If you see that there is no respect or kindness towards you from your partner, you must look at your boundaries again. You can say to them, 'I love you, but I need to take space from you when you speak/act in that way. It's not good for me.'

Unconditional love isn't a binding contract. You aren't forced to continue offering love when your basic needs aren't being met. To love unconditionally means to love now, without being indebted or bound to a situation you aren't happy with. It doesn't mean, 'I offer you my love in the exact same way even if you harm me.' I hope you take that sentence to heart. What it means is that you offered your love unconditionally and freely, but will set boundaries if you need to for your own wellbeing.

> **Unconditional love doesn't mean for ever, no matter what! It means giving love now, in this moment, of your own free will, expecting nothing in return.**

This is the kind of love that allows us and our partners to be ourselves. It allows us to constantly be aware of what is happening and notice any changes that will affect our decision to keep giving our love freely to that person.

Here are some more questions for you to ponder on when you think about unconditional love:

- **What kind of behaviour are you willing to accept** and how unhealthy is your relationship becoming?

- **Are you enabling your partner to act negatively and turning a blind eye to it?** You are culpable if this is the case, and should only accept what is healthy, not what is unhealthy.

- **Pay attention when you offer unconditional love:** are you expecting a certain reaction from your partner? Do you make them feel indebted to you or create dependency on you in some way?

- **How willing are you to be influenced by your partner to change?** Perhaps they can help you to grow, mature, and heal. Do you welcome their efforts or rebuff them in a way that shows you don't value their opinions?

- **How transparent are you?** Do you lay your cards on the table or expect your partner to keep doing all the guesswork? Approaching the relationship with an open deck is essential if you want to avoid misunderstandings further down the road.

If the term unconditional love still confuses you, that's OK. Instead, you can use the term 'wholehearted love'. This may help you to navigate your actions and feelings better. It means leaning into love because you want to. It's a choice; a decision you take. You give it because it feels great to do so and not because you are expecting something in return.

Wholehearted love recognizes your wholeness and the wholeness of your partner. You enter with a full heart, not a half-empty one waiting to be filled by the other person, and vice versa. When two full hearts come together, love flourishes and growth happens for both of you within that wonderful union.

Your relationship goals will become a vision for the future that you both see yourselves sharing. You will nurture, support, and help each other to manifest these goals, both individually and as a team. And there's strength in unity, as you know.

Yes, relationships are often difficult. Yes, they require courage and will absolutely demand all the emotional strength you can muster. But at the end of the day, nothing beats the feeling of the genuine love that's felt in healthy relationships.

When you can say, 'I love you for no reason', you are tapping into the purest form of love where there are no obligations, no expectations, and nothing to be returned in exchange for the love you share. This is the love that liberates you, allowing you to experience it in all its beauty.

Ask me AGAIN if I believe in falling in love, and my answer is, NO. I prefer to believe that we RISE in love.

I hope you can experience that, after reading this book!

After hundreds of pages of challenging your heart and mind with new ways to perceive, navigate, and experience relationships and love, my hope for you is to not complicate your feelings. Lean so deep into self-knowing and intuition that love becomes a visceral experience that you can trust. You are made from and to love. Carry this knowing into every interaction and you will never be without it.

KEY INSIGHTS

- When you live with love, you are living the best life.

- Your capacity to love knows no bounds.

- Love is bigger than me, you, and everyone. It is the Universe itself.

- Choose love in your relationships by validating your partner, practising acceptance, seeing the best in them, and showing genuine interest.

- Love is a right we are all entitled to.

- Setting boundaries is a healthy way to protect yourself and your partners.

- Love can act as a healer and remains steadfast even when you are full of uncertainty.

- Create RICH relationships based on respect, intimacy, communication, and honesty.

- Love is a gift you owe to yourself. Embrace it every moment of your life.

The sun has never asked for anything in return
as it sends its light down below,
Enlightening all that we love and
all that we may wish to hide.
Instead, its rays shine as a gift, an offering.
It's the purest love we know, divine in its ways.
We ought to love like the sun, shining
in all that we are, unafraid to be.
But that kind of love doesn't come easily.
It takes a strength, a selflessness, and a focus
on returning to that sacred, loving sunlight.
We must embrace ourselves fully within its rays,
love ourselves as the sun does,
so that we can illuminate the lives of others
and love them purely, without demands,
without expectations, and unconditionally,
exactly like the sun in all its ways.

ENDNOTES

1   Hamutal Kreiner and Yossi Levi-Belz, 'Self-Disclosure Here and Now: Combining Retrospective Perceived Assessment with Dynamic Behavioral Measures', *Frontiers in Psychology*, 2019, vol.10. https://www.frontiersin.org/articles/10.3389/fpsyg.2019.00558/full

2   Margaret W. Sullivan, 'Approach and Withdrawal in Early Emotional Development', *Encyclopedia on Early Childhood Development* (online), September 2011. https://www.child-encyclopedia.com/emotions/according-experts/approach-and-withdrawal-early-emotional-development

3   *The Upanishads*, translated by Eknath Easwaran, 2nd Edition Paperback, Nilgiri Press, California, 2007

4   Jill Bolte Taylor, *Whole Brain Living: The Anatomy of Choice and the Four Characters That Drive Our Life*, Hay House Inc, London, 2021

5   https://www.betterhelp.com/advice/attachment/what-are-the-four-attachment-styles/

6   Maoshing Ni, *The Yellow Emperor's Classic of Medicine: A New Translation of the Neijing Suwen with Commentary*, Boulder, Shambhala, 1995

7   *New King James Bible*, Thomas Nelson, London, 2017

8   Pablo Neruda, *100 Love Sonnets: A Bilingual Spanish and English Edition*, translated by Gustavo Escobedo, Exile Editions, Toronto, 2014

9   Rudolf Otto, *The Idea of the Holy*, translated by John W. Harvey, Oxford University Press, Oxford, 1958

10 Bowlby, J., 'Processes of mourning', *International Journal of Psychoanalysis*, 1961, 42: 317–339

11 Thich Nhat Hanh, *Buddha Mind, Buddha Body: Walking Toward Enlightenment*, Parallax Press, Berkeley, 2003

12 Norman Doidge, *The Brain That Changes Itself: Stories of Personal Triumph from the Frontiers of Brain Science*, Penguin, London, 2008

13 Erich Fromm, *The Art of Loving*, Thorsons, London, 1995

14 Zygmunt Bauman, *Liquid Love*, Polity, Cambridge, 2003

15 Brian G. Ogolsky, J. Kale Monk, TeKisha M. Rice, Jaclyn C. Theisen, Christopher R. Maniotes, 'Relationship Maintenance: A Review of Research on Romantic Relationships', *Journal of Family Theory & Review*, 2017, 9 (3): 275. DOI: 10.1111/jftr.12205. https://www.sciencedaily.com/releases/2017/09/170911122740.htm

16 https://www.singlesinamerica.com/

17 https://www.theguardian.com/lifeandstyle/2021/may/21/people-are-looking-for-something-more-serious-the-hinge-ceo-on-the-pandemic-dating-boom

18 From one of Nietsche's unpublished notebooks circa 1876, the original German reads 'Nicht die Abwesenheit der Liebe, sondern die Abwesenheit der Freundschaft macht die unglücklichen Ehen'. http://www.nietzschesource.org/#eKGWB/NF-1876,23[72]

19 Leslie S. Greenberg, Rhonda N. Goldman, *Emotion-Focused Couples Therapy: The Dynamics of Emotion, Love and Power*, American Psychological Association, Washington, 2008. Leslie S. Greenberg and Jeanne C. Watson, *Emotion-Focused*

Therefore

Therapy for Depression, American Psychological Association, Washington, 2005

20 Joanne Davila, Jonathan Mattanah, Vickie Bhatia, Jessica Latack, Brian Feinstein, Nicholas Eaton, Jennifer Daks, Shaina Kumar, Edward Lomash, Melody McCormick & Jiaqi Zhou, 'Romantic competence, healthy relationship functioning, and well-being in emerging adults: Romantic competence', *Personal Relationships*, 2017, 24 (1). https://www.researchgate.net/publication/313406102_Romantic_competence_healthy_relationship_functioning_and_well-being_in_emerging_adults_Romantic_competence

21 Esther Perel, *Mating in Captivity: Unlocking erotic intelligence,* Hodder & Stoughton, London, 2007

22 Gary Chapman, *The 5 Love Languages: The secret to love that lasts*, Northfield Publishing, Chicago, 2015

23 Brené Brown, *Daring Greatly: How the Courage to Be Vulnerable Transforms the Way We Live, Love, Parent, and Lead*, Penguin Life, London, 2015

24 Don Miguel Ruiz with Janet Mills, *The Mastery of Love: A practical guide to the art of relationship*, Amber-Allen Publishing Inc, California, 1999.

25 Samantha Joel, Geoff Macdonald & Elizabeth Page-Gould, 'Wanting to Stay and Wanting to Go: Unpacking the Content and Structure of Relationship Stay/Leave Decision Processes', *Social Psychological and Personality Science*, 2018, vol. 9, issue 6

26 Eckhart Tolle, *Practising the Power of Now: Essential Teachings, Meditations, and Exercises from The Power of Now*, New World Library, Novato, 2001

27 Robert W. Firestone, *The Fantasy Bond: Structure of Psychological Defenses*, Glendon Association, Santa Barbara, 1987

28 https://www.gottman.com/blog/are-we-headed-for-divorce/

29 Yasmin Mogahed, *Reclaim Your Heart; Personal insights on breaking free from life's shackles*, IDIFY Publishing, 2015

30 Alaric Hutchinson, *Living Peace: Essential Teachings for Enriching Life*, Earth Spirit Publishing LLC, Cowichan Bay, 2014

31 Stephanie Coontz, *Marriage, a History: How Love Conquered Marriage*, Penguin, New York, 2006

32 A.W. Geiger and Gretchen Livingstone, '8 facts about love and marriage in America', pewresearch.org, February 2019. https://www.pewresearch.org/fact-tank/2019/02/13/8-facts-about-love-and-marriage/

33 Robert J. Sternberg, 'A triangular theory of love', *Psychological Review*, 1986, 93: 119–135

34 Rainer Maria Rilke, *Letters to a Young Poet*, translated by Reginald Snell, Dover Publications, New York, 2002

35 https://www.globalinvestigations.co.uk/infidelity-statistics-uk-infographic/

36 https://www.census.gov/data/tables/time-series/demo/families/marital.html

37 Louis de Bernières, *Captain Corelli's Mandolin*, Penguin, London, 2001

38 James Joyce, *Ulysses*, 1932 revised edition, Wordsworth Classics, Ware, 2010

39 Steven Strogatz, *Sync: The emerging science of spontaneous order*, Penguin, London, 2004

40 https://www.esi-frankfurt.de/research/fries-lab/

41 Ondřej Kučera, Daniel Havelka, 'Mechano-electrical vibrations of microtubules – link to subcellular morphology', *Biosystems*, Sept 2012, 109(3): 346–55. https://pubmed.ncbi.nlm.nih.gov/22575306/

42 Hawkins, David, *Power Versus Force: An Anatomy of Consciousness: the Hidden Determinants of Human Behavior*, Veritas, 1998

43 Harville Hendrix, Helen LaKelly Hunt, *Getting the Love You Want: A guide for couples*, Simon & Schuster, London, 2020

44 Jalāl al-Dīn Rūmī, *The Essential Rumi*, translated by Coleman Barks, HarperCollins, San Francisco, 1995

45 Paulo Coelho, *The Alchemist*, HarperCollins, London, 2012

46 Mata Amritanandamayi (@Amritanandamayi), 'Spiritual love is without limits or boundaries. Worldly love is superficial and fluctuating. #Amma https://twitter.com/Amritanandamayi/status/726569340108038144.' 01 May 2016.

47 https://jkrishnamurti.org/content/chapter-3

48 Oscar Wilde, *An Ideal Husband*: A Play, Public Domain, Project Gutenberg, 2011. https://gutenberg.org/ebooks/885

ACKNOWLEDGEMENTS

Love and thanks to
Kaushal
My family and friends

My social media followers and supporters
Jane and the team at Graham Maw Christie
Carole, Mireille and the team at Bluebird
Gideon and the team at Harper One

Special mention to

Michelle, Jo, Wendi, Amina, Sarah, Debbie and Shanu.

Vex King is a Number 1 *Sunday Times* bestselling author, social media content creator and mind coach. He experienced many challenges when he was growing up: his father died when Vex was just a baby, his family were often homeless and he grew up in troubled neighbourhoods where he regularly experienced violence and racism. Despite this, Vex successfully turned his whole life around and is now leading a revolution for the next generation of spiritual seekers.

As a major voice in the world of personal development, Vex shares deep spiritual knowledge in a way that's easy to understand, with stories from his own life, great inspirational quotes and practical solutions.

@vexking

Accept rejection.
Don't beg.
Never chase.
Know your worth.
Choose yourself.